Historical Fiction for Children

Capturing
the
Past

Edited by Fiona M Collins and Judith Graham

David Fulton Publishers

London

David Fulton Publishers Ltd
Ormond House, 26–27 Boswell Street, London WC1N 3JZ

www.fultonpublishers.co.uk

First published in Great Britain by David Fulton Publishers 2001

Note: The right of Fiona M. Collins and Judith Graham to be identified as the editors
of this work has been asserted by them in accordance with the Copyright, Designs
and Patents Act 1988.

Copyright © Fiona M. Collins and Judith Graham 2001

British Library Cataloguing in Publication Data
A catalogue record for this book is available from the British Library

ISBN 1–85346–768–5

The publishers would like to thank Priscilla Sharland for copy-editing and Sheila
Harding for proofreading this book.

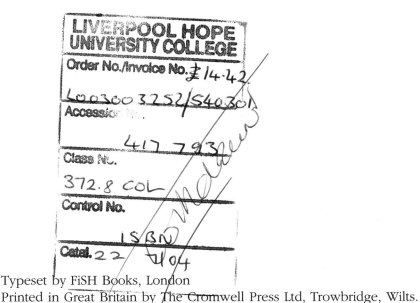
Typeset by FiSH Books, London
Printed in Great Britain by The Cromwell Press Ltd, Trowbridge, Wilts.

Contents

Introduction

Historical Fiction for Children: Capturing the Past is a book dedicated, in its entirety, to exploring historical fiction written for children. We have been prompted to produce this book by twin impulses – increasing interest in the genre mostly because of the emergence recently of some particularly fine authors writing accessibly for young people, and an awareness that the genre has been neglected in recent decades.

Many issues are raised when authors set their stories in the past. First and foremost there is the balance that must be kept between the responsibility owed to historical truth and the need to write a story which in its emotional and narrative truth engages the modern reader. This is as burning a question today as it has ever been when history and imaginative interpretation meet. It is closely connected to the challenge that writers of historical fiction face in exciting interest in unknown and distant eras and in finding a language which suggests the past but which is not dishearteningly difficult for the young reader. Then there is the whole area of shifting interpretations, differing ideological positions, that are both consciously and unconsciously taken up when we write about anything, but particularly about the past.

We invited our colleagues in colleges and universities, some of the 'fine authors' mentioned above and some teachers, from a range of institutions, to contribute their thoughts on these and other matters. The work gathered here examines the nature, and honours the range and richness of historical fiction.

The opening section is intended to reflect the debates about writing responsibly about history while retaining artistic integrity. These debates have taken place whenever historical fiction is discussed. Overwhelming story with too much fact, distorting history, questions of objectivity, bias and didacticism, the marginalisation and silencing of voices are all key issues that are visited. This section is also where a sense of key works, key themes and key authors is offered. Partly, these items are chosen by the contributors to this section from a personal interest and conviction about merit; partly from an awareness of popularity and esteem among readers and partly from an awareness of the place such items have in an overall picture. Historical fiction of the nineteenth and twentieth centuries is tackled – in separate chapters but the task is still formidable! The special contribution made by the time-slip novel is explored as are the ways in which writers use language to give authenticity to their historical stories. Two representative themes are tracked through a selection of novels: the question of child workers and the topic of migration. The historical picture book is discussed and problematised.

The central section is where authors have their say. All are active in the field and all alive, except for Rosemary Sutcliff whose contribution on 'History and time' (Chapter 13) we have been able to reproduce. A wonderfully rich picture of influences emerges – childhood reading, experiences, location, memories, documents. Common themes of openness to ideas, exercising control over the appetite for research and the awareness of ideology characterise the pieces and throughout the writers generously share the ways in which their stories come into being.

The final section concerns children and young people and their enjoyment of historical fiction in the classroom, on the stage, in their reading, writing, research and re-presentation. We meet primary-aged pupils working with some challenging texts in the confines of the ordinary classroom and some other children in the context of a school production, especially written for them, based on Mayhew's nineteenth century characters. We meet middle-school children working in an extended way over several months in a project that links English and history. We see how students in training grapple, through reading, reflection and role-play, with issues underpinning slavery. The perspectives aired by writers in the other sections find further expression here as well as practical application. In schools, teachers need to work with a whole range of genres in order to meet statutory requirements. Many teachers enjoy adult historical fiction and televised period dramas; they may not realise the wealth of fiction available for children nor how enjoyable the classroom experience of working with such books can be for all concerned. It is also exciting to appreciate what a powerful entry into historical understanding fiction can be. The message is clear that history in school need not be restricted to history course books. We hope this section will be inspirational and helpful.

Each chapter is prefaced by an introductory synopsis. Inevitably these summaries cannot do justice to the whole of the writers' arguments and ideas but we hope they help to indicate contents and whet appetites.

Inevitably, we send this book to press aware that we cannot cover everything. At the least, we hope we have raised the profile of historical fiction for children at a time when so much is available to be enjoyed. The combined expertise of the writers here gives us hope that the book will be appreciated by all and excite interest in the field so that new understandings can grow.

Contributors' biographies

Julian Atterton

Julian Atterton was born in 1956 and studied at the Sorbonne, Cambridge and the University of East Anglia. He is the author of five historical novels for readers of 11 and over, and of several stories for younger children, such as *The Shape-Changer* and *Robin Hood and the Sheriff.* He also works in schools as a storyteller and creative writing tutor.

Dennis Butts

Dennis Butts teaches on the MA course in children's literature at Reading University, and is a former chairman of the Children's Books History Society. He has written on various aspects of nineteenth century literature and children's books, including studies of Charles Dickens and Robert Louis Stevenson. He was Associate Editor of the Oxford *Children's Literature: An Illustrated History,* and editions of Francis Hodgson Burnett's *The Secret Garden* and Rider Haggard's *King Solomon's Mines* published by World Classics.

Fiona M. Collins

Fiona M. Collins is Principal Lecturer at University of Surrey Roehampton and coordinator of the Language Teaching Studies Area. Her research interests are in children's literature, popular culture and visual literacy. She contributed to the Roehampton Survey of Children's Reading (*Young Children's Reading at the End of the Century,* 1996) and to *Reading under Control* and *Writing under Control* (both David Fulton, 1998 and 2000 (second edition)) and co-authored *Reading Voices* with Philippa Hunt and Jacqueline Nunn (Northcote House 1997).

Berlie Doherty

Berlie Doherty was born in Liverpool and writes for adults and children. Her first book, *How Green You Are*! was published in 1982 and she has been a full-time, compulsive writer of novels, stories, poems and plays ever since. Her books have been translated into 21 languages and have won many awards, including, twice, the Carnegie Medal for *Dear Nobody* and *Granny Was a Buffer Girl.* Many have been adapted for television, radio and stage both by herself and by other dramatists. She lives in Edale in the Peak District, where she spends her spare time walking and day-dreaming. She has travelled extensively both in Great Britain and in Europe, Australia, America and Asia to work with children in schools and to speak and perform in festivals and conferences.

Andrea Fellows

Andrea Fellows is a deputy head, classroom teacher and literacy coordinator at Linton Heights Junior School in Cambridgeshire. The piece in the book is her first foray into writing in the public arena. Having taken an MEd at the (then) Institute of Education in Cambridge, she returned to take further short courses and it was on one of these that she shared the work she was doing with historical fiction.

Michael Foreman

Michael Foreman has written and illustrated a vast range of books and has collabo- rated with many leading children's authors. His own books include *War Boy* and *War Game*, both winners respectively of the Kate Greenaway Medal and the Smarties Book Prize. His other titles for Pavilion include *Billy The Kid, Michael Foreman's World of Fairy Tales, Michael Foreman's Christmas Treasury* and he illus- trated the American classic, *The Wonderful Wizard of Oz*.

Geoff Fox

For many years, Geoff Fox taught English and drama at the School of Education, Exeter University, where he is now an Honorary Research Fellow. He has also taught on numerous occasions in North America, Brazil, Australia and mainland Europe. Currently, he collaborates in running courses in Eastern Europe using drama, storytelling, poetry and picture books in enhancing the learning of English as a second language. He has written extensively on books and young readers and, for more than 30 years, has edited the international quarterly, *Children's Literature in Education*.

Judith Graham

Judith Graham is Principal Lecturer at University of Surrey Roehampton and has teaching commitments too at the School of Education in Cambridge. Her interests and teaching are in all areas of literacy and children's literature. She is the author of *Pictures on the Page* and *Cracking Good Books* (NATE 1990, 1997) and co-editor (with Alison Kelly) of *Reading under Control and Writing under Control* (both David Fulton, 1998 and 2000 (second edition)).

Linda Hall

Linda Hall established the MA in Children's Literature in Wales at Trinity College, Carmarthen in 1994, where the previous year she had pioneered the first Welsh MA in Women's Writing. She is the author of two books on poetry: *Poetry for Life: A Guide to Teaching Poetry in the Primary/Middle Years* and *Tracing the Tradition: An Anthology of Women Poets* – both published by Cassell. She writes and reviews for the journals *Children's Literature in Education* and *The Use of English*.

Alun Hicks

Alun Hicks is a freelance advisor for English. After ten years as the Head of the English department in a secondary school, he worked as an advisor for English in Dorset. Currently he is a researcher in Media Education for Southampton University, and acts as external moderator for Exeter University PGCE English course. He frequently acts as a consultant for QCA and was joint author of the QCA publication for secondary schools, *Improving Writing at Key Stages 3 and 4*. In collaboration with Dave Martin, he has published a number of articles on teaching historical fiction.

Peter Hollindale

Peter Hollindale retired in 1999 as Reader in English and Educational Studies at the University of York, and is now a freelance writer and presenter of children's literature and drama. He has published widely on children's literature and Shakespearean drama, and is a recognized authority on J. M. Barrie, having produced editions and critical studies of the 'Peter Pan' texts. His most recent book is a study of the terminology of children's literature criticism, *Signs of Childness in Children's Books*.

Gillian Lathey

Gillian Lathey was for many years an infant teacher in a north London school before joining the Education Faculty of University of Surrey Roehampton. She is now Deputy Director of the National Centre for Research in Children's Literature at Roehampton and has particular interest in the translation of children's literature.

Liz Laycock

Liz Laycock is Principal Lecturer in Education at University of Surrey Roehampton where she was Coordinator of Language Teaching Studies for many years. She has taught undergraduate, postgraduate and MA courses. She contributed to *Reading under Control, Writing under Control* and *The Literate Classroom* all published by David Fulton. Her interest in literacy has resulted in several books for Scholastic and children's literature, and literature's place in children's lives has remained an interest for her throughout her career.

Dave Martin

Dave Martin is a freelance adviser for history. After 13 years classroom experience teaching history in a range of secondary schools, he worked for 10 years as Senior Adviser for history in Dorset. Currently he undertakes a mixture of consultancy work for government agencies, advisory work for schools and LEAs and he also carries out school inspections. He is involved in development work on ICT and historical fiction in the teaching of history. In collaboration with Alun Hicks, he has published a number of articles on teaching historical fiction. He is also the author/co-author of a number of history textbooks published by John Murray.

Philip Pullman

Philip Pullman's writing career grew out of the time he spent as a teacher in the late 1970s. He wrote plays for his pupils to perform and it was from one of these that *Ruby in the Smoke*, the first of his historical novels, emerged. More teaching and several books followed and then in 1995 came *Northern Lights*, the first of the now complete trilogy, *His Dark Materials*. These intense and dramatic stories, recipients of several prizes, have firmly established Pullman as a master storyteller.

Rosemary Sutcliff

Rosemary Sutcliff was born in 1920 and died in 1992. From a very early age, she suffered from Still's disease, a poly-arthritic condition that prevented her from completing more than a few years of schooling. Her many historical novels are regarded as one of the most significant contributions to the genre. She is remembered particularly for her stories of Roman Britain but, whichever era she recreates, her regard for honour and loyalty and her interest in place and continuity are characteristics.

Liz Thiel

Liz Thiel is studying for an MA in Children's Literature at the University of Surrey Roehampton. A former newspaper journalist, she gained her first degree as a mature student at Kingston University. Her research interests are varied and include pony stories, children in industry and nineteenth century 'street Arab' stories.

Section 1
Exploring the narrative past

Chapter 1

Dogs and cats: the nineteenth-century historical novel for children

Dennis Butts

Dennis Butts tracks historical fiction's development in the nineteenth century back, in terms of events, to the French revolution and, in terms of writing, to Shakespeare's history plays and the eighteenth century novel The Castle of Otranto. *The major writers, both male and female, of the century are presented and, at the same time, Butts is able to show us how the novel moved from presenting history in somewhat indigestible form, with overt political or religious agendas and formulaic plots, to stories with more engaging juvenile heroes and more entertaining story-lines, such as we find in Robert Louis Stevenson.*

> It was the French Revolution, the revolutionary wars and the rise and fall of Napoleon which for the first time made history a *mass experience*, and moreover on a European scale.
> (Lukács 1969)

> The historical novel seems to fall into two distinct categories. You could call them the doglike and the catlike. The doglike is when the author deliberately looks back and makes his characters subordinate to his history. Generally such books are large and a shade ponderous, but helpful; and they never mind being put down in the middle. The second, or more catlike category, is when the author looks not back but about him and his history is subordinate to his characters. These books tend to be smaller, sleeker, and more self-contained. They don't aim to be particularly helpful, but, once picked up, they grip rather more and firmly resist being put down.
> (Garfield 1970)

As Georg Lukács has argued, the historical novel arose in the early years of the nineteenth century, around the time of the revolutionary wars and the rise and fall of Napoleon, when people began to see in history something which deeply affected their daily lives. Partly because of the spread of literacy and improvements in communications more and more people began to realise that public events and changes in government affected individual destinies (Lukács 1969).

Novels set in the past were to be found in the eighteenth century, of course notably in such Gothic fiction as Horace Walpole's *The Castle of Otranto* (1764), with their antique costumery and melodrama, and some children's writers drew on that tradition in their early attempts at historical fiction, such as we see in Barbara Hofland's *Adelaide; or the Intrepid Daughter* (1823). This tale, set in sixteenth-century France and England, tells of how young Adelaide, who is separated from her parents at the time of the Protestant persecutions, returns to Paris disguised as an English soldier. When some friendly nuns offer her a shelter, and then introduce her to a mysterious lady they have been sheltering for the last ten years, readers will not be surprised to discover that she is Adelaide's long-lost mother. All ends well when peace returns and Adelaide even finds her missing father. But despite the references to Henry IV and Queen Elizabeth, Mrs Hofland is more interested in telling her melodramatic and coincidence-driven story than in giving an accurate picture of the historical period, and the characters are all very much influenced by the time in which the writer was living.

With such novels as *Waverley* (1814), however, Sir Walter Scott not only depicted convincing characters within a realistic historical context, but also portrayed the complex relationships between the actual conditions of life as lived by individuals and the historical events which affected their daily lives. In *Waverley*, when young Edward joins his regiment in Scotland and gradually falls a victim to Jacobite intrigues, Scott develops a story which enabled him to depict the political struggles of eighteenth-century England and Scotland, and show the ways in which ordinary people were affected by a terrible civil war.

Although Scott is rightly regarded as the crucial influence on the rise of the historical novel at the beginning of the nineteenth century, it is also important to recognise the powerful impact of Shakespeare's history plays upon Scott and most historical novelists since him. For it was in that great cycle of plays on British history from *King John* to *Henry VIII*, particularly those dealing with the Wars of the Roses, that Shakespeare revealed that wonderful mixture of private and public worlds, with imaginary as well as real characters.

The towering popularity and influence of Walter Scott's novels in the nineteenth century gradually led to the rise of more serious, more credible, and more carefully-researched historical fiction. Edward Bulwer-Lytton (1802–73) led the way with such novels as *The Last Days of Pompei* (1834), and Dickens's *Barnaby Rudge* (1841) and Thackeray's *Henry Esmond* (1852) all helped to establish the form of the historical novel by the middle of the nineteenth century.

Although women writers, with the exception of Anne Bowman (1801–90), played little part in the contemporaneous rise of the children's *adventure story*, they made a considerable contribution to the development of children's *historical fiction*. This was probably because, while restrictions on their careers meant that most women could not compete with the exploits of such men as the sailor Captain Marryat (1792–48) or the soldier Captain Mayne Reid (1818–83), historical writing depended more upon reading and research than actually experiencing seafaring or military adventures.

Harriet Martineau (1802–76) was the first writer to bring Walter Scott's serious interests to children's historical fiction. Already a successful and respected authoress for her *Illustrations of Political Economy* (1832–34) and such children's stories as *Five Years of Youth* (1831), her early work tended to be too didactic. But there are signs of a more imaginative approach to children's literature in her collection of 1841, *The Playfellow.*

The Playfellow really consisted of four stories, published quarterly in 1841. One of them *The Crofton Boys* is in fact an early example of the school story. But the other tales *Feats on the Fiord, The Settlers at Home* and *The Peasant and the Prince* are historical. *The Peasant and the Prince* consists of two short stories set in eighteenth-century France, one an anecdote about the young Marie-Antoinette, the other a bleak account of the sad life of the Dauphin, who died aged ten in 1795. But there is more anger than history in these brief tales. *Feats on the Fiord* is an imaginative *tour de force*, however. Set in eighteenth-century Norway, the main story describes the adventures of Odda, a mischievous but brave herdboy, and Erica, a timid, superstitious maid, after Erica's lover Rolf disappears and the small rural community is threatened by pirates. The landscape of mountains and water is vividly realised, and in the treatment of Erica and her superstitious fears Harriet Martineau not only reveals insights into endurance under stress, but also successfully evokes the collision between an older folk-culture and a newer but dogmatic Christianity. *The Settlers at Home* is a *Robinsonnade* set in seventeenth-century England during the Civil War, and concerns the Linacre family who are Dutch refugees. They have settled on drained land in Lincolnshire, but are victimised by local people, and are caught up in the Civil War when some of the king's enemies open the sluices and cause a sudden flood. The young children become separated from their parents and are marooned on high ground. The situation becomes desperate and the baby dies, but the children survive the crisis with courage and ingenuity until they are eventually rescued. What is impressive about this story, told with taut narrative skill, is the way in which Harriet Martineau demonstrates the effects of the historical circumstances of the English Civil War upon the lives of ordinary, innocent, and apparently uninvolved individuals.

The history of the Civil War also helped to inspire what is arguably the first enduring historical novel written for children in the nineteenth century, *The Children of the New Forest* (1847) by Captain F. W. Marryat. This tells of the four Beverley children who are orphaned during the war after their father dies fighting for the Royalists. Marryat vividly describes how the children are taken into hiding in a cottage in the New Forest, where they are disguised as the grandchildren of a poor forester, and taught hunting, housekeeping and farming. Dramatic adventures follow as the four children escape capture by parliamentary troopers and their cottage is besieged.

Marryat's storytelling is not without faults. His grasp of dates and the ages of his characters is shaky in places, and his handling of the French political background is unnecessarily detailed. But the tale contains less moralising than the works of his predecessors as Marryat learned to express his ideas more dramatically through his characters. The children not only lose their parents but soon lose their elderly mentor, the forester Jacob Armitage. They have to learn to stand on their own two feet, and in the figure of Edward Beverley, a fiery, arrogant, persevering, sympathetic teenager, we may say that the nineteenth-century juvenile hero had arrived.

Marryat was also successful in relating the individuality and psychology of his characters to the historical circumstances of their age. Thus Edward Beverley and Mr

Heatherstone, the Parliamentary superintendent of the Forest, are both portrayed as individuals, but their conflicts mirror some of the acute problems of seventeenth-century England, the tensions between loyalty to the king and a sense of justice, for example. Marryat brilliantly succeeds in depicting some of the major events of seventeenth-century England by focusing his story on the events of the civil wars as they affect the private lives of a small group of individuals.

An unsuccessful Reform candidate for Parliament who had also served briefly during the 1839 Rebellion in Canada, Marryat is clearly sympathetic to the royalist cause, but is in fact hostile to the extremists on either side. While denouncing the regicides, he is unafraid to criticise the king's absolutism. Edward comes to realise that 'The king was obstinate, the people resolute, until virulent warfare inflamed both parties, and neither would listen to reason' (Marryat 1847 from Butts 1991). Wounded several times in his distinguished naval career, Marryat knew at first hand what war really meant. He was writing in the 1840s at the time of the Chartists, when Britain threatened to become two nations again and the whole of Europe was erupting in revolution. His novel, by contrast, expresses a movement from antagonism between two sides towards reconciliation, a movement suggested not only by Edward's gradual appreciation of the integrity of Mr Heatherstone, the moderate Parliamentarian, but also by Edward's marriage to Heatherstone's daughter Patience, which thus carries a powerful *political* as well as *moral* symbolism, as Marryat suggests the resolution of those self-destructive forces which threatened to engulf Britain in the 1840s as they had in the seventeenth century.

As well as by political controversy, England was also convulsed by religious controversy in the 1840s with the activities of the Oxford Movement, so it is not surprising that one strand of historical fiction for children derives its main inspiration from the impulse to propagate Christian values. Some children's literature had always done that right from such works as James Janeways' *A Token for Children* of 1671.

But writers began to appear who produced more substantial historical fiction in the interests of piety, such as Mrs J. B. Webb, whose *Naomi; or, the Last Days of Jerusalem*, was published in 1841. This story of the Roman conquest of Palestine and the destruction of Jerusalem focuses upon the lives of a Jewish family whose daughter Naomi eventually becomes a Christian, and it contains much detailed history about the Roman invasion and the dissensions of rival Jewish sects. But it is clearly written to attract 'the attention of the young and thoughtless to the wonderful fulfilment of the prophetic word of God' (Webb, Preface, 1841). Though less exotic, the historical novels of Mrs Emma Marshall (1830–99), such as *Under Salisbury Spire* (1890), are similarly pious.

Only Charlotte M. Yonge (1823–1901) really succeeded in animating this sub-genre of the historical novel, however. Famous for such adult novels as *The Heir of Redclyffe* (1853) and children's stories such as *The Daisy Chain* (1856), she also produced over a dozen works of historical fiction including *The Lances of Lynwood* (1855) and *Grissly Grisell – a Tale of the Wars of the Roses* (1893). Writing most successfully about the Middle Ages, Charlotte Yonge, in Suzanne Rahn's opinion, led to a radical rethinking of the historical genre by being the first writer to re-orient history from a child's perspective (Rahn 1991, pp. 1–26). While this may underestimate the achievements of earlier writers, such as Harriet Martineau and Captain Marryat, there is no doubt that Yonge was a novelist of distinction. *The Little Duke; or, Richard the Fearless* (1854) is one of her most enduring tales. Beginning in AD 943 at the Castle of Bayeux, the story focuses on a youthful hero, eight-year-old Richard, son of Duke William of Normandy, and is a tale about a boy growing up amid all the intrigues and violence of tenth century Normandy. When his father is killed, young Richard swears vengeance, but gradually learns not only how to survive in this brutal society but how to forgive his enemies. Although dated in some ways, Charlotte Yonge remains an impressive writer.

By the second half of the nineteenth century historical fiction for children was well established, so that even a successful writer of contemporary adventure stories R. M. Ballantyne (1825–1894), author of *The Coral Island* (1858), was tempted to work in the genre with *The Norsemen in the West or America before Columbus* (1872). But a near contemporary of Ballantyne, George Alfred Henty (1832–1902) was to challenge even Ballantyne's popularity by his distinctive brand of historical fiction in the last quarter of the nineteenth century.

Henty had been a successful journalist and war-correspondent, covering many campaigns and wars in Europe and beyond before publishing his first children's book *Out on the Pampas* in 1870. Henty published his second children's book *The Young Franc-Tireurs*, about two English boys caught up in the Franco-Prussian War, in 1872, and *The Young Buglers* in 1880, a story of the Peninsular War, which evidently gave him the idea for writing other historical novels (Arnold 1980).

Henty's historical fiction is of a familiar but distinctive kind. The plots are extremely formulaic and recur from one book to another, despite being set in different periods. The heroes are 'manly' boys of 14 or so, of no great social or intellectual distinction but endowed with a good deal of 'pluck'. After a crisis at the beginning of the story, perhaps the death of a parent, the young lad leaves home to repair the family's fortunes. He then survives a series of adventures, such as skirmishes, attempted kidnapping and imprisonment before a great culminating crisis, usually a major battle which is successfully won, before the hero returns home triumphant.

Henty's *With Clive in India; or, the Beginnings of Empire* (1884) is typical. It tells the story of 16-year-old Charlie Marryat who leaves home in Yarmouth after the death of his father to obtain employment as a civilian writer for the East India Company in eighteenth-century Madras. On the journey out he distinguishes himself fighting privateers, and then, on reaching India, volunteers for service with Captain Clive, the authentic historical figure, against the French. Charlie performs with distinction over the next ten years, seeing action in such battles as Arcot and Pondicherry. He rises from the rank of ensign to colonel, and returns home rich enough to become a country gentleman and member of Parliament.

Thus Henty's formula usually leads him to place his imaginary boy-hero in a historical situation of some importance, and then to interweave his adventures with those of known public events and personalities. Charlie Marryat not only meets Clive but survives 'the black hole of Calcutta'.

The tales are saturated with facts. Whether the story is set in Revolutionary America, as in *True to the Old Flag* (1885) or dealing with Napoleon's retreat from

Moscow as in *Through Russian Snows* (1896), Henty's books are full of historical, geographical and cultural information about the eras, the countries and especially the battles the hero lives through, sometimes with too many indigestible details, as in the long list of regiments involved in the Crimean Battle of Inkerman (Henty 1883).

Henty's historical range was considerable, ranging from his tale of ancient Egypt *The Cat of Bubastes* (1889) to stories about the contemporary history of the Boer War such as *With Buller in Natal* (1899). He had hoped to treat all Britain's major wars in his prolific career, and almost succeeded as such titles as *At Agincourt* (1897), *With Wolfe in Canada* (1887) and *One of the 28th: A Tale of Waterloo* (1890) indicate.

But whatever historical period he wrote about, whatever the sources of the hero's adventures, they undergo a process of Anglicanisation, and the hero, whether he is an Egyptian prince or a medieval squire, thinks and behaves like a middle-class English boy. Henty was not uncritical of aspects of British conduct, such as Clive's financial greed in India, but he was writing at the peak of British imperialism, and his endorsement of white (British) racial superiority, of social class and of gender-stereotyping has to be viewed from a historical perspective. Henty's stories, whether of Empire or otherwise, are of greatest value for what they tell us not of Roman times or eighteenth-century India but of the late nineteenth century when Henty wrote them. They reveal what late Victorian males made of the past and how they wished to interpret it.

Compared with the solid, densely-packed works of G. A. Henty, the historical novels of Robert Louis Stevenson (1850–94) superficially seem 'catlike' in Leon Garfield's terms. Such novels as *Treasure Island* (1883) and *Kidnapped* (1886) are particularly striking for the vivid, almost poetic episodes which seem to embody a character, a thought or an emotion, such as Ben Gunn's ghostly song amidst the trees, or David Balfour's misery when, shipwrecked on the isle of Erraid, he cries for help and hears himself laughed at.

But, like Henty, Stevenson used many of the elements of the popular romance structure in his adventure stories. The young hero, whether Jim Hawkins or David Balfour, loses his father, leaves home, has a series of exciting encounters and returns safe and prosperous. But Stevenson varies this predictable pattern in unexpected ways. He reveals a good deal of prehistory in *Treasure Island*, for instance, he tells the reader about Captain Flint and the events which led up to the treasure being buried on the island. On another occasion, he transforms the traditional magic of traditional tales into realistic features, as when, in *Kidnapped*, Alan Breck gives David the silver button as a kind of passport through the Highlands. Most strikingly, of course, Stevenson introduces variety into his stories by his moral reversals, by revealing an apparently loyal crew as murderous mutineers, or by exposing David Balfour's uncle as a murderous hypocrite.

But Stevenson was also a historical novelist, deeply interested in Scottish history. In 1881 he actually applied for the Professorship of History at Edinburgh University, and in dealing with the Appin Murder of Colin Campbell, the 'Red Fox' in *Kidnapped*, he was dealing with powerful historical material.

Despite the Act of Union of 1707, which tried to combine England and Scotland into a United Kingdom, many Scots continued to support the House of Stuart and the Jacobite cause. There were numerous risings against the British government, most famously in 1745 with Bonnie Prince Charlie being defeated at the Battle of Culloden a year later. The British government then took punitive measures against Scotland, depriving the rebel chiefs of their lands, forbidding the wearing of kilts, settling loyal troops in the villages, and even trying to ban the playing of bagpipes.

Stevenson is concerned with depicting the state of Scotland six years later, with the clans helpless and humiliated, and much poverty and hardship. What he does most skilfully is to depict these events through the eyes of a non-sympathiser, young David Balfour, who is loyal to King George and the Hanoverian Succession but comes to admire the courage and loyalty of the Jacobite rebels. When he discovers that Alan is collecting money from the loyal Stewart clansmen, who have already been taxed by King George, he reacts generously.' "I call it noble," I cried. "I'm a Whig or little better; but I call it noble" ' (Stevenson 1886).

Stevenson does more than just depict historical events; he analyses them with political intelligence. For though Stevenson depicts the collapse of the Highland way of life, and shows great sympathy for its splendid heroic qualities and the loyalty of the clans, he also shows the weaknesses and contradictions of that system, in the bloodthirsty rivalry between the Campbells and the Stewarts, for instance. Although Stevenson admired many of the achievements of the clans, he does not glorify the past romantically, but sees the reasons for their decline and the inevitable nature of British development.

This is partly achieved by his depiction of the relationship between David and Alan, the other great variation Stevenson introduced into his traditional romance-structure. For Alan is no stereotypical faithful companion of folktale and legend, but a fully-rounded human being, heroic and gallant, but also reckless and vain. He offers to carry the young David over the moors when he is too tired to walk, but does not hesitate to gamble his money away when David is sick. Stevenson's skill in handling the relationship is beyond praise, particularly in the magnificent chapters of 'The Flight in the Heather' when he shows the two friends exchanging heated insults and drawing swords on each other, and only then forced to recognise their fundamental brotherhood and love.

Yet, in depicting the two companions – David, young, Protestant, Whiggish, modest and slightly priggish, English-speaking (an almost surrogate-Englishman) and Alan, older, Roman Catholic, Jacobite, Gaelic-speaking, dashing and reckless – one wonders if Stevenson is not also articulating some of the socio-political tensions between England and Scotland in the eighteenth and nineteenth centuries. Is the tension in the love-hate relationship between David and Alan a reflection of Stevenson's sense of the relationship between Protestant England and Jacobite Scotland?

Stevenson's *Kidnapped* showed what the historical novel could do at its best, and it is perhaps appropriate that it appeared in the last decades of the century which gave birth to historical fiction for children. The Gothic Novel's melodramatic way of dealing with history, and the production of historical fiction for religious reasons gradually declined in the century's closing years. But the writing of historical novels continued. Herbert Strang, the pseudonym of the collaborators Herbert Ely

(1866–1958) and James L'Estrange (1867–1947) continued the tradition of quasi-doglike fiction into the early years of the twentieth century with such books as *Lion-Heart, a story of the reign of Richard the First* (1910). But the poetic catlike tradition of historical fiction was to rise to even greater heights in the magical tales *Puck of Pook's Hill* (1906) and *Rewards and Fairies* (1910) by Rudyard Kipling (1865–1936).

References

The children's books referred to in the above chapter (by title, author and date of publication) amount to too many to be included here in the references. Full bibliographic details are found in some of the references listed below and also on several of the web sites devoted to children's literature.

Arnold, G. (1980) *Held Fast for England: G. A. Henty: Imperialist writer.* London: Hamish Hamilton.

Butts, D. (1991) 'Introduction' in Marryat, C. (1991) *The Children of the New Forest.* Oxford: Oxford University Press.

Garfield, L. (1970) 'History, heavy and light', London, *The Guardian*, October 1.

Henty, G. A. (1883) *Jack Archer: A tale of the Crimea.* London: Sampson Low, Marston.

Lukács, G. (1969) (translated by Hannah and Stanley Mitchell) *The Historical Novel.* Harmondsworth: Penguin Books.

Rahn, S. (1991) 'An evolving past: The story of historical fiction and non-fiction for children,' in *The Lion and the Unicorn,* **15**(1), 1–26.

Stevenson, R. L. (1886) *Kidnapped.* London: Cassell.

Webb, J. B. (1841) *Naomi; or, the Last Days of Jerusalem.* London: Ward Lock.

Chapter 2

The twentieth century – giving everybody a history

Fiona M. Collins and Judith Graham

The published output of children's books in every genre grew decade by decade in the twentieth century. The historical novel was no exception, though the first third of the century produced nothing much that has lasted and was indeed still dominated by the writers of the nineteenth century. But this was to change and, as we write, the sheer number of children's authors, in all countries, who have been attracted to the form, the stretch of history covered, say, from sixth century Byzantium (and earlier) to the Tiannamen Square massacre (and later), and the critical acclaim and number of awards that the genre has received provides an abundance of material and viewpoints which might be adopted when attempting an overview. To do justice to the field is difficult.

In this chapter, we have decided that the twentieth century can best be characterised by considering:

- *the move away from the romantic, heroic, general and idealised and towards the realistic, domestic, miniature and ordinary;*
- *the ways in which women and girls have entered historical fiction as important characters; and*
- *the way in which language is used.*

From the elevated to the everyday

Exciting things began happening to historical fiction in the twentieth century but not, in the UK at any rate, until the mid 1930s when Geoffrey Trease began his long writing career. He is credited with writing the first significant stories which brought together four qualities which we now take for granted in historical fiction: an absorbing story; unclotted language; accurate research; and a concern with how ordinary people were affected by the political and social climate of the time. Gone was the glorification of war, the preoccupation with the upper classes, the racial superiority assumed for the young British gentleman. When *Bows Against the*

Barons (1934) and *Cue for Treason* (1940) appeared, the focus on how peasants, farmers and other ordinary folk fared under and outfaced the rulings of their over-lords suddenly gave historical fiction a new lease of life. It is almost as if Geoffrey Trease asked himself,

What was the texture of life for a young boy or a young girl in past times? What was their relationship with the land, with the world of work, with their parents, with those of their own class and those in another class? How much freedom did they have and how much could they create? How did they react – to laws, to injustice, to political upheaval, to opportunity and to risk? How did they feel when called to defend or leave their country?

Geoffrey Trease went on writing historical fiction for the next 60 years and his many titles live up to his ambition to tell historical stories that create a sense of the past through the lives of the usually unsung members of society. We shall use some of these hypothetical questions that he might have asked to further sub-divide this section.

War: passion and compassion

Writers for children appeared encouraged by Trease's achievements and, by the late 1940s, Rosemary Sutcliff was being published. Her natural inclination was to write in the heroic style and it is quite possible that she would have been closer in style to the much earlier writers of the century without Trease's example of what could be done by exploring the lives and views of the common man and woman as they are caught up in history. One of her particular qualities that, in its turn, has been influential, is her ability to problematise issues to do with war. Her several books about Roman Britain, of which *The Eagle of the Ninth* (1954) is probably the best known, show the reader the complexities and ambiguities of invasion and occupation. Uncomplicated support for one side or another was from now onwards not characteristic of the historical novel.

Johnny Tremain (Esther Forbes 1943), often regarded as a 'classic', is set in 1773 at the time of the American War of Independence. It was published and awarded the Newbery Medal before the mid-point of the century. It follows the fortunes of Johnny, not in the battle but from the sidelines where injury has placed him, reducing his opportunities for glory but thereby sensitising him. The novel nevertheless shares with Sutcliff a respect for the sacrifice of those who die, whichever side they are fighting on.

The Second World War has been visited and re-visited in books for children since the 1950s, several of which are mentioned in the next section. Mostly they strive for a more realistic and less flag-waving view of conflict. As well as books written in the English language, several books about the Second World War have been translated from German for the English speaking market. *Friedrich* (Richter 1961) was the first West German children's novel to tell the story of the Jews during the Third Reich. The story of a young Jewish boy, living in Germany, in the early 1930s, is told through his nameless friend's eyes. The story is linked with the edicts that were passed against the Jews during this time as they affect both of these children. The reader is given a most vivid picture of the mistreatment that was suffered by the Jews and of 'the fear of getting involved and the indecisiveness and inactivity of the German population' (Lathey 1999).

Of novels for children about war and conflict other than about the World Wars of the twentieth century and of the many wars before that, two are worth considering in a little more detail. Lynne Reid Banks uses her personal experiences of living in Israel to great effect in *One More River* (1973) in which she includes descriptions of the Six Day Israeli War in a story of Leslie Shelby, newly arrived in Israel from Canada. Within the story, the two opposing sides are linked by the delicate friendship that develops between Leslie and a young Palestinian boy. *Gulf* (Westall 1992) gives the reader different perspectives on why the recent Gulf War was fought. The story, narrated by Tom, tells of how his younger brother, Figgis, develops telepathic communications with a young Iraqi soldier, Latif. Through taking on the persona of this young soldier, Figgis tells his brother of the young soldier's fears and distress in having to fight at such a young age. Through Figgis, Latif voices the Iraqi side of the conflict. 'The Americans want to eat up the whole world. All the oil, rubber, tins. So they can sit with four cars in each garage.' The brothers' parents reflect British views about the war. The father is gripped by the war and watches the build up on television nightly while the mother takes a more gentle, compassionate stance.

> 'Anyway,' said dad, in a softer, making-it-up sort of tone. 'It won't be our lads that'll get killed. We'll bomb them to bits before we send our lads in.'
>
> 'Bomb them to bits?' Mum went up like a rocket again. 'Don't you think that Iraqi soldiers have mothers as well? Or do you think they're made out of metal, like Daleks?'
> (Westall 1992)

Westall illustrates how easy it would be to think of war as a game, with no acknowledgement of the loss of life that would occur. Although both parents are stereotypical in their representation, through their arguments, Westall succeeds in opening up different views for the young reader, presenting a 'politicised and distinctly non-populist stance' (Fox, in Meek 2001).

Surviving

Surviving is clearly a central part of stories about war but it also features strongly in many historical novels for children, not only because of its basic overriding importance but also because the effort to survive in difficult conditions provides many an adventure. Jan, in *The Silver Sword* (Serraillier 1956), rascal though he is, is essential to the survival of Ruth, Bronia and Edek. Life has taught him necessary canniness and cunning that, up to this point, has not been necessary for the more comfortable Balicki family. He has his antecedents in the children of a different age: 12-year-old Smith in Garfield's novel of the same name (1967) survives (by the skin of his teeth in this nerve-wracking thriller) by sly pickpocketing; Jim Jarvis in *Street Child* (Doherty 1993) also lives a hand-to-mouth existence on the nineteenth century streets of London until he encounters Dr Barnardo; the three children in the New Zealand writer John Lasenby's novel *The Mangrove Summer* (1988) have to survive in the wilderness to which they have decamped, convinced that they are in danger during the volatile times of 1941. Survival, along with the resourcefulness it necessitates, is a focus of interest in many a migration and pioneering story.

Physical survival is one thing. Emotional survival is also significant as people find themselves cut off, exiled, evacuated and generally in places they would rather not be. Handicapped Drem in Sutcliff's *Warrior Scarlet* (1958) is exiled when he fails his ritual wolf slaying. An outcast from his tribe, his sense of self is at risk but the innate courage of the boy enables him to surmount his difficulties and even come to terms with his withered arm. Penelope Lively, in one of her historical books for younger children, *Boy Without a Name* (1975) supplies us with small and convincing details of the life of an orphan in the time of Charles I who has to look out for himself as no one else will. Willie, in *Goodnight Mr Tom* (Magorian 1981) has to grow to mental and physical health after his traumas during the World War II bombing of London and he recovers under the care of 'Mr Tom'. *Sarah, Plain and Tall* (MacLachlan 1985), a very popular novel awarded the Newbery Medal, is the story of a mail order bride who, having travelled out west to the prairies, has to survive emotionally while her heart longs for her Maine homeland and people left behind. Frequently, in historical fiction, mental, physical and emotional survival go hand in hand as the individual sets challenges for him or herself or is driven by circumstance to overcome adversity which arrives in so many different forms in the historical novel.

Growing to political awareness

Ever since Dickon was unjustly whipped by the bailiff in the opening chapter of *Bows against the Barons* (Trease 1934), historical novels have brought issues of social and political justice to the fore. Stories where the rich and powerful exploit the poor in order to line their own pockets have an impact on child readers for whom social justice is a high profile issue. Nowhere is this more apparent than in the stories of slavery which are the topic of Chapter 17 in this book. Geoffrey Trease's more direct descendants are discussed below.

Three novels group themselves around the subject of the highland clearances in Scotland in the first half of the nineteenth century. Land was wanted for sheep-grazing at this time and the rich, the law and the church combined to evict the people from their homes and land. Allan Campbell McLean's *Ribbon of Fire* (1968), Iain Crichton Smith's *Consider the Lilies* (1970) and Mollie Hunter's *A Pistol in the Graveyards* (1975) all have a similar background and tell the stories of men and women as they come to realise and resist the ways in which they are being treated. Peter Carter's novel *A Black Lamp* (1973) set in the iron forges of early nineteenth century Lancashire, Robert Swindells' *A Candle in the Night* (1974) about children working in the coal-mines of Yorkshire 150 years ago and Susan Price's *Twopence a Tub* (1975), which has a similar setting, are three unflinching stories of young boys and men who grow to political awareness through their experience of poverty and oppression in some of the most appalling work conditions.

The change in the lives of ordinary people, as they leave the land and start to manufacture goods in the mills, mines, factories and workshops of the industrial world, has given us such novels as *Granny was a Buffer Girl* (Doherty 1986), *The Rope Carrier* (Tomlinson 1994) and *A Chance Child* (Paton Walsh 1978). Katherine

Paterson's *Lyddie* (1991), about a Vermont girl's efforts to rescue her family from poverty and gain independence by working in the mills of Lowell, Massachusetts in 1843, is notable for the way in which the reader's political awareness grows with that of the main character.

This achievement is characteristic of the best of historical fiction. Recent titles keep our consciousness raised. Henrietta Branford's *Fire, Bed and Bone* (1997) tells her tale of the Peasants' Revolt of 1381 through the first person narrative of an unnamed dog who lives with the focus family and Jonathan Croall's *Sent Away* (1993) tells of those children, sent to Australia to start new lives after their Second World War experiences, who were in fact exploited and seldom reunited with their families.

Young people in and out of their families

Setting the fortunes of families against the events of history is the basic structure of much historical fiction. The Laura Ingalls Wilder stories discussed later revolve around family; indeed, it is Laura's family security that enables her to endure great physical hardship and respond to ever new challenges. The Logans in Mildred C. Taylor's trilogy (which starts with *Roll of Thunder Hear My Cry* (1977) and is set in the Mississippi of the 1930s) are a proud and dignified family who struggle together at their different levels in the face of the oppression and racial bigotry they encounter. Families who migrate together (see Chapter 8) such as Judith O'Neill's in *So Far from Skye* (1992) need each other to survive. This story of migration to Australia after the failure of the potato crop on the Scottish island of Skye draws on records kept by the author's family. Judith Kerr's novels, starting with *When Hitler Stole Pink Rabbit* (1971), also draw on first-hand experience of her family's escape from Nazi atrocities and subsequent life as refugees. Their family unity enables survival. Dorothy Edwards' *A Strong and Willing Girl* (1980) gives us the story of ten-year-old Nan who is chief breadwinner for her family, supporting them through her work as a servant in Victorian times.

Both Barbara Willard and K. M. Peyton are interested in the portrayal of social inequalities, and in their work they frequently raise questions about differing value systems. Both writers have written what might be called family 'sagas': a series of novels in which the fluctuating fortunes of families are the focus. K. M. Peyton's 'Flambards' books (1967 onwards, popularised on British television) are notable for their independent women and non-stereotyped male characters. These stories, set pre- and post-World War I, reveal Peyton's interest in social and class differences which was to surface again in her later titles which she sets mostly in the nineteenth century. Willard's 'Mantlemass' novels exemplify the way in which a writer can give the reader an account of the ordinariness of daily lives, touched but not dominated by the great events of the time.

The other side of the coin to these family stories, where essentially the home, however needy, stressed or restrictive, still functions, are the stories of families that neglect and abandon their children. Two stories, *Ask Me No Question* (Schlee 1976) and *Coram Boy* (Gavin 2001) expose true stories of child abuse and cruelty. An outbreak of cholera in 1849 at Bartholomew Drouet's workhouse school killed 180 children. Drouet was tried but acquitted of neglect. Ann Schlee tells this sad true story through her heroine, Laura, who cannot make her superiors believe her appalling stories. *Coram Boy* tells the tale of one boy at least who survived the 'dying houses' which Thomas Coram strove to eradicate by opening his hospital in 1741.

Girls and women come into their own

If the historical novel in the twentieth century aims to convey the texture of the lives of ordinary people living either in extraordinary or ordinary times, it follows that the lives of women and girls start to figure more prominently. And this is indeed the case. But not immediately. As we have seen, it took time for the nineteenth century to loosen its grip. If the British child was still reading the novels of Henty, Kipling and Stevenson in the early years of the century, the American child was being offered books such as the 'Little Maids' series by Alice Turner Curtis (*A Little Maid of Old Philadelphia*, 1919) which honoured girls' roles in the Revolutionary War. Curtis also wrote the 'Yankee Girl' series, set during the Civil War.

But of greater quality and ultimately of more impact were the novels that started to emerge that followed the lives of ordinary American women. Rachel Field's *Hitty, Her First Hundred Years* (1929), memoirs of an independent minded wooden doll and her owners, and her *Calico Bush* (1931), the story of strong, resourceful Marguerite Ledoux, who travelled, in 1743, from France to be an indentured servant of a Massachusetts' family in Maine, have strongly drawn female characters though we may now blanche at the author's representation of indigenous people. Elizabeth Coatsworth's *Away Goes Sally* (1934), moving house, literally, from Massachusetts to Maine, and Carol Ryrie Brink's *Caddie Woodlawn* (1935), Wisconsin frontier life in 1864, based on her grandmother's memories, were all casting the historical novel less in heroic and more in the personal style and giving women a place in the accounts. The most lasting of such historical stories are those written by Laura Ingalls Wilder, the first of which is *Little House in the Big Woods* (1932). Seven semi-autobiographical books tell of the family's pioneering and settling experiences from the perspective of curious and spirited Laura. The books could be said to have brought pioneering to life for child readers. The 'Little House' stories describe how ordinary people, who struggle through life, can maintain dignity and strength through times of hardship.

Rahn (1991) argues that feminism was a significant factor in this tendency to feature strong girls as the central character. These women writers, 'born into the first emancipated generation, established a claim through fiction to a place in history which textbooks were not to recognise for another forty or fifty years' (Rahn 1991). The trend continued. Elizabeth George Speare, in *The Witch of Blackbird Pond* (1960), writes the story of 16-year-old Barbadian girl, Kit Tyler, who rebels against the restrictions of life with Puritan relations in Connecticut and befriends an outcast Quaker woman which brings accusations of witchcraft against her.

The Newbery prize was awarded to several of these titles. In 1961, it was awarded to *Island of the Blue Dolphins* (O'Dell 1960), a moving survival narrative based on the real story of the Lost Woman of San Nicolas. Karana, a young Native American Indian girl tells of how she wishes to avenge her brother's death by killing the wild dog who has ravaged him, but she has a dilemma: as a woman in her society she is not allowed to make weapons. 'As I lay there I wondered what would happen to me if I went against the law of our tribe which forbade the making of weapons by women.' However, necessity pushes her to make the weapons in order to protect herself. O'Dell's fine writing helps the reader to understand the choices that Karana has to make, her strength of will and her genuine love for the island and its many animals. The book takes the reader back to a pre-industrialised time through the many Native American traditions and customs that are described, from the making of bows and arrows, to collecting and drying abalone and making a shirt from cormorant skins.

In the work of Mildred Taylor (her first novel, *Song of the Trees* was published in 1975 but she is better known for *Roll of Thunder, Hear My Cry* which won the 1977 Newbery Medal) we are introduced to spirited young Cassie, and, through her, to some of the injustices meted out to black people in America. Wanting to fight back after the racial insults she endures, Cassie learns a hard lesson from her father that she has to balance her own hurt against the possible violent repercussions there may be for the whole community. In the end, however, there are times when she must stick to her beliefs and convictions.

Across the Atlantic in Britain *Cue for Treason* (Trease 1940) was published. An exciting if unlikely story, set in Shakespeare's times, the main characters are thought-ful young Peter and a strong young girl, Kit, who has to masquerade as a boy to take girls' parts on stage. ('Do you know, you're the first boy who hasn't murdered that speech?' Shakespeare compliments her.) Together these two foil a plot against the Queen. Trease reveals something of Elizabethan attitudes to women as well as intro-ducing a strong and feisty female character into the story.

After the Second World War, it became common to find writers including girls and women in their stories. In the first highly respected book about the war, *The Silver Sword* (1956), Ian Serrailler tells the story of three Polish siblings, who with the waif Jan, travel across Europe trying to find their parents who have been taken away by the Nazis. Ruth, the eldest, is portrayed as a steady, intelligent, resourceful young woman. *Carrie's War* by Nina Bawden (1973), a very different and quieter book, signals in its title its focus on the experience of Carrie, evacuated with her brother Nick. Carrie has to remain tactful but strong during a difficult time and grows in our estimation as she resists the meanness and bullying of Mr Evans with whom she is billeted. Many another 'war' story in the twentieth century has focused on girls' experiences, including *The Little Riders* (Shemin 1963), *In Spite of All Terror* (Burton 1968), *When Hitler Stole Pink Rabbit* (Kerr 1971), *The Upstairs Room* (Reiss 1972), *Number the Stars* (Lowry 1989), *Stepping on the Cracks* (Hahn 1991) and *A Candle in the Dark* (Geras 1995). These titles speak variously of girls who have had to go into hiding, separate from their parents, re-establish lives in new countries, maintain friendships with those forbidden to them, conceal secrets, bear the unwanted effects of war and meet challenges which would be unimaginable in peace-time. Of course there are equally powerful novels about the Second World War which focus on boys and men but it is notable how many of those that are still read with interest are about girls' experience.

Two women writers at work in the UK in the 1960s and 1970s who wrote well of women and girls in the historical past are Hester Burton and Barbara Willard. Burton creates, in *Time of Trial* (1963), *In Spite of All Terror* (1968) and *To Ravensrigg* (1976), pivotal and thoughtful heroines in Margaret Pargeter, loyal to her imprisoned father, the orphan evacuee Liz and bereaved Emmie carrying on her father's anti-slavery mission. Barbara Willard's heroines in her 'Mantlemass' novels which cover the years between the death of Richard III and the end of the Civil War, are no less determined and principled, a 'formidable tribe, expecting no pity or excuses, tender and loving and much more clear-sighted than the men' (Meek 1980). Lilias Rowan, in *The Iron Lily* (1973) is nothing less than the Master of the iron foundry.

It will be apparent that many – but not all – of the writers mentioned so far are women. Scott O'Dell and Geoffrey Trease need now to be joined by Philip Pullman whose 'Victorian' trilogy, *The Ruby in the Smoke*, *The Shadow in the Plate* and *The Tiger in the Well*, (1985–91), follow the fortunes of Sally Lockart, as she involves herself in high adventure, the supernatural and growing social awareness. We should also recall *The Wreck of the Zanzibar* (1994), Michael Morpurgo's novel, centred on the diary kept by Laura as she endures the hard life on the Scilly Isles at the end of the nineteenth and beginning of the twentieth century. Two of the novels of the Greek writer, Alki Zei, *Wildcat under Glass* (1963) and *The Sound of the Dragon's Feet* (1979) explore the feelings of their girl heroines as they each face truths about their families.

The Canadian writer, Barbara Smucker follows, in *Underground to Canada* (1978), the perilous journey of two slave girls as they escape to freedom from slavery. Two other Canadian novelists, writing about very different periods, put women in the centre of their historical fiction. Jan Hudson tells the stories of strong Blackfoot women in *Sweetgrass* (1984) and in *Dawn Rider* (1990), and Kit Pearson writes, in *The Sky is Falling* (1990) and sequels, about Norah, sent to safety with her brother from occupied Holland but suffering nonetheless. Janet Lunn, another Canadian writer, has written a memorable time-slip *The Root Cellar* (1981) in which orphan Rose has to make a new life in Ontario but travels in time back to 1862 and the Civil War in America. Saving a relative enables her to return to the present-day more at ease with herself.

In *Tangara* (1960), the Australian writer Nan Chauncy explores Tasmanian history in a fantasy/time-slip novel in which Lexie, a contemporary nine-year-old meets Merrina from the early nineteenth century. With the coming of the white man, Lexie foresees the massacre of islanders. In the event, her brother Kent becomes involved, both as a victim and ultimately as a survivor. *Mathinna's People* (1967) continues Chauncy's concern for the original inhabitants of Tasmania. Ruth Park's time-shift novel *Playing Beatie Bow* (1980) has a 14-year-old heroine, Abigail Kirk, who spends a reluctant but ultimately rewarding year in the seedy Sydney slums of the nineteenth century.

Before we leave this section, two further points need to be made about women and girls as characters in historical fiction. Firstly, it may be argued that the further one goes back in history the less is known about any lives, and least of all those of women. Henry Treece, Rosemary Sutcliff, Ronald Welsh and others, who wrote about Romans and Vikings and other distant periods, certainly have few women playing any sort of roles. When Rosemary Sutcliff 'thumps the tub' and declares that 'history is people' (in Haviland 1973) she really does mean 'men', though her *Song for a Dark Queen* (1978) tells the rather violent story of Boudicca and there are one or two titles – *The Armourer's House* (1951) and *Flame-coloured Taffeta* (1986) for instance – which include girls. The reasons for the absence of female characters has less to do however with available evidence; after all, much has had to be imagined about these distant times anyway. Much more to the point, both Treece and Sutcliff were unable to shape their stories without the values that they lived by and that they had imbibed with their own nineteenth century reading. Lonely determination, male comradeship, growing to greatness, dying for one's country and one's beliefs – it was hard for Treece or Sutcliff to invest women with these traits. However, we need to remind ourselves that a writer such as Henrietta Branford, in *The Fated Sky* (1996), can paint a powerful picture of a young woman's life during Viking times. Branford allows us to find out about Viking life, events and experiences through skilfully letting 16-year-old Ran tell us the story of her growth to womanhood via terror, loss, hardship, love and resignation. The break away from the 'heroic tradition' with its inevitable male narrative viewpoint is undoubtedly one of the reasons why this novel is so fresh and riveting.

The second point to make is that, while all the women and girls in the novels mentioned above, tend to be unimportant people living in past times, sometimes witnessing famous people, sometimes being caught up in situations that we now, from our positions, can give names to – The Boston Tea Party, The Children's Crusade – there has also been a strong strand of writing about well-documented women. *Grace* (Paton Walsh 1991) tells the story of Grace Darling who, on 7 September 1838, with her father, rescued survivors from a shipwrecked paddle steamer. The book thus fits into Paton Walsh's own category of historical fiction being 'wholly or partly about the public events and social conditions which are the material of history' (Paton Walsh 1972). Paton Walsh's novel tells the well-known story of Grace's bravery in saving the men's lives; she also explores, with great insight, the resentment and downright hostility that Grace had to endure after the event from the local community. The whole is much more than a biography. Joan of Arc, Pocahontas, suffragettes, various queens, including Catherine the Great of Russia, are other heroines who have found their place in fiction of the twentieth century. But, in truth, the famous are far outnumbered by the humble and their stories.

There has been a distinct growth in the numbers of books that detail women's experiences and this may be, in no small measure, because women are using personal and family memories. There are still plenty of novels which rely on research and imaginative re-creation of an era and women's lives within it. Whatever the source, the writer's task is always to understand and balance the ideology of the time as far as women's roles in society were concerned and the view of women in the time in which he or she is writing. This is a difficult task in which a keen eye for research and an awareness of one's own preconceptions should always be at the fore to give a balanced view for the young reader.

Writing forsoothly

I try for a middle course, avoiding both Gadzookery and modern colloquialism; a frankly 'made-up' form that has the right sound to it...It is extraordinary what can be done by the transposing of a single word, or using a perfectly usual one in a slightly unusual way: 'I beg your pardon' changed into 'I ask your pardon'.

(Geoffrey Trease)

Writers of historical fiction have, through their use of language, a means not only of encoding a story as any novelist has, but also a means of suggesting the strangeness and distance of the past. Linguistic devices such as the use of 'thee', 'thou' and 'ye'; verb endings that are now only preserved in dialect or biblical language, such as 'dost', 'shalt' and 'hast'; variations in word order, now lost to modern English along with the loss of inflections ('took you out the chest?', 'Give me leave the child to kiss'); and numerous archaisms, double-barrelled, compound words, kennings ('whale-road', 'pity-pleading eyes') and slightly poetic/heroic phrases ('giver of gold', 'ten summers old') – these devices and many others signal the past and they have their uses. They may not be linguistically accurate or faithful to their times and they may be over-used and irritating and they can certainly be mocked and were as early as 1902, as we see in the passage that follows.

In the following passage, from *Five Children and It*, E. Nesbit pokes fun at 'pish-tushery', the language of 'historical romances'. Robert is attempting to join his brothers and sisters who have been granted their wish for a beseiged castle. Two long-legged soldiers in steel-caps approach him and Robert, realising that he has no chance of running away from them, stands still and awaits capture.

'By my halidom,' said one, 'a brave varlet this!'

Robert felt pleased to be called brave, and somehow it made him feel brave. He passed over the word 'varlet'. It was the way people talked in historical romances for the young, he knew, and it was evidently not meant for rudeness. He only hoped he would be able to understand what they said to him. He had not always been able to follow the conversations in the historical romances for the young.

'His garb is strange,' said the other. 'Some outlandish treachery, belike.'

'Say, lad, what brings thee hither?'

Robert knew what this meant, 'Now then youngster, what are you up to here, eh?' – so he said:

'If you please, I want to go home.'

'Go, then!' said the man in the longest boots; 'none hindereth, and nought lets us to follow. Zooks!' he added in a cautious undertone, 'I misdoubt me but he beareth tidings to the besieged.'

'Where dwellest thou, young knave?' inquired the man with the largest steel-cap.

'Over there,' said Robert; and directly he had said it he knew he ought to have said 'Yonder!'

(Nesbit 1902, p. 114)

These archaisms of vocabulary and grammar give Nesbit an enjoyable opportunity to satirise the language she associates with historical novels of the nineteenth century.

Twentieth century writers of historical fiction have not dispensed with the advantages of an altered language use to suggest a past age, what John Stephens calls 'defamiliarising devices' (1992), but there has been a noticeable avoidance of obvious archaisms, as if Nesbit's satire has been taken to heart. One guiding realisation seems to be that clear modern usage is essential at those points in the story where the plot and the historical information need to be conveyed without muddle.

Here is Cynthia Harnett, writing in the mid twentieth century (1959) about fifteenth century England and specifically about Caxton and the establishing of the 'new' printing techniques.

> I can print a hundred books in the time it takes a scribe to copy one. But a hundred books use a hundred times the paper, and paper has to be brought across the sea. There are paper-mills in Flanders, where I learned my printing; but none is made in England and the few reams stocked by grocers are soon swallowed up. Nowadays my press is idle half the time. (Harnett 1959)

Harnett keeps her language extremely accessible when she is conveying information such as this that must be understood if the historical context and story-line is to be followed. She reserves her defamiliarising language for such exchanges as greetings and courtesy remarks ('I am honoured', 'Ah, mistress, your pardon', 'If it would please you to go home') and for phrases, reminiscent of Shakespeare, that are strange in their word order but instantly clear in their meaning: 'Look not so scared, boy. I do but think aloud.' This sensible mixture of languages seems to be a solution to the age-old problem of keeping the story and the detail vivid but sustaining the illusion of a past time. Many successful novels have been written in the twentieth century with no particular modification of language but those authors who have steeped themselves in literature, documents and records of the period of which they are writing and who then allow cadences and echoes of those times to flavour their writing achieve something rather special. Rosemary Sutcliff and Jill Paton Walsh are clear forerunners in this respect, as, in their different ways, are Joan Aiken and Leon Garfield.

It is not only a sense of a past time that can be conveyed through different language rhythms, vocabulary and word order. As in all fiction, the speech of characters conveys their age, class, status, character, state of mind, country or county of origin and much else. Not least, a character's particular language can be a source of humour in stories that are often serious and sombre. Here is old Cemetery Jones in Robert Westall's *The Machine Gunners* (1975). Rather than the Anderson for shelter from the air raids, he takes his family to a tomb in the graveyard.

'Where are we going, Cecil, are you mad?'

'We're going to t'graveyard, woman.' Mrs Jones shrieked, but Cemetery Senior took her by the hand firmly and led her out of the Anderson, round the Cemetery Lodge and out among the tombstones. The guns were silent, the bells still chimed, the moon rode high, and the angels on the graves flickered white as they passed.

> A larger bulk loomed up: a marble block as big as a garage, with white ionic columns and marble urns on top. It had a huge bronze double door.
>
> 'The Irving Tomb,' announced old Cemetery, in his best undertaker's tones. 'Those doors is best bronze and three inches thick, and the marble's best quality and two foot thick. Stop a howitzer, that would.' He fished in his pocket and produced an elaborate bronze key which he thrust into the double door.
>
> 'But,' screamed Mrs Jones, 'what about them dead Irvings?'
>
> 'Moved them in with the Ibbotsons there months ago. People must learn to accept smaller accommodation in an emergency . . .'   (Westall 1975)

These characters may be in a tomb but they are 'alive, warm and tangible' as Geoffrey Trease says they must be (in Fox 1995). As with characters much further back in time, they need to speak in ways that are understandable but just sufficiently different to make the child reader realise that they are not of our time. The characters need to be able to throw an atmosphere around themselves and their readers, 'like a magic pavilion' (Trease in Fox 1995). Not to attempt echoes of distant times, with their different linguistic and rhythmic tunes, is to offer 'a threadbare carpet' (Joan Aiken's metaphor in Fox *et al.* 1976). We are fortunate that few writers this century offer their readers threadbare carpets.

Conclusion

> The first thing I noticed once I reached land was the space.
>
> It made me feel nervous. I'm a Londoner, used to safe, narrow streets, houses crowded nicely together, small rooms, dark passages, plenty of rafters, skirting boards, holes, drains, useful piles of this and that everywhere. This place had no boundaries, if you understand. No edges. I felt I could set off in any direction and just keep going, with no way of knowing why any place was different from the last.   (Hooper 1988)

The Diary of Watkin Stench, from which this extract is taken, is a rather splendid logical conclusion of the shift that has taken place throughout the twentieth century. Upheavals of one kind or another have always been the stuff of historical fiction but here we have an upheaval, seen from the point of view of a rat. The fact that Watkin Stench is a rat and that the diary kept is by him is, as we say, only a logical result of a process of democratisation that has enabled the flow of history to be experienced, recorded and reflected upon by the ordinary person. The narrative device here is extremely effective as rats live close to humans and are likely to be affected by similar occurrences; in this account, the rat convincingly records all the departures, hardships, fears, celebrations and mysteries that accompanied migration on a convict ship to Australia in 1788. In recording rat impressions, the life of the settlers is believably unfolded before us.

There is a case for hoping that we will go no lower than the rat as narrator in historical fiction. We end this chapter with a rather more sublime quotation from the American writer, Laurence Yep. He uses the phrase 'a child's history' where we have been using the history of the ordinary person, but the emphasis he puts on the shift that occurs when the view of history accommodates itself to its child readers, by focusing on the intimate and immediate is one that we believe has helped to make the historical novel a more accessible and enjoyable genre in the last century.

> Adult history thunders on a grand scale like a movie in Cinemascope but for all of its size it is still flat and its actors are like ants except for a few close-ups of the stars. On the other hand, a child's history is like a hologram that can be held in the palm quiet and small but three dimensional. It treats its subjects with an immediateness that makes them seem to live and breathe.
>
> (Laurence Yep in Silvey 1995)

References

Fox, C. (2001) Conflicting Fictions in M. Meek, (ed.) *Children's Literature and National Identity*, Stoke on Trent: Trentham Books.

Fox, G. *et al.* (eds) (1976) *Writers, Critics and Children*. London: Routledge.

Fox, G. (ed.) (1995) *Celebrating Children's Literature in Education*. London: Hodder and Stoughton.

Haviland, V. (1973) *Children and Literature: Views and Reviews*. New York: Scott, Foresman and Company.

Lathey, G. (1999) *The Impossible Legacy Identity and Purpose in Autobiographical Children's Literature set in the Third Reich and the Second World War*, Berne: Peter Lang.

Meek, M. (1980) 'The fortunes of Mantlemass' *The Times Literary Supplement*, 18 July.

Meek, M. (ed.) (2001) *Children's Literature and National Identity*, Stoke on Trent: Trentham Books.

Paton Walsh, P. (1972) History is Fiction, *Horn Book Magazine*, February 1972.

Rahn, S. (1991) An Evolving Past: The Story of Historical Fiction and Non-Fiction for Children, *The Lion and the Unicorn* **15**(1).

Silvey, A. (ed.) (1995) *Children's Books and their Creators, New York: Houghton Mifflin Company*.

Stephens, J. (1992) *Language and Ideology in Children's Fiction*, London: Longman.

Children's books

Only those children's books which are actually quoted from in the above overview chapter are included in the reference list that follows. All others mentioned in the chapter (by title, author and date of publication) can be found in the Title Index and Author Index.

Harnett, C. (1959) *The Load of Unicorn*. London: Methuen.

Hooper, M. (1988) *The Diary of Watkin Stench*. London: Lutterworth Press.

Nesbit, E. (1902) *Five Children and It*. London: T. Fisher Unwin.

Westall, R. (1975) *The Machine Gunners*. London: Macmillan Children's Books.

Westall, R. (1992*) Gulf*. London: Methuen.

Chapter 3

The silent ages: prehistory and Peter Dickinson

Peter Hollindale

Intrigued by the absence of books for young readers set in undocumented time, Peter Hollindale sets out to consider A Bone from a Dry Sea *and* The Kin *two books by Peter Dickinson. He traces influences on Dickinson's writing to William Golding, and even further back, to H. G. Wells. Through these connections, he illuminates all three writers. He reveals the exciting way in which Dickinson offers imaginative space to readers, rewarding them with enhanced understanding of their origins and animal natures, and an oppportunity to sense the enormity of time.*

In 1961 Professor Helen Cam wrote a paper called *Historical Novels* for the Historical Association. Near the end of a thoughtful and well-informed survey she wrote: 'There is no doubt that the generally high standard of fiction today corresponds with the widening field of history', and stressed the influence of 'research in archaeology and anthropology', (Cam 1961). Even so, her extensive bibliography of historical novels for both adults and children stretched no further back into undocumented history than two stories of the Bronze Age, Rosemary Sutcliff's *Warrior Scarlet* (1958) and part of Kipling's *Puck of Pook's Hill* (1906). Otherwise her list began, as one might expect, with ancient Greece and Rome.

Forty years on, the Western mindset is essentially the same. History, for most people, begins with the Graeco-Roman and Judaeo-Christian traditions. It accommodates archaeology but not palaeontology, and effectively begins four thousand years ago with the beginnings of modern 'civilization'. Even ancient Egypt is a marginal inclusion. The ages before that are rarely conceived as ancestral times; they are considered, if at all, as the province of biological science. Glyn Daniel and Colin Renfrew remind us that 'Prehistory deals with man and not with nature and is not part of the natural sciences...Prehistory is then a humanity; it is the earliest phase of historical study...Prehistory is part of human history' (1988).

Unsurprisingly, it is a part of human history which has not much interested historical novelists. The reasons are clear. Once past the Bronze Age in our retrospective journey – and the Bronze Age is on our historical doorstep – there is no documentation, no precise historical record, no language, nothing but an ever more sparse assemblage of bones and artefacts. Only a short distance into the past, we must engage with the fact of evolution, which a century and a half after Darwin and Wallace is still a provocative and unaccepted concept for many religious believers. In his novel *Healer* (1983) Peter Dickinson's main character, Barry, reports a confrontation with one of his teachers, Mr Elias, on just this question:

> 'I'd been reading in a magazine about evolution, about how when a new species starts to evolve somewhere, the same sort of thing happens other places in the world, no connection…but it was evolution I had the row about. I just mentioned the idea and Mr Elias blew up. It was like if I'd spat in his face or something.'   (Dickinson 1983)

The character Barry is speaking to, Mr Freeman, responds: 'New ideas are always seen as threats, especially by those whose profession it is to teach old ideas. You are threatening both their self-esteem and their livelihood' (Dickinson 1983). Later, in *A Bone from a Dry Sea* (Dickinson 1992), Dickinson showed this human trait not just among conservative teachers but scientific fossil-hunters, whose intellectual rigidity and careerist prudence combine to dismiss out of hand Elaine Morgan's sea-ape theory of human origins, on which the novel is based. Evolution, long after it has changed from theory to proven truth, continues to challenge humanity's sense of identity, and the standard strategy for coping with it has been to exclude it from history and assign it to scientific palaeontology. This is reflected in the record of historical fiction. The only writer for children who has made a significant attempt to demonstrate through story that 'prehistory is part of human history' is Peter Dickinson, in *A Bone from a Dry Sea* and *The Kin* (1998), and his mentor is one of the great innovative novels of the twentieth century, William Golding's *The Inheritors* (Golding 1955). Together they look, as Dickinson memorably put it in *A Bone from a Dry Sea*, 'through the lenses of time, right at the edge of imagination's eyesight'.

Golding's antagonist, in the intellectual contest underlying *The Inheritors*, was H. G. Wells, whose progressive view of evolution in his *The Outline of History* (Wells 1920) provides Golding's novel with its epigraph. Wells is a rationalist, and in his study of Golding Samuel Hynes compares their respective views: 'The two positions are essentially antithetical ideas of the nature of evil: the rationalistic, and the religious. Golding has used a view which he deplores as a foil for his own' (Hynes 1964). In considering Dickinson's two highly original excursions into fictional prehistory for children, it will be important to determine where he stands (as it might be between Wells and Golding) on the question of evolution and human progress, and I shall suggest that with admirable integrity he rejects short cuts and easy answers, and instead presents young readers with an unresolved ambivalence.

In a pessimistic late book, *The Outlook for Homo Sapiens* (1942), Wells himself sets out the revolution which modern palaeontology has produced (or should have produced) in our conception of time and human history. It is an excellent statement of the case for treating prehistory as history, and fictions of prehistory as historical fiction. Writing in 1942, he noted 'the modification of time values' as a striking difference between mid-twentieth-century humanity and its grandparents:

> By the measure of our knowledge their time-scale was extremely shallow. They had scarcely any historical perspective at all. They looked back to a past of a few

thousand years and at the very *beginning* of time, as they conceived it, they saw human life very much as it is now . . .

our historical imaginations, quite as much as our geographical imaginations, live today in a vastly enlarged system of perspectives. We know that the ever-lasting hills are not everlasting, that all our working conceptions of behaviour and destiny are provisional and that human nature and everything about it is being carried along upon an irreversible process of change. Our historical ideas reach back now through vistas of millions of years, we see humanity emerging from sub-human conditions, from the life of relatively solitary apes, at distances in the nature of a quarter of a million years, we know with increasing precision of the onset of a social hunting life in those distant ages.   (Wells 1942)

Both the time-scale and the biological self-image that we now inhabit are at once exhilarating and intimidating. Richard Leakey and Roger Lewin point to the collapse of our sense of *Homo sapiens* as a uniquely separate species:

the long-held notion that our ancestors were essentially human from the begin-ning of the human family has . . . crumbled. From the evidence of the fossil and archaeological records, and from data from molecular biology, we now know that, although the first human species evolved about 5 million years ago, the cher-ished attributes of an enlarged brain and technological ability did not appear until about 2.5 million years ago. For a long time in our prehistory, we were bipedal apes, and no more . . . From this perspective, *Homo sapiens* may be blessed with special traits, but we are not separated from the rest of the world of nature by an enigmatic gulf; we are joined to it by a succession of ancestors in whom these traits developed gradually.   (Leakey and Lewin 1996)

In the Preface to his study *The Palaeolithic Age*, John Wymer links this new dimension of historical time to the accelerating speed of change in our own:

All of us now die in a world far different to that into which we are born. It is little wonder that we should ponder on how it all started, and this means retracing the history of Man to the time when it becomes difficult to be sure whether we are really dealing with our own species.   (Wymer 1982)

These are the perspectives in which Golding and now Dickinson are working. *The Inheritors* (Golding 1955) explores the extermination of Neanderthal Man by Cro-Magnon Man, in Europe a mere 40,000 years or so ago. Dickinson's *The Kin* (1998) is set in Africa a notional 200,000 years ago. Its 'people' are clearly *Homo sapiens*, a little earlier than the date of 150,000 years ago that Leakey gives for their emer-gence. *A Bone from a Dry Sea* is placed in Africa a staggering four million years ago, with a conjectural and controversial imagining of humankind's earliest biological origins. The depth of years gives us imaginative vertigo. Twice in *A Bone from a Dry Sea* Dickinson touches on its physical effects. In the present-day half of the story, a palaeontologist called May Anna says 'I still wake up nights and think about all those years and my skin crawls', and later the book's young modern heroine, Vinny, says 'It makes my skin prickle, thinking about all that time' (Dickinson 1992).

For young readers Dickinson's fictions open up imaginative spaces, and are an important corrective to our historical parochialism. They offer three essential enlargements of experience. One is a personal sense of the unbroken bloodline which leads each one of us back to our ape-like distant grandparents, but for whose procreative success we would not be here. Another is the altered sense of time itself, as Wells described it. A third is the understanding that *Homo sapiens*, though undeniably a large-brained and ingenious animal, is still at root an animal like any other. Resistance to this truth dies hard, even among prehistorians, as Leakey and Lewin observe:

> Only in the relatively recent past have anthropologists begun to discuss human origins as they would the origin of oysters, cats, and apes. Nevertheless, a desire to maintain a boundary between us and our biological relatives can, even now, be discerned in some scholars' theories on human prehistory, particularly in the matter of the origin of modern humans, people like you and me.
>
> (Leakey and Lewin 1996)

The founding fictional text for this imaginative exploration is Golding's *The Inheritors*. Told almost to the end from the point of view of Neanderthal Man, it is partly a fable of the Fall, partly an imaginative reconstruction of a crucial point in the emergent dominance of modern humankind. Golding's Neanderthals are innocents, with a natural reverence for non-human life (they themselves *are* human), which precludes killing for food. Their religion permits them to take the leftovers of animal kills, because then 'There is no blame'. They are capable only of clumsy and elementary attempts at consecutive thought, and they have no language in our sense of the word. Instead they communicate by a telepathic exchange of 'pictures', joined to the very beginning of verbal sound. Golding resolves the problem of expressing the exchange of thoughts between virtually wordless people with great technical brilliance. Wherever possible he accompanies the Neanderthals' 'words' with actions and gestures, themselves implicitly expressive of the verbalised meanings, and he avoids the conventional 'said' in favour of 'spoke', varied by 'cried out', 'chattered' and other expressions plausibly indicative of 'speech' by a pre-verbal hominid. These are people at the very brink of language as we know it, and also at the edge of ratiocinative thought. When Lok and Fa, two of Golding's Neanderthal family group, find a rich food source at an inconvenient distance from their camp and fire, the intelligent Fa has a 'picture', fleetingly, of transplanting the nutritious vegetation so that it is nearer. She cannot 'hold' the thought, and it goes, but she is generating innovative ideas, and in this way is a prototype for Li in *A Bone from a Dry Sea* and Tinu in *The Kin*. Golding's Neanderthals, unlike Dickinson's sea-apes and Kin, are in a biological cul-de-sac, but both writers link potential survival and evolutionary change to the creative intelligence of mutant individuals, and this is one of many respects in which Golding's influence is evident.

The Inheritors is a major book. In their study of Golding, Kinkead-Weekes and Gregor suggest that 'nowhere in our literature has either the primitive man or the Natural Man been realized more imaginatively' (Kinkead-Weekes and Gregor 1970), and Hynes suggests that it satisfies Golding's own criterion for the point of writing a novel, namely that it does what 'you are pretty certain that nobody else has tried before' (Hynes 1964). Yet compared with the abundant fictional progeny of *Lord of the Flies* (Golding 1954), its influence has been limited, and transposing its achievement to children's literature has rested with Dickinson alone.

Kinkead-Weekes and Gregor suggest four ways in which *The Inheritors* can be read: as 'a fictional essay on prehistory', as a 'fictional *tour de force*, taking us to an otherworld and othertime that we enjoy for their own sake', as an allegory, and as an act of discovery, a displacement of modern consciousness through which Golding contrives 'to see things new, not merely to see new things'. Dickinson's two books can also be read in all four ways, though their methods are dissimilar and each makes compromises in order to be intelligible to young readers.

A Bone from a Dry Sea is closer to *The Inheritors*, but in some respects Dickinson's feat of atavistic imagination is even more daring, going back 4 million years instead of a mere 40 thousand. Vinny, the modern teenage child of a broken marriage, visits her father, a palaeontologist, on a dig in east Africa. Her story alternates with that of another girl, Li, living 4 million years ago in the same place, one of a community of sea-apes from whom humankind descended. The 'reality' of the prehistoric story is the subject of unorthodox and rejected theory in the modern one. Vinny's father summarises for her the zone of uncertainty in the fossil record of evolution.

> 'Well, about ten million years ago there were ape-like creatures, walking on four legs and so on, with just enough to show that they're probably our ancestors, and then there's a huge gap to about three-and-a-half million years ago when there are creatures something like us, with smaller brains than ours but walking on two legs and with jaws much nearer to ours and so on. Between those two points there's one doubtful tooth and one even more doubtful bit of jaw.'
>
> (Dickinson 1992)

Before her visit Vinny has read books recommended by her father and one that he did not recommend, Elaine Morgan's *The Aquatic Ape*, which suggests 'that we're really half sea-animals'. Vinny has found this 'really interesting'.

> 'The sea rose and there must have been an island which got cut off with a few apes on it, and they had to get most of their food out of the sea, so they learnt to walk on their hind legs and they lost their fur and used stones to crack shells open...'

From her father's reactions and those of his colleagues, Vinny soon finds, as Barry did in *Healer* (Dickinson 1983), that these new ideas are seen as threats to 'their [intellectual] self-esteem and their livelihood'. Meanwhile, the prehistoric story of Li enacts through imagination the 'truth' of the rejected theory.

The book's extraordinary achievement is its re-creation of this imagined prehistoric life. As in *The Kin*, with its more recent setting, Dickinson is impressively successful in representing plausible physical conditions for early life. He shows the tribe's precarious hold on existence, its meagre food-supply, the need for constant movement because food and fresh water do not exist in the same places, the asset-stripping economy of survival. Community, hierarchy, prestige and leadership are shown in action. They resemble in one direction the known behaviour-patterns of current animal species and in another the (hugely more sophisticated but still analogous) practices of modern human groups. Li's people are on the cusp of a new order of biological success, and we are their distant beneficiaries.

Li 4 million years ago and Vinny now are the key figures. In some ways Li is like Fa in *The Inheritors*. 'She had no words for [her new-found] knowledge. Thought and understanding were for her a kind of seeing' (Dickinson 1992). Unlike Golding, however, Dickinson is interested in successful progress. Li can organise her 'pictures' into a sequence, forming a temporal series of possible events, so at a very simple level she can theorise and predict. She can relate one 'picture' to another and make analogies based on observation. She is not only able but, more important, willing to diverge from the communal mind-store. In some respects Dickinson is obliged to make her unrealistically 'modern' in order to make her comprehensible, but only so that his readers can perceive that human evolution must be tied to single untraceable 'thought events' such as Li's.

Dickinson does not *inhabit* Li's mind continuously, as Golding does that of his Neanderthals for most of his story. He openly intervenes with a modern narratorial voice. ('Her head is the shock, tiny to our eyes, with a face more monkey than human. What room can there be in that cramped skull for thoughts, imaginations, questions, wonders, for all that makes us human? Can this be where we came from?') And the present-day plot is itself an intellectual commentary on the prehistoric one. But it serves a more complex purpose. The academic debate, professional competitiveness, fierce politics of leadership, desire for authoritative display, among the 'tribe' of modern palaeontologists are a contemporary equivalent of the tribal behaviour of Li's people 4 million years ago. Unknowingly, except to narrator and reader, they mimic the human primitives they are studying. The very search for bone fragments is itself a modern and luxurious counterpart of Li's people's search for food.

The comparisons mainly cluster on Li and Vinny, sisters across the epochs. Vinny's rebellious willingness to defend Elaine Morgan's heretical sea-ape theory – to defy the adult professional establishment, including her father – is a small modern counterpart of Li's willingness to discard her inherited mind-map. Vinny is lucky enough to discover significant bone-fragments which have not been previously seen, but as with Li (and with Ko in *The Kin*), her success allows Dickinson to both affirm and query the very concept of 'luck'. What we call 'luck' can be a strange compound of boldness, intuition, and lack of restrictive mental baggage – not fortuitous circumstance but personal quality. In both Li's world and Vinny's it is important enough for leaders to be eager to grab credit for it.

The parallel is left in no doubt. When Li in old times befriends the dolphins, bringing food to the tribe, the leader Presh must find a way of using her to enhance his own prestige.

> Watched in silence and alarm by the rest of the tribe he turned and raised her to sit on his shoulder... He was telling the tribe that he, Presh, Leader, had sent his niece Li out to ride in deep water with the dolphins... So he made her triumph into his triumph.

When Vinny has 'luck' with the modern-day fossil-hunt, the expedition leader, Dr Hamiska, does just the same. 'Without warning he bent and picked Vinny up and set her on his shoulder like a three-year-old', diverting her achievement to himself by treating her as a mascot. Across the millennia, huge biological, intellectual and cultural changes join in one instinctual continuum. When Nikki, an expedition member, draws Vinny:

> It showed a sort of ape-child sitting cross-legged and bashing a huge clam-shell...The body was half-way between ape and human, but the head was completely human, only too small.
> 'Is that me?' said Vinny.

And at the deepest level of biological history, it is Vinny, and every child. The human inheritance includes powerfully enhanced intelligence, but also destructive aggression (the violent outcast Greb in Li's world, military politics in ours) and hunger for power in both times. Dickinson is ambivalent. Like Wells, he shows us evolutionary progress; like Golding, the unchanging darkness of man's heart.

The four-part epic novel *The Kin* is very different in fictional method, but ideologically similar. Set a mere 200,000 years ago, its characters are all recognisably *Homo sapiens*, though the various groups of 'people' exhibit profound linguistic and cultural differences. As in the earlier novel, Dickinson powerfully re-creates the likely physical conditions for early life. A major volcanic eruption is a central event in both books, and the Kin – loosely connected sub-groups, somewhere between tribe and family, united by a shared culture – live a precarious nomadic existence on the plains, deserts and volcanic landscapes of prehistoric Africa. The Kin, each group named after a patron animal deity such as 'Snake' or 'Fat Pig', are largely peaceable groups with developed practices for intermarriage, developed rituals for celebration, praise and mourning, and a simple but thought-rich language. They have been evicted from their traditional 'Good Places' by murderous invasive groups of other humans, and on their odyssey they meet another group of 'demon people', who kill and rape, and prize the skulls of their victims. (Parallels with modern history are not signalled, but are there for readers to infer.) The Kin also meet human groups *without* language but still with developed wordless cultures. Their status is ambivalent. Unlike the 'demons' or killer-groups, they are not to be feared or despised, but the immensity of advancement tied to human language is still dramatically clear.

The Kin is both an imaginative re-creation of the life of early hunter-gatherers, and an allegory of human biological constancy across the ages. We follow the Kin called Moonhawk, and in particular five children. At the start the Moonhawk group, expelled to the wilderness by murderous incursions, have abandoned the four weakest of their small children. Two of the others, the boy Suth and girl Noli, desert the family group in order to retrieve these four from certain death. Of the six children one is a baby, but the other five become in turn the central figures in a story covering many years. Suth is the good leader, decisive, protective, resourceful and kind. Noli is the 'priestess', the chosen voice of Moonhawk, gifted with second sight – each of the Kin groups has one such figure. The boy Ko is the dreamer, the imaginer, the risk-taker, the insou-

ciant explorer. The girl Mana is, so to speak, the moralist and nurturer, the very opposite of the killer instinct which drives other human groups. Each of these four has his
or her own story, in which each special gift and viewpoint is the one that drives
Moonhawk forward – in its journey, and in its evolution. And then there is the fifth
child, Tinu, who is the equivalent of Li. Tinu is the thinker, the exploratory intellect,
the key to survival and change. She has no story of her own because she is indis-
pensable to all of them. Without Tinu, as without Li (and Vinny) there is no beneficent
evolution. The five together are the five keystones of desirable humankind.

If Tinu is always needed, Mana is finally crucial. At the end the demon people
have been defeated, and Mana, who has killed one of them, makes reparation by
adopting and mothering a surviving demon baby, whom they call Okern. (Okern's
adoption by Mana is Dickinson's reverse image of Cro-Magnon Man's 'adoption' of
the last surviving Neanderthal baby at the end of *The Inheritors*.)When an old
'demon man' attempts to seize him:

> Mana snatched him away. She was filled with sudden fury, fury at this fearsome
> old man, and all the demon men, and what they were – what they had allowed
> themselves to become. It had been their choice. The demon was theirs. They had
> chosen it.

But what of the baby Okern? Born 'demon', brought up by Mana's love in
Moonhawk's civilised care, what will become of him? 'Okern would one day
choose.'

The choices of prehistory are still those of modern children. The split personality
of Dickinson's 'people' is still evident in the evolved modern human group. The
mingling of blood, and of cultural blood, happens both then and now. Mana realises
that all are 'people', and so does Dickinson's reader. We are their kin, and if we
choose to be, their Kin. There is a difference, and a choice. Again the ambivalence
is there in Dickinson's creation. Like Golding, in opening up remote prehistory, he
opens up the present and the future. *The Kin* is intercut with the people's legends
of their origins, the stories through which they understand themselves, and
Dickinson's books, like Golding's, perform the same mythopoeic service.

References

Cam, H. (1961) *Historical Novels*. London: Historical Association.
Daniel, G. and Renfrew, C. (1988) *The Idea of Prehistory*. Edinburgh: Edinburgh
    University Press.
Dickinson, P. (1983) *Healer*. London: Victor Gollancz.
Dickinson, P. (1992) *A Bone from a Dry Sea*. London: Victor Gollancz.
Dickinson, P. (1998) *The Kin*. London: Macmillan Children's Books.
Golding, W. (1954) *Lord of the Flies*. London: Faber & Faber.
Golding, W. (1955) *The Inheritors*. London: Faber & Faber.
Hynes, S. (1964) *William Golding*. New York: Columbia University Press.
Kinkead-Weekes, M. and Gregor, I. (1970) *William Golding: A critical study*, 2nd
    edition. London: Faber & Faber.

Kipling, R. (1906) *Puck of Pook's Hill*. London: Macmillan.

Leakey, R. and Lewin, R. (1996) *The Sixth Extinction: Biodiversity and its survival*. London: Weidenfeld and Nicolson.

Sutcliff, R. (1958) *Warrior Scarlet*. Oxford: Oxford University Press.

Wells, H. G. (1920) *The Outline of History*. London: Newnes.

Wells, H. G. (1942) *The Outlook for Homo Sapiens*. London: Readers Union and Secker and Warburg.

Wymer, J. (1982) *The Palaeolithic Age*. London: Croom Helm.

Chapter 4

A havey-cavey business: language in historical fiction with particular reference to the novels of Joan Aiken and Leon Garfield

Gillian Lathey

For Joan Aiken and Leon Garfield, the two authors on whom the spotlight is turned in this chapter, historical accuracy is not the declared aim. But Aiken and Garfield are passionate about 'getting things imaginatively right'. Gillian Lathey tracks this 'rightness' to the wit, the eye for detail and the ear for sound shown by both writers. She suggests that, in fact, history, in the widest sense of the term, is not dishonoured in their work. She examines their linguistic playfulness, and reflects on the rather different but equally powerful language use of Rosemary Sutcliff and Jill Paton Walsh.

When judged by their intentions, authors of children's fiction set in the past seem to divide into two groups. In the first group are those driven by a passion for history and a desire to make a historical period live and breathe for the child reader. Writers who belong to the second group cannot be so easily described; for them a histori-cal setting acts as a catalyst for the imagination, a pretext, or a refuge from the demands of contemporary realist fiction. Comments made in interviews and essays clearly place Joan Aiken and Leon Garfield in this second category. Aiken has declared that she writes 'fantasy – not serious history', arguing that the past is 'a region where the writer may be secure from interference' (Aiken 1996a). For Leon Garfield, too, the past provides an essential alibi. In an invented conversation with a young 'punter', Garfield acknowledges the role of the past in his work, but confesses to a dislike of history. Responding to an accusation of 'cowardice before the world of today', Garfield explains that he needs 'to go away into another age before I can act out my fantasies' (Garfield 1975). Historical accuracy, then, is not a primary concern in the novels of Aiken and Garfield. Yet for both writers historical language is central to their art. Period language does not fulfil an overtly didactic purpose in their novels, nor is it designed to alienate in order to remind readers that people thought differently in a given historical period (Stephens 1992). What, then, is its function? The role of the language of the past in the novels of Aiken and Garfield is best approached in the first instance by way of contrasts. I intend to begin with a brief discussion of the pursuit of historical authenticity through language, then to review the subordination of history to a writerly purpose in a novel by Jill Paton Walsh. Finally, a more detailed exploration of the language choices of Garfield and Aiken will reveal the position of history in their fiction to be more paradoxical and intriguing than their anti-historical assertions imply.

At its most basic, period vocabulary becomes a stage prop to indicate costume, food, trades, military equipment and the like. Historian Trevor John, who regards 'details of time and place' as central to the didactic aim of making history live in children's fiction, praises Barbara Willard and Henry Treece for their 'clever' use of archaic vocabulary, citing items such as: 'pattens, snood, mantle, palfrey, trouba-dour, solar...' (John 1989). A sprinkling of obsolete terms may be supported by a restructuring of syntax in dialogue or in written narrative which creates an illusion of authenticity. Pseudo-historical language is also an important feature of the desire to create entertainment from history in the historical romance, a genre dating back to Walter Scott or, in children's fiction, to Charlotte M. Yonge. Readers of these romances enjoy the linguistic archaisms and inventions summarised by both Hollindale and Janet Fisher as 'gadzookery' (Hollindale 1997, Fisher 1996).

The quest to make the past live in the mind of the child reader reaches a high degree of artistry in the carefully wrought language of the novels of Rosemary Sutcliff. Sutcliff's work is underpinned by a serious historical intention. She has described the filling of red exercise books with notes in pursuit of answers to her questions: 'What houses do my people live in, what food do they eat, what weapons do they carry, what songs do they sing?' (Sutcliff 1990). That last question is of course the most difficult to answer, since songs – and by extension all language of the era – are ephemeral, espe-cially when Sutcliff chooses historical periods set far back in time. Her solution is to invent that 'register of antiquity' named and illustrated by John Stephens (Stephens 1992). As Stephens points out, this rarefied language registers the contemporary values of the author, creating a mismatch between past and present. This is particularly clear-cut in one of Sutcliff's early novels. The Armourer's niece Tamsyn in *The Armourer's House*, first published in 1951, wears 'sensible shoes', her cousin Giles keeps insects in boxes, and the children are allowed to stay up late when relatives visit. The house-hold, in other words, resembles nothing so much as that of a 1950s' middle-class British family. Archaisms in the novel add a patina of historical romance to the re-inforcement of familiar values. Young Tamsyn, on finding a magical spot by the Thames, runs down to a stream: 'she kilted up her green kirtle and ran down through the golden cups of the Mary-buds...'. Sutcliff combines a romantic vision with a didac-tic intention realised in the narrator's occasional explanation of unfamiliar terms: 'Mary-buds (marsh marigolds we call them nowadays)'.

Sutcliff's intentions are transparent, but what is the position of past language when the quest to make a historical period real for the child becomes only one aspect of the author's artistic purpose? In Jill Paton Walsh's *A Parcel of Patterns* (1983), past language becomes the structure of modern thought patterns in a beau-tifully constructed artistic conceit. The language of narrator Mall Percival is based on

research into the syntax and vocabulary of contemporary documents from the plague village of Eyam in Derbyshire. Mall guides us through the plague years; her thoughtful, earnest nature chimes with the sonorousness of the record she feels compelled to write and leave behind before setting out for a new life in America. Mall's purpose is to free herself from the emotional legacy of the plague years; the twentieth-century concept of writing as therapy is disguised as a 'ridding charm' to remove troubles by writing them down. Convincing as this narrative strategy is, Mall's written record is no simple country girl's charm: the reader is privy to a modern consciousness couched in period language. Thus the affecting rhythms of Mall's concluding words highlight the novel's artifice:

> With tears and with difficulty have I written it all, set down as best I might, and as it came to mind, all that I know, or that anyone told me ... And now, at last, it is brought to a conclusion, I shall lay it in my mother's linen chest, where let who may find it. It will lie heavy enough on the heart of who may read it, but writing of it has lightened mine!   (Paton Walsh 1983)

This marriage of past and present does not jar as it sometimes does in the work of Sutcliff, because the reader is aligned with Mall and there is no mediating adult narrator. Mall's fictional voice is convincing for the duration of the novel, as is the historical detail the reader perceives through her eyes. Despite the undoubted quality of the research involved and the historical information conveyed, Mall's story does not demand to be explained or measured against standards of historical accuracy.

Although it is based on an anachronistic premise that writing is a therapeutic act, *A Parcel of Patterns* is regarded as a historical novel. The same cannot be said of the work of Joan Aiken and Leon Garfield. Carpenter and Prichard in *The Oxford Companion to Children's Literature* state emphatically that: 'In no sense at all are Joan Aiken's books historical novels' (Carpenter and Prichard 1984). In her James III series Aiken takes a renegade attitude to the past which is unsettling for those who privilege the aim of historical accuracy. Similarly, Joan Fisher names Garfield as the best of a number of writers who write about the past: 'but not in a way that can be considered as pure historical fiction' (Fisher 1996). Indeed, the non-historical nature of Aiken's and Garfield's work leads to frequently cited affinities. Carpenter and Prichard propose the title of 'gothic fantasies' for Aiken's James III series, while John Stephens (1992) uses the same term of Garfield. Both writers employ the 'gothic' strategies of exaggeration and melodrama to explore the terrors, humour and irrationality of human society and both have been compared to Dickens: Aiken, for example, absorbed Dickens in readings by her mother from the age of seven and acknowledges his 'terrific influence' (Rosen and Burridge 1993). Finally, and of particular significance for this chapter, both writers are attracted to the comic and sinister language of the underclass, to the thieves' cant of the eighteenth century and Elizabethan times. Aiken and Garfield may not fit the standard definition of the historical novelist, but each has designs on the past expressed in a linguistic flamboyance that shares some common origins and purposes.

Joan Aiken has traced her love of unfamiliar language to her early childhood experience of stories (Aiken 1982). She can recall the pleasure and difference of the words 'blue-gums' and 'spinifex' in a story about Old Man Kangaroo read to her when she was three. Aiken's lasting delight in stories by the Comtesse de Ségur – read to her by her mother in French – led her many years later to translate one of them, *The Angel Inn* (Aiken 1976), for the benefit of an English audience. To translate is to become a wordsmith, so it is not surprising that Aiken should have seized on the language of the criminal underworld and employed it throughout most of her James III sequence. She has spoken of her joy at discovering a book entitled *The Elizabethan Underworld* while writing the second volume of the series, *Black Hearts in Battersea* (1965), a lexicon which contained: 'reams and reams of the most marvellous thieves' cant, and it just seemed to be a terrible waste that these words weren't brought back into circulation' (Rosen and Burridge 1993).

Aiken loves words, but she is not a pedant. On the contrary, she has warned would-be children's writers against the temptation to display historical knowledge for its own sake (Aiken 1982). She qualifies her expression of gratitude for Georgette Heyer's notebooks of information on eighteenth-century slang, costumes and carriages, by adding: 'but one salad and cucumber in *Pride and Prejudice* carries more conviction than all the products of careful research' (Aiken 1996a). Research, Aiken argues, should take second place to an invention which is imaginatively right; she is a writer with an eye and an ear for any detail which can be elaborated to delight her readers. This imaginative urge is realised in language in a rich mixture of cant, cockney, and specialised professional terms. The Italian, Dr Subito, in *The Cuckoo Tree* (1971), for example, speaks exclusively in musical directions. Typical of Aiken's linguistic excesses is the following passage from the fourth volume in the sequence, *The Stolen Lake* (1981), where the sea-voyage back to England of young cockney heroine Dido Twite is diverted to the eastern seaboard of America. Once ashore, the ship's captain commandeers two sempstresses (in a whimsical touch Aiken also refers to them as 'modistes') to make dresses for an unwilling Dido. The dialogue of the mother and daughter sewing team soon spirals into a parody of their craft:

> Mrs Vasavour said, 'both gowns oughter be white. Mull for daytime wear – a round gownd over a silk pettingcoat, ingbroidered with cat-tails in turkey-work –'
> 'And –' struck in her mother, 'french knots round the neck, and the border round the sleeves ingbossed –'
> 'A pink sash –'
> 'Then, for evening wear, a white silk taffety gownd, pinstriped with cream, and a lace pettingcoa –'
> 'A sash of the same, ingbroidered with silver sequing fronds –'
> 'She'll look like a Hangel from Heaving, that she will!' (Aiken 1981)

The comedy of this scene lies in the contrast in register between the arch fabrications of this pair with their nasal 'ing' intonation, and the sceptical cockney voice of resourceful street urchin Dido. After the dressmakers use their pincushion to chloroform her, Dido is furious at her own gullibility: 'How could I be sich a nodcock as not to twig their lay from the first minute? Any addlepate could see they was a pair of downy ones' (Aiken 1981). Didospeak, with which the reader soon becomes familiar, is an anachronistic mixture of the Cockney still in use and colloquialisms which, according to Partridge (1973) date back to the eighteenth and nineteenth centuries ('twig': to understand, C18; 'lay': a plan, as in a planned robbery, in use from *c.* 1705; 'downy' meaning 'artful' 1820–30) or even to Elizabethan times ('pate': head, C13; 'addlepate': fool, late C18–19). The language of Dido resonates with sharp, streetwise responses.

Aiken continues to draw on Elizabethan and eighteenth-century slang in later volumes of the James III sequence; two lines of telepathic transmission from Is, who displays the same wary cunning as her sister Dido, drive this point home. Is wants to warn her cousin Arun that she has spotted pistols and handcuffs hidden in the carriage in which they are travelling: 'Hey! Arun! They've got duke-irons aboard! What kind of a havey-cavey start is this? What do they want famble-snickers for?' (*Cold Shoulder Road*, Aiken 1996b). 'Famble' (hand) dates back to the mid-sixteenth century, while the synonym 'dukes' is a coinage based on rhyming slang (Duke of Yorks – forks – fingers – hands), and havey-cavey is a late eighteenth century expression for doubtful, uncertain (Partridge 1973). It can take time to get used to the voices Aiken creates, and there is always the danger that her linguistic playfulness can become tiresome or off-putting for the young reader. Aiken has admitted that her Dido books are 'probably too self-indulgent, full of dialect and adult wordplay' (Aiken 1986a), and there is surely a wry reference to her own word-spinning abilities in the cats with extracts from Dr Johnson's dictionary concealed in their collars in *The Stolen Lake* (Aiken 1981).

Leon Garfield is not so fanciful in his use of language, nor are his narrative inventions quite so wild as Aiken's. It is impossible to imagine such episodes as the transportation of St Paul's on giant rollers (*The Cuckoo Tree,* Aiken 1971) or the introduction of telepathy in *Is* (Aiken 1993) and *Cold Shoulder Road* (Aiken 1996b) in Garfield's altogether more geographically limited and plausible settings. Garfield's exaggeration is confined to figurative description; he is not attracted by obsolete and arcane vocabulary for its own sake. Nevertheless Garfield, too, fabricates a vernacular voice for his apprentices, pickpockets, highwaymen, swindlers and street children. In passages of dialogue reminiscent of Dido and the two sempstresses, Garfield writes to comic effect in the stylised cockney of the nineteenth-century music-hall and pantomime. Both Peter Hunt (commenting on *The Pleasure Garden,* 1976) and John Stephens (1992) finds this phonetic representation of Cockney irritating. Commenting on the spelling of 'dockiment' in a passage from *Smith* (Garfield 1968a), Stephens concludes that it conveys little information about the speaker and is phonemically ineffective. Stephens seems to ignore the role of this spelling as part of a comic creation; in the utterance from which it is taken, Smith's sister Miss Fanny is telling him to be careful: 'or you'll be coming down them steps stone dead! And *then* where will our dockiment be!' (Garfield in Stephens 1992). This may not be authentic eighteenth century cockney, but it is not meant to be – no more than the voices of Dickens' characters are consistently representative of the language of their day. By taking certain linguistic features and exaggerating or attributing them to one character, a characterisation is achieved which is part of a greater panorama of human types and individual variations. The visual effect of this spelling on the page adds to the caricature of Smith's sister whose eye for the potential financial gain from the 'dockiment' outweighs any concern for her brother's welfare.

Equally reminiscent of Dickens are the malapropisms of Hatch in *Black Jack*, (Garfield 1968b) or of Mrs Branch in *John Diamond* (Garfield 1980). Hatch is a dastardly character who presents proof of a kidnapping as: 'Me Boney-Fridays, m'am' (Garfield 1968b). Mrs Branch describes the ramblings of the injured William Jones as 'deleterious...Poor Mr Branch was like it in 'is cups. Very deleterious' (Garfield 1980). A combination of the mispronunciation of delirious with a collo-quialism for drinking dating back to the sixteenth century renders Mrs Branch's feigned concern for William ridiculous. Humour and cruel indifference or even violence are closely linked in these novels. The manipulative Mrs Gorgondy in *Black Jack* calls herself a 'mint-new widder' (1968b) to gain sympathy, pretending to be the widow of hanged men so that she can take and sell their bodies. Garfield, who admires humour in books (1975) uses linguistic comedy to reinforce his chilling vision of human behaviour, but also to temper it for the young reader.

Garfield's adoption of historical slang associated with robbery of various kinds – his second affinity with Aiken – is well-documented in John Stephens' analysis of *Smith*. Stephens (1992) points to the influence of Henry Fielding, an author much loved by Garfield, as a source of the cant in *Smith*. Garfield's range is not so wide as Aiken's, since he prefers to repeat a chosen set of terms throughout any one novel – for example 'nubbed' (in use from 1670 to 1840, Partridge 1973) for 'hanged' in *Smith* (Garfield 1968a); 'snick-and-lurk' (early nineteenth century, Partridge 1973) for pickpocketing in *John Diamond* (Garfield 1980), and 'bluebottles' for police in *Blewcoat Boy* (Garfield 1988a). In Garfield's novels this language remains tied to the criminal practices and codes dating back to Elizabethan times by which an entire section of society lives. Innocent, well-to-do Hertfordshire boy William Jones in *John Diamond* first encounters this social stratum when he meets all manner of wrong-doers and swindlers in the dank streets of London. He has to be taught – by means of mime since his friend Shot-in-the-Head can think of no words to describe the practice – the meaning of 'snick-an-lurk' (Garfield 1980). Within this underworld there are further hierarchies: a prowling pickpocket who darts from the shadows operates at the opposite end of the spectrum from the confrontational 'high toby' (highway robbery, early nineteenth century, Partridge 1973) in *Smith*.

Aiken and Garfield, then, employ their own distillation of the cockney and underworld slang of the past for comic effect. Comedy and the grotesque arise from the historical and social forces interacting beneath the surface of their novels; the linguistic codes Aiken and Garfield have chosen indicate multiple, alternative social realities. At the very edges of society, spoken codes become a deliberate strategy of opposition and survival. Such 'antilanguages' are defined by the linguist M. A. K. Halliday as codes generated by those who operate beyond the norms of society at any given time. New language is generated in opposition to the standard language in a display of linguistic creativity which defies the prevailing social order. In a prob-ing essay on the subject of antilanguages, Halliday argues that they should be taken seriously 'but not solemnly' (Halliday 1978), since humour is a significant aspect of their social purpose. In his analysis of three examples of antilanguages associated with criminality, one of which is the language of the criminal underworld in Elizabethan England, Halliday identifies the function of antilanguages as a means of social cohesion among subversive groups. Although the syntax is largely that of the standard language, the secrecy and speedy communication necessary to commit crimes gives rise to an alternative vocabulary. Indeed, overlexicalisation results from the rapid turnover and constant search for originality characteristic of all slang, so that synonyms abound. Joan Aiken's extensive use of thieves' cant as an inspiration leads, for example to the alternatives 'duke-irons' and 'famble-snickers' for hand-cuffs in the passage already cited from *Cold Shoulder Road*. An ever finer differentiation of criminal acts also leads to a proliferation of new terms, hence the distinction noted earlier between 'snick-an-lurk' (opportunistic pickpocketing) and the 'snaffling lay' (planned robbery).

Antilanguages only come into existence when there is a social structure which is perceived to be either culturally or politically oppressive. Mikhail Bakhtin analysed the effects of social polarity in language, taking into account the complete spectrum of registers. He noted in the unconstrained language of François Rabelais the: 'unof-ficial side of speech used by the dregs of city and country (but primarily the city)' (Bakhtin 1996). According to Bakhtin's interpretation of speech genres, the centrifu-gal force of variety, openness and creativity in language – the language of the 'dregs' – counteracts the centripetal force of official codes. At its most free, spinning away from the centre, the non-standard language of opposition expresses the humour, vitality and verbal dexterity of peripheral social groups, the kind of language which first caught the imagination of Joan Aiken and Leon Garfield. Indeed, Garfield on several occasions directly represents the tension between these forces and between different registers. As soon as Smith begins to learn to read he 'acquires a fanciful taste in words' (Garfield 1968a), addressing the muffin man in a mixture of cockney syntax and recently acquired vocabulary: 'd'you know the two ladies what reside in its nether regions?' An awkward phrase highlights the comedy of linguistic aspira-tions, but it is the language of the law at the outermost limits of the centripetal spiral that enshrines ultimate social power. The plot of *Smith* is driven by the words of a legal document which at one point appears to disappoint all hopes, since it contains: 'Not even a "whereas" or a "felonious" or a "property" to justify a family's dreams' (1968a). Smith places his faith in the talismanic power of individual words – even though 'felonious' is inappropriate in this context, it is imbued with the power of the law. Mr Jenkins, the lawyer in *John Diamond*, is a comic figure who has completed a social transition but retains command of the language of different social spheres. Confident of his cockney roots in ''oundsditch', Jenkins defends his linguistic shortcomings: " 'My haitches may be in default', said Mr Jenkins solemnly, 'but my 'eart is in the right place' " (Garfield 1980). In his profession as a lawyer he supports the *status quo*, yet he playfully subverts its static, Latinate language by call-ing young William his 'little Habeas Corpus' and 'rosy-faced Assumpsit' (1980).

Does this attraction to an historical antilanguage and the interplay of different speech genres indicate that there is, after all, a serious historical dimension to the work of Aiken and Garfield? A further examination of the underlying preoccupations of both authors indicates that there may well be considered evaluations of history at work. John Stephens (1992) argues that Garfield's perspective is governed by an awareness of the 'social abyss' which lies beneath the behaviour and language of his characters, an ideological gap which prevents Garfield from offering the kind of optimistic closure we expect from children's fiction. There is, to be sure, a hopeful conclusion to some of Garfield's novels (the escape of Belle and Tolly to the New World at the end of *Black Jack*, or the return of William's purse by pickpocket Shot-in-the-Head in the final chapter of *John Diamond*). These are positive resolutions but the mood of mistrust created earlier in both narratives is never completely dispelled. In *Smith*, every single character is unmasked as self-seeking and duplicitous to some degree. Garfield's protagonists live in a world where deception is a necessary life skill. Indeed, he has expressed his lack of faith in any development towards a more humane society in an essay on historical fiction. Garfield cites Ambrose Bierce's definition of history as: 'an account mostly false, of events mostly unimportant, which are brought about by rulers mostly knaves, and by soldiers mostly fools' (Garfield 1988b). Yet Garfield is not a diehard cynic; he believes that his historical writing should resurrect the hidden and silent majority: 'far from touching too closely on actual historical figures, whose course is well known, I'd try to bring out of the shadows – ourselves' (1975). He has even expressed a didactic conviction that if young readers discover the repeated pattern of the misuse of power through historical fiction, they will recognise it in their own times; 'and possibly they will do so before they vote' (Garfield 1988b). This statement, however, is not entirely convincing. Bakhtin's concept of 'unfinalisibility' seems more appropriate to the tenor of Garfield's recreation of the eighteenth century than a rousing message to young voters. Since the forces of the prevailing social order can never reach into every corner of society, the world remains messy and chaotic and there will always be a multitude of competing voices and registers. By bringing 'ourselves' – ordinary individuals – out of the shadows and parodying our historic voices, Garfield acknowledges the creativity and linguistic resourcefulness of individuals and fluid social groups.

Joan Aiken's lighter tone makes her delight in archaic language appear to be simply a surface feature of her fantasies. *The Wolves of Willoughby Chase* (1963), the first novel of the James III series, espouses the traditional happy ending in a world which, despite the machinations of fraudsters, is essentially a safe, comfortable and reliable place. Yet from *Black Hearts in Battersea* (1965) onwards – coincidentally the point at which she claims to have discovered *The Elizabethan Underworld* – Aiken addresses the comic and cruel extremes of human behaviour. She, too, does not entertain the notion of historical progress; underlying her imaginative, sometimes overblown excesses is a meandering current of deception, exploitation, plot and counter-plot. In her 'Reflections of an historical novelist' Aiken cites Gibbon rather than Ambrose Bierce, but the sentiments are similar: 'History...is little more than the register of the crimes, follies, and misfortunes of mankind' (Aiken 1996a). Certain novels in the James III series stand out in conveying the scale and nature of these follies. In *Dido and Pa* (1986b) there is a parody of literary workhouse scenes which hovers between comedy and pathos. A Mrs Bloodvessel allows street children to stay in her basement for a farthing a night; the children sleep suspended by their waists over loops of rope, their feet trailing on the ground. Aiken's exaggeration draws on a reservoir of past misery which was real. Historical fact is further exploited in *Is*, where kidnapped children are worked to their deaths in mines and foundries, and Dido Twite and her sister Is witness apocalyptic scenes of early industrialisation in the northern town of Blastburn. Their cockney twang becomes the voice of resistance as they scheme to rescue the children. After the sickening sights of a local infirmary, for example, Is tells Dr Lemman: 'I gotta go off a minute and lob me groats –' (Aiken 1993). Aiken's use of the vernacular of the past both offers the reader the release of black humour and identifies Is with the underclass of exploited children who call themselves 'the Bottom Layer' (1993). These children communicate telepathically with Is as one entity, a collective named TomJimNanMarySuePhilPatEllenDickCharlie. It is not simply another act of whimsy on Aiken's part that this anonymous mass sends subconscious messages; just as Garfield recognises the presence of the 'people of the shadows', she is fully aware of the weight of unresolved dialogues.

> Like the subconscious, the past lies all around us; and we ignore it for most of the time. In fact, inso far as the subconscious is the aggregate of all our former wishes, experiences, and frustrations, it could be said that history forms the mass subconscious, the underlying source of all our actions.   (Aiken 1996a)

If, as Jacques Lacan has asserted, the subconscious is 'structured like a language' (Lacan 1968), then the anachronisms and metaphoric connections in the language of Aiken's characters offer glimpses of the collective unconscious and the relentless momentum of history. Despite the happy endings of individual novels, the James III sequence as a whole does not appear to move towards a resolution.

Joan Aiken and Leon Garfield are often regarded as eccentric novelists captivated by the surface features of language, plot or the grotesque. But sometimes the play of surfaces can reflect what lies beneath more effectively than the results of any amount of earnest excavation. Both writers, however bizarre their vision may be, connect with the unconscious and the unresolvable in human history. It is at this subconscious level that the most interesting parallels with Dickens – who has also been accused of superficiality – can be drawn. Dickens relishes the range and comedy of human voices and, beneath a veneer of sentimentality and optimistic resolutions, conveys the relentlessness, fallibility and inhumanity of the social engines we create. This is the deeper significance which attracted a darkly allegorical novelist such as Franz Kafka to Dickens; there are moments when Garfield's London can be compared both to that of Dickens and to the Prague of Kafka:

> Here, the houses reared and clustered as if to shut out the sky, and so promoted the growth of the flat, pale and unhealthy moon-faces of the clerks and scriveners, glimpsed in their dark caves through dusty windows, silent and intent.
>
>   (*Smith*, Garfield 1968a)

For Dickens, Aiken and Garfield, the creative voices of the past, whether those of pale scriveners, cockney waifs or pickpockets, are essential to their artistic enterprise. By writing against the grain of authenticity and thus breaking the rules of the genre known as historical fiction, Aiken and Garfield have touched a linguistic vein running through history which is often neglected. Language is indeed a havey-cavey business, uncertain, unreliable and marked by sleight-of-tongue; in the hands of novelists who allow their imaginations free play, it has become a conduit for the echoes of unrecorded voices. As Russell Hoban has written in his 'Thoughts on being and writing': 'Language does, of course, carry the past in it, but the man of words need not always turn back, or need not *only* turn back' (Hoban 1975).

References

Aiken, J. (1963) *The Wolves of Willoughby Chase*. London: Jonathan Cape.

Aiken, J. (1965) *Black Hearts in Battersea*. London: Jonathan Cape.

Aiken, J. (1971) *The Cuckoo Tree*. London: Jonathan Cape.

Aiken, J. (1976) *The Angel Inn*, tr. from the French of the Comtesse de Ségur. London: Jonathan Cape.

Aiken, J. (1981) *The Stolen Lake*. London: Jonathan Cape.

Aiken, J. (1982) *The Way to Write for Children*. London: Elm Tree Books.

Aiken, J. (1986a) Interview with Nettell, S., *Books for Keeps* **39**, 12–13.

Aiken, J. (1986b) *Dido and Pa*. London: Jonathan Cape.

Aiken, J. (1993) *Is*. London: Jonathan Cape.

Aiken, J. (1996a) 'Interpreting the past: reflections of an historical novelist', in Egoff, S. *et al.* (eds) *Only Connect: Readings on children's literature*, 3rd ed., 62–73. Toronto: Oxford University Press.

Aiken, J. (1996b) *Cold Shoulder Road*. London: Red Fox.

Bakhtin, M. (1996) 'Forms of time and of the chronotype in the novel: notes towards a historical poetics', in Holqvist, M. (ed.) *The Dialogic Imagination: Four essays by M. M. Bakhtin*, 84–258. Trans. Emerson, C. and Holqvist, M. Austin: University of Texas Press.

Carpenter, H. and Prichard, M. (1984) *The Oxford Companion to Children's Literature*. Oxford: Oxford University Press

Fisher, J. (1996) 'Historical fiction', in Hunt, P. (ed) *International Companion Encyclopaedia of Children's Literature*. London: Routledge.

Garfield, L. (1968a) *Smith*. London: Puffin.

Garfield, L. (1968b) *Black Jack*. Longman: London.

Garfield, L. (1975) 'Bookmaker and punter', in Blishen, E. (ed.) *The Thorny Paradise: Writers on writing for children*, 81–6. Harmondsworth: Kestrel.

Garfield, L. (1976) *The Pleasure Garden*. London: Kestrel.

Garfield, L. (1980) *John Diamond*. Harmondsworth: Kestrel Books.

Garfield, L. (1988a) *Blewcoat Boy*. London: Gollancz.

Garfield, L. (1988b) 'Historical fiction for our global times', *The Horn Book Magazine* **LXIV**(6), 736–42.

Halliday, M. A. K. (1978) *Language as Social Semiotic: The social interpretation of language and meaning*. London: Edward Arnold.

Hoban, R. (1975) 'Thoughts on being and writing', in Blishen, E (ed.) *The Thorny Paradise: Writers on writing for Children*, 65-76. Harmondsworth: Kestrel.

Hollindale, P. (1997) '"Children of Eyam": the dramatization of history', *Children's Literature in Education* **28**(4), 205–18.

Hunt, P. (1980) The Good, the Bad and the Indifferent: Quality and value in three contemporary children's books in Chambers, N. (ed.) *The Signal Approach to Children's Books*. London: Kestrel 225–246.

John, T. (1989) 'Children's Historical Fiction and a sense of the past', in Atkinson, D. (ed.) *The Children's Bookroom: Reading and the use of books*, 101–6. Stoke-on-Trent: Trentham Books.

Lacan, J. (1968) *Speech and Language in Psychoanalysis*. Trans. and ed. Anthony Wilden. Baltimore: Johns Hopkins University Press.

Partridge, E. (1973) *The Routledge Dictionary of Historical Slang*. London: Routledge.

Paton Walsh, J. (1983) *A Parcel of Patterns*. London: Kestrel/Viking.

Rosen, M. and Burridge, J. (1993) *Treasure Islands 2: An adult guide to children's writers and illustrators*. London: BBC Books.

Stephens, J. (1992) *Language and Ideology in Children's Fiction*. London: Longman.

Sutcliff, R. (1990) 'History and time', in *Travellers in Time: Past, present and to come*. Proceedings of the summer institute at Newnham College, Cambridge, 150–6. Cambridge: Children's Literature New England/Green Bay.

Sutcliff, R. (1994, first published 1951) *The Armourer's House*. Oxford: Oxford University Press.

Chapter 5

'Time no longer' – history, enchantment and the classic time-slip story

Linda Hall

Linda Hall picks up where Dennis Butts left off by considering Kipling and Nesbit, and the ways in which their seminal works have influenced the time-slip form of the historical novel. While Kipling demonstrates a serious respect for the past, his child characters are simply an audience for history rather than active participants as in Nesbit. But Kipling's introduction of the ordinary individual paved the way for the more democratic and domestic stories of the twentieth century. Writers such as Boston, Lively and Pearce share a focus on gardens, houses and possessions that for all three symbolise a conservationist reverence for the past (not unconnected with their alarm at twentieth century events). While their time-slip novels are possibly more illuminating about time than history, Linda Hall argues that they have an inestimable role in helping us 'apprehend' the past.

When Rudyard Kipling in *Puck of Pook's Hill* and Edith Nesbit in *The Story of the Amulet* came by chance, in the same year, 1906, to write the first time-slip stories, they wove together two hitherto disparate elements: incidents and characters from our national past and the time travel popularised ten years earlier by H. G. Wells' science fiction story *The Time Machine* (1895). The result is a curious new form, utterly removed from scientific rationalism, which for the first time touches English history with the aura of enchantment.

This magic is most evident in Kipling, because his child characters in their games inadvertently evoke Shakespeare's Puck, the last of the ancient earth spirits, who then conjures up their various encounters with the past. But Kipling's sense of the seriousness of history means that there is a deeper magic at work in the continuity that he traces across several thousand years from the prehistoric pagan gods to the signing of Magna Carta. Through all the rootless changes that come and go, including key moments like the Roman occupation and the Norman Conquest, Kipling reveals the things that persist, rooted in the land and the people and by so doing defines the essential core of Englishness.

It is not hard to see why, of all the writers of her childhood, Rosemary Sutcliff regarded Kipling as having made the greatest impact on her. His genius is to show how, in T. S. Eliot's words, 'history is now and England' (Eliot 1959). As Sutcliff recognised, children have a tendency to see history 'as a series of small static pictures all belonging to THEN and having nothing to do with NOW' (1960). *Puck of Pook's Hill*, on the other hand, helps children to 'link past and present in one corner of England' (Sutcliff 1960). Even the narrative structure of the book reinforces this for each separate story is linked with previous and following ones so that there is no escaping the interpenetrating of the past in future events. For example, the sword that the old god, Weland the Smith, makes in the first story for the courteous novice, Hugh, wins the treasure of gold in the third story, while the casting away of that gold in the final story ushers in the Law and Justice. Hence, Kipling weaves an inextricable link between personal courtesy and respect for the Law and defines both as essentially English.

Kipling's method of time travel, unlike Nesbit's, involves bringing the past into the present. His child characters, Dan and Una, sit in a magic ring in the garden of Kipling's house on the Sussex Downs. Before them Puck summons imaginary characters, like Sir Richard Dalyngridge, who came with William the Conqueror, and Parnesius, a Roman soldier who is posted to Hadrian's Wall to defend the Empire from Pictish incursions, to tell their stories and be questioned by the children. Such a technique did not engage child readers always, probably because the child characters seem more physically passive, though they are certainly intellectually active in their questioning and comments.

Nesbit, on the other hand, sends her child characters back in time to enter the past by means of a magic token, like an amulet, so that they actually take part, in an apparently more active way, in the events known to them (and the readers) from their history books. In this manner she set the pattern that has been followed since, most notably in Alison Uttley's *A Traveller in Time* (1939). The main character, Penelope, who lives in Thackers, an old Derbyshire farmhouse that had once sheltered Mary, Queen of Scots, finds herself returning to the Elizabethan period in order to save the doomed Queen.

It is curious, given his conservatism, that Kipling's form of time-slip should be more radical than Nesbit's, given her socialist politics. This is because he looks between the cracks of the great events of the past to winkle out the unsuspected influence of ordinary individuals, whom the actual historical record does not include but whose actions made a difference to our island story, even in its most defining moments. The final story in *Puck of Pook's Hill*, 'The Treasure and the Law', is a fine illustration of this. King John's momentous acceptance of Magna Carta, which is the very foundation of our present constitutional freedoms and reasserted the paramountcy of English respect for the Law, is traced back in a chain of small links to an outsider, the Jew, Kadmiel, whose action of sinking the gold, which would have assured the King's resistance to baronial pressure, forces John to agree to the barons' terms.

This story, like the whole novel, is a perfect example of Peter Hollindale's category of 'creative history' (1979), in which the imagination of the artist has to be particularly active to make up for the paucity of the written record. Though he cites

Rosemary Sutcliff as the prime exemplar of this category because he had in mind less well documented historical periods like the Bronze Age and Roman Britain (both of which feature in *Puck*, of course), *Puck of Pook's Hill* is a brilliantly imaginative, and pondered work, not least in its presentation of the power-brokers of our past. The implications are entirely democratic. Whoever we are, we can make a difference.

The nature of Nesbit's time slippage back into the past, exhilarating though it is and giving rise as it does to children's personal involvement in exciting events, makes nonetheless for a conservative form. This is because history is, by its very nature, fixed; events have already been determined. Nesbit's child characters are impotent, however much they try to intervene to prevent what we know has already happened. Elfrida in *The House of Arden* (Nesbit 1908) meets Anne Boleyn out riding and tries in vain to warn her of her impending fate at the executioner's hands, but Anne's death is a donnée of history. The 'magic' of Nesbit's form of time travel carries with it, therefore, an inevitable plangency, something like the emotion that attaches itself to lost causes. The characters' efforts to help are always frustrated.

As the time-slip story developed after the Second World War in the hands of some exceptionally talented women writers, such as Lucy Boston, Philippa Pearce and Penelope Lively, it came to jettison Nesbit and Uttley's concern with famous historical characters and to adopt Kipling's interest in more ordinary, unknown individuals. There was a shrinking away, however, from his exploration of power and cunning. In the wake of the Second World War, time-slip also lost this interest in matters of public moment; instead, it became more personal, and undertook more intimate and domestic excursions into the past of a particular family or place – often a house and garden – unaccounted for in the national historical record, but nonetheless representing those continuities over time, 'though dynasties pass' (Hardy 'In the Time of the Breaking of Nations' cited in Grigson 1969), that also exercised Kipling's imagination.

It is significant that in 1976 Penelope Lively published an introduction to the history of landscape called *The Presence of the Past* (Lively in Townsend 1979). Because of a continuous history of over 5,000 years, the landscape of England carries an almost electrical charge; it fairly bristles with other, previous lives and wherever we look we see their signs. Stonehenge (4,500 years old), Hadrian's Wall (2,000 years old), and the old well from which Kipling dredged up a Neolithic axehead (6,000 years old), all testify to 'the continued life of the past in the present' (Townsend 1979). Writers of time-slip stories are particularly alert to this sense of place and people through time which at the national level used to be part of school history. It is no accident, perhaps, that at the time Lively began writing in the 1970s, the Schools' Council's History Project replaced the traditional approach to school history with 'discontinuous history', breaking that sense of continuity that Lively sees as essential to the life of the imagination and to a sense of being part of an unfolding story.

At the same time the traditional structures of family life were also breaking down through greater economic mobility and divorce, so that the vital contact with the old, 'the grandmother at the fireside' (Lively in Townsend 1979), as Lively put it, was being lost. The old, familial stories ceased to be passed on. All recent time-slip authors recognise the vital role of the older generation in the building of the child's sense of place, purpose and identity; like Kipling's Puck books, they are 'full of mutual respect of young and old – of children for the "old things" and vice versa' (Hunt 1994). It actually becomes the source of the remarkable, emotional depth of The Green Knowe stories (Boston 1954, 1958, 1976), *Tom's Midnight Garden* (Pearce 1958) and *The House in Norham Gardens* (Lively 1974). Recognising that memory, time and continuity- 'the four dimensional wholeness of life' (Townsend 1979) – are the key concerns of time-slip, Lively writes:

> It may be that books attending to memory, both historical and personal, are more important to children than ever before...Children need to sense that we live in a permanent world that reaches away behind and ahead of us and that the span of a lifetime is something to be wondered at and thought about...Children have to be told about these things because...they can't yet place themselves in a wider framework of time and space than *today* and *here*. But they have to, if they are not to grow up enclosed in their own personalities.   (Lively 1973)

The distinctively magical or mystical atmosphere that imbues time-slip stories stems largely from this emphasis on time, a much less easily defined concept than history. Indeed, scientists are still hypothesising about it, although what time-slip writers seek is not a scientific or rational explanation of time. Time for them seems to represent the opposite of what we understand by the word 'history'. Whereas history is about change, time becomes the focus for intuitions about the changeless, timeless matters of human existence and for fears of the loss of such necessary continuities. As a result, time-slip occupies a philosophical-cum-poetic terrain that the materialist nature of history has largely denied itself. It is inevitable therefore that time-slip engages with more intangible matters than historical fiction does. These matters are profoundly serious because they address compelling emotional and psychological needs. As Peter Hollindale (1997) suggests, 'We depend for our identity on our sense of personal continuity in time.' It is this sense of identity and of personal and cultural inheritance that time-slip stories, in the aftermath of the Second World War, seem deeply concerned to explore.

Time-slip, which may be defined as a story with its feet in the present but its head and heart in the past, seems far removed from any interest in the future. But if personal and cultural continuity is the shaping theme of the form, as I think it is, then present and future are bound together in an inextricable bond with the past; they are not safe if the past is forgotten or obliterated. In the late 1940s and early 1950s when *The Children of Green Knowe* (Boston 1954) and *Tom's Midnight Garden* (Pearce 1958) were being gestated and written, there was a real threat to the past. Post-war reconstruction in Britain did not follow the pattern of the continent. Whereas the Poles, Germans and Belgians showed a reverence for their respective pasts by replacing their razed cities with faithful replicas of what had been destroyed, Britain set about sweeping away the remains of the architectural gems and medieval city centres that had fallen foul of bombing. Coventry, which had been badly bombed, but not flattened like Ypres in the First World War, lost not only its medieval cathedral but an impressive and ancient town centre to the craze for the modern. As these women writers realised, buildings are more than just bricks and mortar; they evoke ghosts, symbolise what we were and provide 'an historical locus against which to measure unpalatable change' (Lowerson 1992).

It is hardly surprising, then, that these levelling processes, also at work in the social sphere through the election of a Labour government, should be reflected in the work of a number of cultivated, middle-class, women writers. Their collective sense of the England they knew being under threat led to a series of time-slip stories that nowhere overtly address contemporary national change, yet, in their portrayal of old houses and magical gardens, evoke a world on the edge. Haunted by a sense of loss, these writers attempt to recapture and preserve, in an inhospitable present, a past that seems to be as much under threat as the present.

The threat is manifested in the destruction not simply of buildings which are the arena for our social and public lives, and which can enhance or degrade those civic interactions. The threat is also perceived as directed at the countryside itself, which during the war had served as a potent symbol of the nation, the collective identity, and for many English people is still the well-spring of their spirituality, as the 'outdoor walking boom' (rambling) attests. For Lucy Boston, who was an environmentalist long before it was fashionable, the loss of the countryside is almost the greater loss. At the centre of her later book *The Stones of Green Knowe* (1973) lies an environmentalist concern with the garden that was once England. Roger D'Aulneaux, half Saxon and half Norman, travels 850 years forward in time from 1120 to visit Tolly and is utterly stricken by the litter-strewn, malodorous, tarmacadamised desolation he encounters almost everywhere he looks.

A house and its garden is the central focus of that feeling for the past generated in the major examples of time-slip story since Nesbit. The greatest of these texts since the war have been essentially conservative, in the best sense of the word, meaning, as Peter Hollindale (1990) puts it in relation to Lucy Boston, conservationist, historically and environmentally. Environment and history in fact unite in that 'sense of place' on which the structure of feeling in these stories is so often focused. This is usually manifested in the concern with the fate of a particular house and is most memorable in Lucy Boston's Green Knowe, which is based on her own house, the manor of Hemingford Grey; while *Tom's Midnight Garden* is a loving memorial of the garden of the mill house in which Pearce grew up. The house that is both the setting and the subject of Boston's novels seems almost more important than the people who have lived within its walls, if only because it transcends their individual mortality by its lasting power and so can become the symbol as well as the receptacle of that continuity without which all human effort seems purposeless. But not all houses have the power to withstand change, as Pearce makes plain in *Tom's Midnight Garden*. There the old house in which Tom spends his quarantine from measles had been subdivided into small flats, in tune with a less hierarchical age. It no longer resembles the grand Victorian family house of Tom's dreams and Mrs Batholomew's memories, while its magical garden has disappeared altogether, eaten up by encroaching 'development'. All that is left of the garden is an ugly, paved backyard as a space for dustbins.

This physical loss has its social parallel and is actually emblematic of the differences between then and now. The modern inhabitants of the house hardly know each other and live in fear or resentment of the old lady owner on the top floor. Though apparently more democratic than the past, the present is a more fragmented, atomised world. The tenant in the ground-floor flat is known only by his most prominent feature, 'the ginger beard', while to him Tom is nameless – 'the boy' (Pearce 1958). There is a greater sense of community during the Victorian heyday of the house, which despite its inequalities involved people in a web of relationships. For example, it is Abel, the gardener, who acts as the protector of the young orphan Hatty and tries to resist Tom's trouble-inducing presence. We correctly infer that he is the only other person who sees the ghost of Tom, because he cares for her.

In *The Children of Green Knowe* (1954) and *The Stones of Green Knowe* (1971), Lucy Boston's feeling for the spirit of place and the living continuity of her Norman manor-house conquers time by making past and present one. The novel is about Tolly's making contact with the past, gradually seeing the three ghostly children of the house, only after sensing them, hearing stories about them and touching their toys. Eventually and in one of the most moving episodes of the story, Tolly makes contact with Feste, the phantom horse, that once belonged to Toby and that Mrs Oldknow has never seen. The whole movement of the story is toward this 'realisation' of the past, not in the usual realistic sense of that word, but in a much more poetic sense of 'apprehending' it through one's senses and developing an openness to, and a feeling for, the past.

In detail after detail Boston stresses the continuity and sense of belonging that are so important to the young child Tolly who at the beginning of the novel is alone and outcast. He shares his Christian name with his father, grandfather and great-grandfather and, to prove how much he belongs, with three local villages. Distinctive features and traits of character persist and tie the generations together in one unbroken chain. One detail after another embeds Tolly in a rich historical and familial pattern stretching back four hundred years.

It is not just in the genes but in unconsidered, cultural practices that the ties with the past are maintained and become sustaining. The traditional songs that Mrs Oldknow teaches Tolly were also taught to the three ghostly children by their mother over three hundred years before. Mrs Oldknow later hears her grandmother's voice singing a cradle song in her bedroom and it moves her to tears. It is then taken up by a voice she hardly knows from more distant times. As she plays the song on the spinet, Tolly sings it and joins the magic web of continuity: 'Tolly who sang alone while four hundred years ago a baby went to sleep' (Boston 1954). It is in such intensely moving moments, where past and present intersect at a still point, that time itself is conquered. This is the promise from the *Book of Revelations*, which is also engraved round the dial of the grandfather clock in *Tom's Midnight Garden*. Its fulfilment is made possible in both Boston and Pearce by the deep magic of rootedness and attachment to 'the old things'.

The beauty of the house and garden make Green Knowe seem an arcadia. It is also an ark of values vital for a humane and civilised life. But Lucy Boston was not blind to the threat to this arcadia from the outside world. Both natural disasters, such as flood and disease, and man-made forces, such as political change and war, can, and do, inflict devastating change and suffering. The outside world embodies those forces which would break the continuity Lucy Boston cherishes. What her novels offer readers is a vision of natural and social harmony in which, in Hollindale's words, 'the responsibility of the individual being is one of care, respect and intelligent transmission – from the past to the present, from the present to the future' (1990). Lucy Boston's almost mystical sense of guardianship of both the natural and the built environment is not a simple, didactic environmentalism, for her writing has the power to invest images of continuity with a sensuous magic that appeals to the imagination of children and adults alike.

In *The Stones of Green Knowe* (1973), her last novel in the series, Boston brings together all the children that have lived in the house and sets it, as it is being built, just 50 years after the Conquest. The two stones of the title resemble thrones. They have been in the landscape from time immemorial and have a magical power to transport Roger in 1120 forward (or back) in time. Mainly he moves forward to trace the continuity of his beloved house. He meets his descendants, Tolly in 1970 and Alexander, Toby and Linnet in the 1660s, as well as Susan from *The Chimneys of Green Knowe* (1958) in the late 1800. Each period alters his house a little, but he is shocked that the whim of Susan's mother, a silly woman wedded to fashion's requirement for 'the new', presents the gravest danger to the house's continuity.

Though he finds that the house has survived into our present, the Garden of Eden that once was England has not. In some ways an achingly sad novel, it plots the magic of the natural world – 'in iron and wells, in stone and wood and hawthorn trees, and rings' (Boston 1973), in the virgin forests, in hares – and its gradual despoliation by modernising man. Roger's attitude is one of reverence for 'the old things', so that when he comes across the stones for the first time, he goes down on his knees to them.

Boston concludes the novel with a moving scene in which past and present fuse in a ring, as well as in the house itself. All the children, his descendants, meet under the copper beech, where Roger is given a vision of his role – 'He was one of many, but he was the first' (Boston 1973). Tolly's 16-year-old grandmother-to-be hands Roger a gold ring which she asks him to give to his wife, so that it will eventually come down to her, as a family heirloom, as it has already done. This is the magic circle of transmission, the 'pattern of the dead and living' from old to young. Like the skates in *Tom's Midnight Garden*, it is the token that confirms the defeat of time. She also promises to keep the house safe and hand it on to Tolly, for 'Where should we be if it was gone?' (Boston 1973) she asks, a question that lies at the core of all time-slip. It is the tangible reminder of their own, all too brief, lives.

It is this relationship of young and old that lies at the emotional and moral centre of *Tom's Midnight Garden* (1958), Philippa Pearce's finest novel. Employing a dual form of time-slippage in which Tom is a 'ghost' from the future in Hatty's late-Victorian world, while she is a 'ghost' from the past in his 1950s' present, Pearce explores the mysterious nature of time. Through the changes wrought to a house and, more importantly, to its lovely garden, she shows linear time in action. But it is the novel's distinction to suggest that the linear concept of time may not be the whole story, a view that is gaining ground even among scientists today, though Pearce's intuitions about time are poetic rather than scientific.

The Biblical quotation, from the *Book of Revelations*, on the dial of the grandfather clock in the hall – 'Time no longer' – is fulfilled in Tom's ghostly visits to the beautiful Victorian garden, long since sold off and built over, in that timeless period after midnight when the clock strikes 13. The mystery of this is held in perfect equipoise with the ordinariness of the characters by the structure of feeling that imbues the story: a Wordsworthian sense that human beings can 'exchange Time for Eternity' as a memorial tablet in Ely Cathedral says of a gentleman. They can exchange Time for Eternity not in death but by the deep magic of memory and the power of the imagination. The mystery is sustained without any sense of strain or contrivance, while every ingredient in each magical event is accounted for and is, surprisingly perhaps, very ordinary in itself. Just as supernatural explanations of the events of the story are invalidated by narrative evidence, so the rationalist explanations of Tom's uncle are shown to be simply inadequate.

It has been suggested that such rich evocations of our Victorian heritage of large houses and gardens are part of the nostalgia industry. If by this we mean a sentimental longing for a supposedly better world, we would be wrong, for Pearce does not take sides; she simply records what was and is now, with the kind of objectivity summed up by Keats in his idea of 'Negative Capability'. The loss of the garden is in fact distanced. Instead, Pearce simply creates the beauty of the arcadia that once was, with its secret places, stately trees and beguiling possibilities beyond the garden walls, in such a way as to recall the childlike, first stage of Wordsworth's enjoyment of nature such as we find in 'Tintern Abbey'. The story records in passing the unwelcome changes to the countryside, wrought by the modern world, and includes equally obliquely the atomisation of people, but does not stress them, so that on a first reading they hardly register. The links with the past – the trees, the house, the clock – remain, but though they have suffered the depredations of linear time and are barely what they were, we do not recall these changes when we have finished reading the novel. It is 'the glory of the garden' (Kipling 1994) and the profoundly moving ending, which highlight the fine, human qualities that can bridge the generations, that colour our memories of the novel.

John Stephens (1992) waives his critique of historical fiction only when considering Penelope Lively's work, for in *The Ghost of Thomas Kempe* (1973), for example, she shows how different from us people were in the past. However, like all classic time-slip authors, she is also determined to unveil those continuities over time that we share with the past, despite its intractable otherness. *The House in Norham Gardens* (1974) is a deeply serious meditation on the spiritual and psychological losses involved in the passage of time. Through the life of 14-year-old Clare Mayfield, for whom time seems to stand still, especially during a particularly snowbound winter, Lively traces the forces of dissolution, what the African lodger calls 'cultural disintegration'. However, there are telling signs signalled by the other lodger, Maureen, that respect in English culture for what is old, be it people, places or stories, is on the wane. The women's magazines that she reads elevate the young over the old and trivialise life – 'all uncertainties resolved by a change of shampoo' (Lively 1974).

An orphan and a sensitive only child, Clare is deeply attached to the Victorian house she lives in with her great aunts, for, unusually, it has been occupied by four generations of her family and still houses the memorabilia of her great-grandparents' lives. In a school essay she fearfully envisages the demolition of her house and connects it with damage to her own psyche. Intercut with this demonstrable sense of her own rootedness, and its importance for her psychological stability, is her reading of an ethnological account of a tribe of New Guinea bushmen whom her great-grandfather had been among the first Europeans to discover in 1905. These primitive people had lived in a timeless world in which the present was seamlessly interwoven with the past through ancestor worship, as represented by a tamburan or shield like the one in Clare's attic, which begins to haunt her.

The bushmen's sense of timelessness was encapsulated in their contact with the spirits of their ancestors, for they kept them alive by passing on stories of them to their young. In the same way, the stories we tell of our familial or national ancestors which we call 'history' are memories that build the foundations of our sense of who we are. The bushmen also believed that their ancestors 'live on, protective and influential, represented by objects' (Lively 1974) such as the tamburan. Clare's feelings about the objects in her house that once belonged to her own ancestors have a similarly non-materialist derivation 'If you keep things you can go on being sure about what's happened to you' (Lively 1974) and, by extension, to your family or your tribe or your nation. Without such cultural signposts, human beings, whether primitive or advanced, suffer disintegration.

Clare at the age of 14 lives in an equally ancestral world in Norham Gardens and the fineness of her life in harmony with her great aunts and the old house makes her wish that time would stop. But the more she reads about the bushmen and the more she considers the advancing years of her great aunts, the more that time's ineluctable whirligig makes her feel everything is slipping from her. The sensation fills her with panic and 'a sudden desolation' (Lively 1974), which mirrors the apathy which had overcome the bushmen on losing their traditional ways. As Clare's dreams are more and more troubled by the 'small brown men', she becomes convinced the shield should be returned to them because of its spiritual significance to them. But it is now too late to save them, for the culture shock of the twentieth century has made them forget their past.

The parallels that Lively draws between Clare and the bushmen in their reverence for, and their spiritual attachment to, their respective pasts remind us, of course, of Lucy Boston. This is inevitable, as it is in the nature of time-slip to touch history with an aura of enchantment, although such a word seems inappropriate for the particular sadness that pervades Lively's novel. By enchantment I do not mean the facile magic of fairies, but the more serious sense of the spiritual dimension inherent in our lives. The ghosts of those who have gone before, 'hands behind hands' (Hardy in Lively 1974), 'the multitudes below the iceberg's crest' (Ridler 1997), on whose lives cultural memory relies, link in an extended and inextricable network back in time to build the foundations of personal, local and national identity. Only Lively, of the three writers considered closely in this chapter, has pinpointed the dangers to the individual and collective psyche of the loss of such necessary continuities.

The House in Norham Gardens, complex and profound, is a salutary warning to those who would rewrite our cultural history and is Lively's most accomplished time-slip story to date.

A feeling for the past, for nature and the imagination were 'widely shared elements in English literary culture' (Rustin and Rustin 1987) in the days when the Leavisite critique of materialism was influential in academia. Now Marxist critics would equate such a cluster of attachments, and especially the emphasis on heritage, with a conservative, middle-class ideology. But such conservatism (with a small c) is today a radical response to a decultured present and an even more glob-alised future. Its conservationism confronts municipal and corporate despoliation of traditional and beloved townscapes, landscapes and ways of living. It presents an inevitable challenge to a consumerist ideology in which a culture – those irreducible continuities of a people and a place over time – has been debased to the deraci-nated pursuit of the latest novelty.

From secret places in nature, and an ancient university town, to old houses and magical gardens, the receptive individual can encounter the sense of both the distant past and of the transcendent in human life. Without such a sense, something very fine would be lost, something which Fred Inglis has referred to as 'a richer moral vocabulary' (Inglis 1975). The classic time-slip story sets out to recapture that fine-ness and to remind us of the price we have paid for losing it. Within its unassuming domesticity, time-slip became a surprisingly flexible sub-genre of historical fiction; it managed to address key social and economic changes in the post-war period that were undermining traditional ways of life, while simultaneously restoring a sense of the numinous in an increasingly materialistic world.

References

Boston, L. (1954) *The Children of Green Knowe*. London: Faber & Faber.

Boston, L. (1958) *The Chimneys of Green Knowe*. London: Faber & Faber.

Boston, L. (1976) *The Stones of Green Knowe*. London: Faber & Faber.

Eliot, T. S. (1959) *Four Quartets*. London: Faber & Faber.

Grigson, G. (1969) *A Choice of Hardy's Poems*. London: Macmillan.

Hollindale, P. (1979) *Choosing Books for Children*. London: Elek.

Hollindale, P. (1990) 'The darkening of the green', *Signal* Jan., p. 61.

Hollindale, P. (1991) 'Lucy Boston, storyteller', *Signal* January p. 64.

Hollindale, P. (1997) *Signs of Childness in Children's Books*. Stroud: Thimble Press.

Hunt, P. (1994) *An Introduction to Children's Literature*. Oxford: Oxford University Press.

Inglis, F. (1975) *Ideology and Imagination*. Cambridge: Cambridge University Press.

Kipling. R. (1906) *Puck of Pook's Hill*. London: Macmillan.

Kipling, R. (1994) 'The Glory of the Garden' in *The Works of Rudyard Kipling*. London: Wordsworth Poetry Library.

Lively, P. (1973) *The Ghost of Thomas Kempe*. London: Heinemann.

Lively, P. (1974) *The House in Norham Gardens*. London: Heinemann.

Lowerson, J. (1992) 'The mystical geography of the English', in Short, B. (ed.) *The English Rural Community: Image and analysis*. Cambridge: Cambridge University Press.

Nesbit, E. (1906) *The Story of the Amulet*. London: T. Fisher Unwin.

Nesbit, E. (1908) *The House of Arden*. London: T. Fisher Unwin.

Pearce, P. (1958) *Tom's Midnight Garden*. Oxford: Oxford University Press.

Ridler, A. (1997) *'Nothing is Lost', (Collected Poems)*. Manchester: Carcanet.

Rustin, M. and Rustin, M. (1987) *Narratives of Love and Loss: Studies in modern children's literature*. London: Verso.

Stephens, J. (1992) *Language and Ideology in Children's Fiction*. Harlow: Longman.

Sutcliff, R. (1960) *Kipling*. London: Bodley Head Monograph.

Townsend, J. R. (1979) *A Sounding of Storytellers*. London: Kestrel.

Uttley, A. (1939) *A Traveller in Time*. London: Faber & Faber.

Wells H. G. (1895) *The Time Machine: An invention*. London: Heinemann.

Chapter 6

The historical picture book – is it a 'good thing'?

Judith Graham

Judith Graham asks if we take the helpful nature of the illustrations in a historical picture book too much for granted. Having identified the key visual markers of era in pictures, she examines two books where visual markers are meticulously researched. Without background knowledge however, or if the story and emotional truth of the story are not convincing, the detail may be lost on the child reader, especially if time to look, question, reflect and revisit is limited. The picture book that makes direct links with present times, however, may aid access to the remote past and build more secure historical understanding.

There is, I think, a widespread assumption that the historical picture book must be a 'good thing'. If pictures are more easily 'read' than the written word and if historical detail can be presented in picture form, then the information may be slipped painlessly and efficiently into the child reader's mind. A similar argument is used for historical artefacts in the classroom to give children more immediate experience. Kath Cox and Pat Hughes acknowledge the helpful presence of pictures in *Seeing Red* (Garland and Ross 1996): 'The children were quick to agree that this was a story about the "olden days" ... The reasons given were the clues given in the illustrations – the clothes worn, the design of the warships, the weapons shown, objects such as a candlestick and bellows' (Cox and Hughes 1998). Anna Davin is positive about her own early use of pictures: 'Cynthia Harnett ... includes her own sketches of all kinds of everyday objects which figure in the text, which I remember made it much easier to visualise how things were different in medieval England' (Davin 1978) and Janet Fisher confidently asserts, 'Illustrations can play an important part in a historical novel, helping to clarify details and events and some of the very best artists have worked in this genre' (Fisher 1994).

These comments suggest that pictures are helpful in indicating the past and putting flesh on verbal descriptions but, in fact, we know very little about what children make of the pictures in historical picture books. What we do know is that the creators of historical picture books face the same challenge as writers of historical fiction: how to combine an accurate historical context with absorbing storytelling. Many writers of historical fiction have written about the dangers of clogging their stories with too much fact. Is it perhaps similar for the illustrator? Is it possible that pictures include too much detail? That the illustrator's assiduous industry is lost on a child reader who lacks the context into which to put new information? Pitfalls abound for writers and illustrators and it may be no easier for an illustrator to present his or her material accessibly than for a writer.

The visual indicators of period are much the same whether one is writing or illustrating. The illustrator of course has more decisions to make about the actual representation in his or her image: for instance, whether to simplify, exaggerate, magnify, shrink or in other ways distort for the sake of presenting information. It is useful to remind ourselves briefly of what the main visual indicators are.

Visual markers of period

Buildings and interiors, streets and bridges, furniture, cooking implements and other artefacts, clothes, hairstyles and jewellery, certain forms of transport are all relatively easily represented in images and are among the most common indicators of period. The absence of any of these is also informative. But only some of these are strong visual markers.

Ancient buildings on their own do not necessarily signal the past; because they are all around us to this day (there can hardly be many readers of these pages who could not walk from their front door and pass buildings which are several decades, if not centuries, old) and because they are frequently still in use, their presence is no automatic key to the past. Narrow, cobbled streets and absence of traffic can also mislead: some pedestrianised city centres may look pretty old these days. Old kitchen fittings, ranges, coppers, mangles, ancient kettles, heavy old furniture, brass bedsteads, cast-iron baths – such items are still to be found all over the world, either still in use or deliberately placed in re-created interiors. The historical illustrator cannot rely on such items alone.

It seems that all the above can only be utilised effectively to illustrate the historical past for young readers if they are shown in conjunction with characters whose clothing is different from that in the modern day. Clothes are a major and inescapable visual marker of period. Not for nothing are many historical films and dramas on television called 'costume dramas'. One of the reasons for this salience is that clothes from the past are never seen in taken-for-granted use in current-day life. The only place one could see period clothes other than in theatre, film or picture would be in museums where they may be statically displayed on dummies. In all picture books one has to dress the characters somehow. In a historical picture book, an illustrator usually takes pains to do it accurately and historians will require this. Even in books set in the rather recent past, such as Shirley Hughes' *The Lion and the Unicorn* (1998), the small evacuated boy is set well apart from his modern equivalent in that he wears what appears to be school uniform (rather long grey shorts) at all times. Casual clothes just were not part of that world. (Though crutches can hardly be called clothes, it is careful research that enables Shirley Hughes to show us crutches in this book that one no longer sees in the post-NHS world.) In *Peepo!* (1981), Allan and Janet Ahlberg's book set also in the 1940s, and in Raymond Briggs' *Ethel and Ernest* (1998) which takes us from 1928 to 1970, the signalling of era by clothes (again in settings that are also period) is most successful, whether it is knitted woollen shorts for toddlers or print dresses and pinnies for their mums.

There is only one other strong visual marker that comes close to clothing and that is transport and it does so for similar reasons. Transport is a prominent indicator of period because it has changed so very radically over time. Wooden sailing ships with rigging, masts, billowing sails, flags and much else are surprisingly common in historical picture books for children and instantly signal 'olden times', as the children reading *Seeing Red* (Garland and Ross 1996) were able to point out. Whether one is sailing with Columbus, with Napoleon or with the Dunkirk flotilla, great ships with sails instantly signal the past. But other forms of transport are equally signifying, from the horse and chariot in Roman stories to the first aeroplanes in the sky in books set in the twentieth century. A book such as *I Go with My Family to Grandma's* (Levinson and Goode 1986) illustrates a whole range of now 'dated' transport as five families (including 24 children) cross an uncrowded, early twentieth century New York by tandem bicycle, trolley, horse and wagon, trains and ferry to grandma's.

Having problematised the presence of pictures in historical stories for children and reflected on key and secondary visual markers of era which may or may not be understood by child readers, I want to turn to the first of the books I consider in this chapter.

Five Secrets in a Box

Here is the complete text of the picture book *Five Secrets in a Box* (Brighton 1987).

> My name is Virginia. I am the daughter of Galileo. My father studies the sky at night. I sleep.
>
> In the day he sleeps behind a fine curtain. Our house is quiet. My silent slippers creep.
>
> My afternoon seems long. I rustle to his study, up wide stone stairs.
>
> His desk is covered with things. I look, but I don't touch. His papers. His instruments.
>
> There is a box. I lift the lid. I peep inside. There are five things in the box . . .
>
> . . . two round pieces of glass. One piece makes things look bigger. Look at his writing!
>
> I hold the first piece next to the second. The countryside comes towards me. I see the children in the bell tower! I see the golden oriole!
>
> There is another fragment in the box. It is blue. The world turns to night.
>
> The red glass sets the world on fire. The prince's falcon flies to the lure.
>
> Last in the box is a feather. Soft and white. Why does my father keep a feather?
>
> I go to him. He is awake. His book slips to the floor. The feather floats after it. He says the feather is important to his work.
>
> I pick up the feather and he puts it in my hair. I parade like a proud bird all day. Galileo sleeps.

As a story, this seems to be for the youngest children, with its first person narrative, simple sentences, childish preoccupations, queries and pleasures. The older reader can enjoy what is *not* said in the understatement concerning the telescope glasses and the feather that we know were at the heart of Galileo's thinking and experiments and that were to lead him into so much trouble with the authorities. The pleasure an adult may take in this text may not be available to the youngest reader as it comes from prior knowledge. Without this prior knowledge, young children may find themselves unexcited. Conversely, they may be intrigued and be lucky enough to have an adult at hand to explain.

But of course this is a picture book. We must consider it as a composite text. If you chose to create a picture book about sixteenth/seventeenth century Italy and Galileo in particular, you are going to have to think about interiors and exteriors of the time, dress, hairstyles, artefacts, scientific instruments and much else. It would I suppose be possible to illustrate this story in a rather out-of-focus, nondescript way but in the end that would seem rather pointless to most illustrators for this type of text. Catherine Brighton, as in all her historical picture books, has done her research thoroughly. She gives us clear images of Renaissance scientific and domestic life and paraphernalia. Galileo's globe, instruments and telescope, a page or two of his work, *Sidereus Nuncius* published in 1610, sit on a table with heavy, leather and brass bound books, an inkwell and quill pen, a candle and a tiny jewelled box, in which are kept the five 'secrets'. More generally, throughout the book we are treated to vistas through the medieval house, of stone arches and windows, of rich patterned curtains and coverings, of tall-backed chairs, carved furniture and curtained beds. And through the magnifying glasses that the child Virginia holds up to the outside world we see children in the leaning tower of Pisa, the golden oriole bird, the prince training his falcon. When we look at the characters (Virginia, her father, the maid) we take in their clothes, their hairstyles, their jewellery, spectacles and keys hung at the waist.

When I say 'we', I really mean readers who are 'in the know'. What is unclear is how the child reader takes in these details. I try to put myself into the heads of six-year-olds. What they will respond to is the tender relationship between father and daughter that the cameo on the title page instantly establishes. They will notice that mice, a hare, a parrot and other birds have entered the house, that Virginia is very small in relation to doors, tables, chairs and window ledges and that she is given to peeping, prying and playing. These are the elements that one might say are salient, fantasised about or universal and timeless in child experience. They have little historical import but they may well enrich the child's response and enable a bond with the book to arise.

Undoubtedly children will also notice that Virginia wears elaborate long dresses and has beads threaded into her hair and that Galileo wears a hat in the house. We, as experienced readers, know that what is being suggested here is Renaissance Italy but this is a learned response and is not to be assumed in young readers. Long dresses, hats and jewellery may equally readily suggest fancy-dress parties or eccentricity in the child's mind. If they do suggest the past, it is not at all clear that any one period of the past would be understood: 'olden days' might be as far as we'd get. We also need to ask how will our child reader view Virginia and Galileo's home? Utterly different from yours or mine or that of the average reader, with its wide stone staircases, arched windows open to the elements, interconnecting rooms, high, beamed ceilings, it may nevertheless not impose problems as it is still recognisably an interior. In addition, if the child has entered older buildings it may chime with first-hand memories but, again, whether he or she will recognise these aspects as signalling 'history' and any particular period is questionable.

Most young readers are challenged in their reading (or listening/looking) the further the story departs from their known experience. Much of the historical information in these pictures may be unregistered or misconstrued, despite the accurate research and meticulous detail that Catherine Brighton has presented. I want to suggest however that her industry is by no means all a waste of time. Children, as we know, are given to poring over pictures, pondering, speculating and musing. There is no question that they use their eyes, perhaps more sharply than we do. They are curious and form conclusions. They lay down images that they can interpret much later when they have had more experience of life. There is a case to be made for the adult to allow a book such as this to sit with all its mysteries and trust that the images are being stacked up against future understanding. The question to ask is not whether the illustrations will inform the child of the period in which it is set, but to ask whether the book has enough story and emotional resonance for the child to stay with it and return to it.

The next picture book I examine helps confirm some of these points.

When Jessie Came Across the Sea

When Jessie Came Across the Sea (1997) by Amy Hest, illustrated by P. J. Lynch, is set some three hundred years later in time than *Five Secrets in a Box* and is a story where the much longer written text allows a story to unfold over several years. The very length of the text suggests an older readership than for *Five Secrets in a Box* but the challenge is the same: the reader has to move from the known experience of his or her own life into the fictional world of someone else, with the added complication that this other person lived a long time ago.

It is not absolutely clear where 13-year-old Jessie and her grandmother are living at the start of the story, but an Eastern European country would fit. We follow Jessie through her early happiness with her grandmother, her dismay at being chosen by the village rabbi to go to America, her hardships and friendships on the voyage, her work, study and courtship in New York and her eventual reunion with her grandmother and the excitement of an anticipated wedding. Happiness and loss, work and pleasure, fears, struggles and determination – these propel the story as they do many another. This picture book echoes the themes explored by Fiona Collins in her chapter on novels of migration (Chapter 8).

As always, if the text is illustrated, the illustrator has no choice but to clothe his or her characters and set them against some sort of setting and have them interact with objects and artefacts of the time. How does P. J. Lynch clothe this story? On the cover, Jessie looks out from the rail of a ship as it comes into the harbour of New York, the Statue of Liberty just perceptible in the background. (Versions of this image may well be common to many illustrated migration stories. It is on the front cover of Adele Geras' *Voyage* (1983).) Boats with sails circling round the Statue of Liberty, together with the polished mahogany rail of Jessie's ship and her thick woollen scarf and double-breasted coat hint at another era for those who know that nowadays things are different. It is indeed clothes and transport along with representations of activities that are Lynch's chief indicators of period. He is skilled enough to show how the clothing in Jessie's home village is simple, warm, dark-coloured, probably hand-woven and hand-made compared to the New York fashions which are brighter, more elaborately designed and worn with a belt to emphasise the waist, at least by women. Hair, mostly hidden by a shawl in the village and on the boat, is swept up and piled on the head in New York. The sailing ships, the horse and carts clinch the era as, to some extent, do the scenes of occupations: Jessie sewing lace, her sweetheart cutting leather shoes for a baby on the deck of the transport ship, vendors selling from stalls. Incidental details such as interior lighting, Jessie's treadle sewing machine, luggage (leather suitcases with triangular protectors on each corner and string to keep them shut), heavy, leather-bound books, dip pens and inkwells are there quietly in the background, adding to but not absolutely defining period.

What is 'readable' by all, however, is the tenderness between Jessie and her grandmother as heads touch over lace-making, the affection between the travellers on the ship, the sense of new experience on arrival in America (symbolised by the searching look in Jessie's eyes as she presses towards the rail) or the sense of a happy ending for Jessie with her sweetheart whom she originally met on the ship. Above all, we rejoice for Jessie and her grandmother whom we see in a final emotional embrace in the rain on the New York dockside. The shape of the whole story, the investment we put in our heroine, the pull of the ending keep us with the book. We take in the historical information according to experience; impact will inevitably vary and one cannot rule out delayed appreciation of significance. The emotional strength of this book is such however that most readers will want to remain browsing in its pages where the images can do their work.

New approaches

All the books mentioned up to this point, including the two discussed in detail, could be described as picture books whose authors and illustrators have set their stories firmly at a specific time in the past. The illustration which sets the period relies, quite properly, on key visual markers such as clothing as outlined in the opening section. *Five Secrets in a Box* is set four hundred years ago and, to those readers who 'know' the detail is accurate and interesting. *When Jessie Came Across the Sea* is set one hundred years ago and the story probably lasts over a period of ten years and the illustration, again to those in the know, confirms the visual changes that would have occurred.

Both of these stories are told in a straightforward linear fashion. They work within a closed world of a specific period in history. In this final section I want to consider titles that are the closest we come to time-slip fantasies and experimental work in picture book form.

For the youngest children, Ruth Brown's book *One Stormy Night* (1992) gives a great sense of the past-in-the-present in what is essentially a ghost story. An effigy of a King Charles spaniel detaches itself from under the feet of his master and, descending from the tomb, revisits, as a ghost, the home where he lived three hundred years earlier. Through the window he sees a newspaper dated 1992, a television and the current, living, canine occupant asleep in front of the fire. Above the mantelpiece is an old oil painting of the children of the Tudor family embracing our spaniel as he used to be. A long, lingering look and then the spaniel races past the stables and other outbuildings (just as they were in his time) and back to his position under the feet of his master. The past, the present, continuity and change seem encapsulated in this brilliantly simple idea. Ruth Brown also achieves a similarly striking – and for many readers profound – sense of the past in her retelling of the true story of *Greyfriars Bobby* (1995), the terrier who remained faithful to his dead master's memory by living for several years at his graveside. The book begins in modern-day Edinburgh as a brother and sister examine the water fountain memorial to the small dog in Candlemaker Row. They move to the graveyard and ask the gardener if they would have seen Bobby 150 years earlier. As we turn the page, the modern day dissolves into the past, we live for several pages in Victorian Edinburgh and its countryside, and then, again as we turn the page, we return to our brother and sister of the present. Some things stay the same; many buildings link the two eras (see my earlier points about the unreliable nature of buildings). The contrasts in the illustrations are in the clothes worn in the two centuries (T-shirts, baseball cap, jeans, trainers, rucksacks compared with bonnets, dresses, sailor suits, boaters, buttoned boots, wicker baskets) and in the changes in the street scenes (cars, yellow lines, advertisement for pizza compared with carts, cobble stones, gas lights, advertisement for tea rooms, ices). The book is superbly successful at suggesting how different eras are connected. The visual markers of period have become successful by contrast and comparison. Moving between eras has the effect of drawing our attention to change, making picture-scrutinising essential and leaving us very aware of history.

Several books by Michael Foreman have also broken boundaries (see his chapter, Chapter 11, in the next section for some of them). I want to consider two he has not mentioned. *Angel and the Box of Time* (1997) begins very much in present-day New York, with skyscrapers, road signs, pylons, kids on skateboards, derelict cars, a multicultural population and baseball caps worn back-to-front. Angel and her grandfather have a small travelling show that involves a goat dancing to pan pipes and a very ancient box, inscribed with dates. Each time Angel and her grandfather pack up their show, Angel peeps into the 'box of time' and is metaphorically and literally transported back in time, to 1918, to 1876, to 1720 and earlier. Her grandfather helps her understand her roots in the past and, as the book ends, he takes his travelling road show away, with Angel, towards her future. There are visual markers in plenty of the several periods but, over and above that, Foreman implants a sense of what the passage of time really means. *Grandfather's Pencil and the Room of Stories* (Foreman 1993) also plays with time and history in complex but accessible ways. The story involves generations of the same family who remain over time in the same family house. Items lost between floorboards provide a sense of the past and of continuity here (as they do in many another story). The illustrations invite detective work. From the carriages crossing the bridge and the scene in the stationery shop, it is clear that the story starts in the early years of the twentieth century. Conceivably, as the boy has a photograph of his father in army uniform, the period may be the 1914–18 war. The boy grows up and older and retires to St Ives. His grandson Jack visits him and then returns to a London of today, with its red buses and skyscrapers. Again, the engagement with historical change is aided by the author/illustrator and, while it is still important to inspect, ponder and revisit these books as with all complex picture books, the security of the more familiar present and the intrigue of time-slip makes engagement more likely.

The final book for discussion is *Memorial* by Gary Crew and Shaun Tan, an Australian picture book published in 1999. This book leaves one with the strongest sense of times past, of times changing and of the role of families in retaining memories. Four generations of one family, roughly spanning the twentieth century, reflect, through the book, on the enormous Moreton Bay fig tree that was planted at the crossroads of their town in 1918 to commemorate the Great War. The narrator's great-grandpa and Betty, the young girl who was to become his wife and the narrator's great-grandma, played their part in the planting. Great-grandpa, his blue eyes milky with age, touches his war medals as they transform themselves in front of our eyes into photographs of his fellow soldiers and then into falling leaves. The narrator's grandpa takes up the story of the tree, recalling hiding in its branches to avoid a visit to the barber shop and courting under it when he in turn came home from a war, the Second World War, in 1946. Then Dad and Mum recollect the tree-house they made there and yet another memorial service when Dad returned from Vietnam in 1972. By this time the tree is in the centre of a busy road and is viewed by the council as a road hazard. The young narrator, having heard the tree's stories from his family, is full of protest but the tree is felled anyway. Pictures are understated at this point: half a dozen tiny cameos as a tree-feller makes preparations, a beetle leaving the tree, a mass of birds flying out from its branches, a swirl of falling leaves, a fleeting vision of an old soldier leaning on his rifle, ducks eagerly gobbling up the fallen figs. Great-grandpa offers consolation: 'Memories, now they're different. Memories, they're ever-livin' things.'

Collage illustrations in this book, using bandages and hessian (the hessian that the roots of the original tree had been wrapped in), painted boards, simulated old photographs, including a shot of soldiers reflected in the muddy puddles at Ypres, canvas (that the tree-house had been made with), road markings and a cross-section of the enormous, felled tree's trunk with its myriad rings, are punctuated with dramatic double-page spread oil paintings of the tree's roots and branches. The accumulated effect seems to give the very texture of memory. The book is about war and the pity of war and the way in which war has affected lives; it is also about how the past is held in memory and of how it is passed on from generation to generation. It is a most powerful picture book.

The books I have presented in the final part of this chapter require decisions about story and central characters as well as meticulous research and shrewd judgements about which visual markers to include and exclude to indicate period. As in all winning books, they strive to get the emotional truth right too. In this way, they are no different from those books set firmly in just one period of the past. They are more demanding perhaps in that they involve the writer and illustrator in research across several time spans. Moreover, in introducing a fantasy element, a time-slip element, that will not detract from the 'truth' of the facts presented, they have to control a more complex narrative. Reading these books left me, as an adult, with an enhanced appreciation of history, memory, time, continuity and change. What of the intended child readers? I want to suggest that such books also have more chance of deeper understanding as the links made with the times we live in now, the surreal slipping and the leaps of imagination are of intrinsic appeal and interest to children. Many of the more straightforward historical picture books are perfectly informative and certainly engage the reader when the story and the emotional truth are right; it is the links with the present, made by the books that I have considered in the final section, that tip the reader into greater understandings. In the process, I believe, the interests of history are ultimately served more truly. Somehow, the more daring literary approaches open up a channel from our own lives lived now towards an understanding of those lives lived in past times. The difficulties we have with 'reading' the visual markers seem to be fewer; it is as if we are held by the hand as we make our journeys rather than being left to travel alone. Every well written, accurately illustrated historical picture book can be considered a 'good thing' if the reader brings enough background knowledge to the task and is lucky enough to share the reading with helpful others. Those books I have considered, in the second half of the chapter, seem to have built-in support and work a rather special sort of magic.

References

Ahlberg, A. and Ahlberg, J. (1981) *Peepo!* London: Kestrel.

Briggs, R. (1998) *Ethel and Ernest.* London: Jonathan Cape.

Brighton, C. (1987) *Five Secrets in a Box.* New York: E. P. Dutton.

Brown, R. (1992) *One Stormy Night.* London: Andersen Press.

Brown, R. (1995) *Greyfriars Bobby.* London: Andersen Press.

Cox, K. and Hughes, P. (1998) 'History and children's fiction', in Hoodless, P. (ed.) *History and English in the Primary School: Exploiting the links*, 87–102. London: Routledge.

Crew, G. and Tan, S. (1999) *Memorial.* Port Melbourne: Lothian.

Davin, A. (1978) 'Historical novels for children', in Grugeon, E. and Walden, P. (eds) *Literature and Learning*, 72–84. London: Ward Lock Educational in association with The Open University Press.

Fisher, J. (1994) *An Index of Historical Fiction for Children and Young People.* Aldershot: Scholar Press.

Foreman, M. (1993) *Grandfather's Pencil and the Room of Stories.* London: Andersen Press.

Foreman, M. (1997) *Angel and the Box of Time.* London: Andersen Press.

Garland, S. and Ross, T. (1996) *Seeing Red.* London: Andersen Press.

Geras, A. (1983) *Voyage*. London: Hamish Hamilton.

Hest, A. and Lynch, P. J. (1997) *When Jessie Came Across the Sea*. London: Walker Books.

Hughes, S. (1998) *The Lion and the Unicorn*. London: The Bodley Head.

Levinson, R. and Goode, D. (1986) *I Go with My Family to Grandma's*. New York: E. P. Dutton.

Chapter 7

Beyond expectations: historical fiction and working children

Liz Thiel

Liz Thiel's chosen books tell the stories of children working in grim factories, coal-mines and mills. While such books put reform and working towards a better future firmly on the agenda not all of the characters in the stories discussed are represented as victims and Liz Thiel shows how many of them are both independent and self-, and indeed whole family-supporting, compared with Western children of today. Liz Thiel constructs a strong base for arguing that the reader needs to understand narrative history, not through present day ideologies, but in relation to the ideologies of the time.

Child labour has long been a subject to arouse the emotions in the Western world. Victorian writers and politicians campaigned vociferously to legislate against the employment of young children in mines and factories; modern sensibilities are outraged by news of child workers in other lands. As Anna Davin (1996) comments, 'Because of our expectations about "proper" childhood experience and our knowledge of how children suffered and were exploited in early industrialisation (or in Californian agriculture or in third-world situations today), the idea of child labour rouses immediate moral indignation.'[1] It would seem that a veritable minefield of cultural bias and preconception confronts historical novelists who choose to locate their tales for young readers in a bygone world of children at work. To conform to modern concepts of 'proper' childhood necessitates condemnation of 'the shameful practice of child labour' (Cody 1987) and implies rejection of the past – and, occasionally, a novelist *does* appear to conform in this way by 'saving' a labouring 'victim' and magically transporting him or her to a nurturing new life. Yet, and more commonly, other writers eschew assumptions about child workers of the past by disallowing enduring visions of exploited, helpless beings. The protagonists of such texts are rarely portrayed as heroic[2] but, more frequently, as ordinary individuals, existing and progressing, albeit to varying degrees, within realistic social and economic parameters. All of them remain workers and few could ultimately be characterised as victims. Indeed, it might be argued that the central characters of many of these novels possess a level of independence that contrasts with, exposes and implicitly questions the dependency of today's Western child.

While the contrast between past and present is an inherent characteristic of historical novels generally, the immensity of the contrast between the working child of past ages and the Western child of today has continued to entice authors of historical children's fiction to the subject. A storehouse of stories encompassing a wide variety of juvenile occupations has been produced, ranging from the seventeenth century stonemason of Penelope Lively's *Boy Without a Name* (1975) to the eighteenth century rope-makers of Theresa Tomlinson's *The Rope Carrier* (1991) to the 1700s' London apprentices of Leon Garfield's series *Apprentices* (1976–78). The texts are not always entirely focused on work; child labour may be foregrounded to enable social comment but at other times work is a backdrop for a mystery, fantasy or study of family life. There are tales of young orphans adrift, seeking work wherever they can; encounters with notable historic figures; texts which link present and past.[3] The 1800s are a favoured location; adjacent to our own recent history, yet alien in their concept of childhood, particularly that of working-class children, they provide rich territory for a novelist. Child employment in factories, coal-mines and mills so clearly contradicts contemporary beliefs in a sheltered, educational childhood, that nineteenth century industrial Britain might be perceived as horrifying – especially if it is judged on contemporary criteria and denied contextual explanation. But when authors focus beyond such bias, the poverty, hardship and working lives of children of the past can be explored as much more than merely a horror tale.

To progress beyond the horror that accompanies the notion of child labour in nineteenth century Britain and so circumvent reader bias might seem a complex manoeuvre, but it has been, and continues to be, a popular approach. Authors writing 'against the grain' and publishing in the 1970s were particularly drawn to the 1800s' world of factories, mills and coal-mines, prompted, possibly, by the industrial unrest that was prominent at the time. Neither horror nor nostalgia prevail in these texts; there is, rather, a sense of re-examination. Suzanne Rahn (1991) asserts that 'the only types of historical novel to flourish in the seventies' had moved towards revision, rather than total rejection, of the past. 'Some were stories of...the lower classes which consciously attempted to correct what had been distorted or omitted in the classroom', she comments. Rahn's statement is of particular relevance to a number of novels published in the 1970s. Some explore the beginnings of reform, others trace individual characters as they work to survive within a hostile environment, be it in underground mines, with lethal factory machinery or in the polluted atmosphere of a cotton-mill. Their settings and story-lines may be varied, but many of these novels share a commonality; they attempt to reappraise the 'bad old days' of the nineteenth century from a social and cultural perspective that is markedly different from that of the here and now. And this trend of reappraisal of the past is one that continues to be pursued.

Different perspectives

While it may be a psychological impossibility for any contemporary author to reappraise the past, or child labour, from a true nineteenth century perspective, a quasi-realistic point of view would, at least, appear attainable. Joan Aiken (1996) points out that 'writers of fiction make a profession of projecting themselves into other people's minds and positions and their imaginative grasp can help make a reality of the past'. However, those texts that achieve the illusion of a nineteenth century perspective are more clearly revealed when compared with one whose judgemental viewpoint would appear to be located in the present. Catherine Cookson's *Our John Willie* (1974), set in 1852, follows orphans Davy and John Willie Halladay from the coal-mine to homelessness and thence to the shelter of the abrasive Eleanor Peamarsh, a minister's daughter, who finally resolves their parentless situation by offering to adopt them. Rescued from the working-class world of the nineteenth century, the boys prepare to assume new identities by becoming David and John William Halladay Peamarsh. Davy is assured of a future beyond the mines – 'I need never worry about going below again', he says – while 'puny', deaf and dumb John Willie, virtually unemployable and condemned by his father as 'no good for nothing', is acknowledged as a valuable individual. 'He has more common sense...than all of us...he will be a great help to us as he grows older', comments Miss Peamarsh. Cookson's story is rich in pathos and conforms to twentieth century cultural bias by implicitly rejecting the past. Its protagonists are transported from a grim, labour-based life of poverty and hardship to an existence that much more resembles the modern concept of a 'proper', nurtured childhood and although Davy will work part-time, he will be 'labouring' towards the restoration of the family estate. Paradoxically, Cookson's earlier text, *The Nipper* (1970), similarly located in the industrial 1800s, appears to arise from a less contemporary perspective. Central character Sandy Gillespie, nearly 16 when the novel begins, finds contentment through more realistic means and within the working world; he regains his adored pony, The Nipper, initiates talks to improve conditions at the mine where he has been employed, and returns to his preferred role of farm worker. Sandy's experiences in the mine and its surrounding community are sometimes extraordinary, but, overall, 'help make a reality of the past' (Cookson 1970). In comparison, *Our John Willie* might be considered a fantasy. In fact, Davy perceives his tale as such: 'Things like this didn't happen to lads like him', he reflects.

This tendency towards fantasy is largely absent from the work of many other writers of both the 1970s and beyond; their acceptance of the past is characterised through protagonists who, like Cookson's Sandy Gillespie, may escape from undesirable situations, but find some degree of satisfaction within seemingly realistic boundaries. These children frequently perceive work as a normal, necessary phenomenon; as Liz, a central character of Margaret Lovett's *Jonathan* (1972) understands, 'only the children of the gentry did not have the satisfaction of contributing to the general wellbeing of the family'. But, as orphan Liz, her brothers, sister and friend Thomas learn, work can be more than merely a means of survival. Jonathan, the teenage reformer who 'adopts' the children, suggests that economic viability can also lead to self-sufficiency and freedom. 'There's no freedom without life, and you're not fit to live yet except sheltered and cared for and taught. Talk about freedom when you can support yourself', he tells Liz's brother Jemmy. Jonathan also stresses that even a supposedly 'unbearable' job can be preferable to unemployment; when Jemmy talks of leaving the pottery to go 'on the roads', Jonathan warns him, 'You'd still freeze before midnight…what's so unbearable about your life that death in a ditch looks better?'[4] Although Jonathan and Jemmy suffer through work – Jonathan becomes critically ill as a result of his work as a pottery 'runner' and Jemmy dies when he is caught by mill machinery – work remains an accepted and integral feature of the children's existence. The closure of the novel finds the group contentedly under the auspices of Robert Owen, a real-life industrialist and social reformer, who founded a model industrial community in the early 1800s, with four of the 'family' working for Owen, and Liz and Jonathan pledging to strive towards a better future for children.

Taking control of the future

The theme of working towards an improved future underlies Susan Price's *Twopence a Tub* (1975), a tale of strikes and divided loyalties. The cover notes report that 'family memories' contributed to 'the startling authenticity' of the book, and Price convincingly portrays nineteenth century mining community life through the viewpoint of miner Jek Davies. Jek's age is unspecified, although he and his similarly-aged friend are described as 'young men', but he is a former child worker growing to manhood, and Price's narrative offers an insight into the mentality of a boy whose life is inextricably bound to the mining community. No miraculous escape route is offered, but despite the superficial pessimism that permeates the novel's closure, there is, ultimately, a sense of progress towards a better future for Jek, although he cannot yet perceive it. Beyond the pit lies his relationship with Rachel: '…he had to work through the next days with as little thought and…feeling as possible, until Sunday. Then he could see Rachel.' Moreover, his experience of the strike has awakened a new consciousness; he has learned to distrust the bosses and has witnessed the eviction of the union man's wife from her home: 'Driven out of their home by the Wicked Gaffer. Jek wouldn't forget that, and he wouldn't let anyone else forget it either.' If *Twopence a Tub* forbears to proffer an overtly optimistic conclusion, it at least hints at future resolution. Already unconvinced by his grandfather's argument that 'if [God] put thee to live like this, then this is how He wants thee' (Price 1975), Jek's anger at the miners' plight will inevitably engender rebellion. The reader feels confident that change will come.

To allow that change to emanate from an unlikely outside source, rather than from the protagonist himself, encourages contemporary assumptions about nineteenth century child workers. Davy of *Our John Willie* may be resourceful, as Miss Peamarsh acknowledges but he and his brother are clearly rescued; Davy tells his benefactress, 'you've given us everything, everything we'll ever want…you've made it possible for me to see daylight all me life'. In contrast, both *Jonathan* (Lovett 1972) and *Twopence a Tub* portray the child, or older child, much more as the agent of his own destiny. All authority, including that of God, is questioned; Jonathan tells Robert Owen's Quaker partner 'that he preferred being a heathen to believing in a God who…allowed [children] to be deformed and killed by men's wickedness in a factory, mine or workshop' (Lovett 1972), and Jek challenges his grandfather's religious stoicism (Price 1975). This emergent independence of mind is compounded by a desire and aptitude for mobility; if the work is intolerable, the child moves on. Geoffrey Kilner's Joe, the 11-year-old miner protagonist of *Joe Burkinshaw's Progress* (1979), leaves the pit in which his brother Jud drowns, is bound in service to the pit owner and runs away, and is enslaved into coal shifting before finally finding a new home and satisfactory work with a blacksmith. Joe is not a victim, nor is he helpless; he sees 'the hopelessness and resignation' of the other coal shifters but determines to escape, and refutes the notion that, in service, he 'could've been set up...if he'd behaved'. For Joe, satisfaction lies not in Jud's vision of a heaven where 't'sunleets all yeller and shinin' an' there's no night, no dark', but in freedom of choice and of occupation. He tells his dead brother's ghost, 'I don't want to behave...I want to be free.'

Family matters

Freedom of choice is achieved, sometimes, by severing or loosening family ties. Joe leaves his miner father and industry-crippled mother to forge his own way, although he visits the family home once his new life is established: 'He was proud to visit his mam to...enjoy her pride...and her relief that he had found the freedom and the purpose he had been seeking for so long' (Kilner 1979). Mudlark Jamie, of Melvin Burgess's *The Copper Treasure* (1998), an 11-year-old Victorian Londoner who scavenges along the Thames and is 'proud to be a working man' (Burgess 1998), buys himself a berth on a ship with his hard-earned money and leaves his family of eight. 'I felt bad...I never even went to say goodbye which I regretted...but father would never have let me take all that money away', he says. In each of these texts, family ties are a barrier to a potentially better future. In order to survive and progress, the independence of the protagonist is paramount.

Yet, as Theresa Tomlinson's novels suggest, the family, and the community-as-family, can also be a source of strength that enables the working child to achieve independence. Tomlinson's *The Flither Pickers* (1987), its companion text, *The Herring Girls* (1994), and her tale of nineteenth century ironstone mining, *Ironstone Valley* (1998), are a blending of fiction and fact, and focus on the children of fishing villages in the North of England. Neither *The Flither Pickers* nor *The Herring Girls* is strictly nineteenth century; the first is set around 1901 and the second is a sequel, but, nevertheless, they would seem to represent a way of life that has remained largely unchanged. Both books feature the photographs of Victorian/Edwardian photographer Frank Meadow Sutcliffe, and the inclusion of these photographs – with their children at play, social groupings and working women and men – further develops the sense of community that permeates *The Flither Pickers* and *The Herring Girls*. These are tales of communities and of families that work together and offer mutual support in times of hardship, and, while the protagonists achieve independence, they do so within the auspices of a caring environment. Liza Welford, the central character of *The Flither Pickers*, who appears in a secondary role in *The Herring Girls*, resists schooling, preferring the notion of work: 'I'm not wanting schooling. I want to be...doing the work, fetching bait for my dad's lines', she tells her grandmother, although eventually she defers to family encouragement, becomes a pupil teacher and, in *The Herring Girls*, travels away from home. Thirteen-year-old Dory Lythe, the protagonist of *The Herring Girls*, becomes a fish gutter in order to provide for her family when her mother is taken ill: 'I must go away and earn us some money, or we'd all be sent to the workhouse', she realises. She is encouraged in her decision and offered support from Miriam, an older neighbour: ''Tis terrible hard work for a little lass, but...I can certainly see to the bairns and nurse her mother.' Having left home, Dory becomes an independent wage-earner, confident of her own abilities. On her return, she tells her family, 'I'm a herring girl...I can do anything!'

Like Dory, Ned Nicholson of *Ironstone Valley* is keen to realise his economic value: 'I'll be working like a man. I'll be bringing home a proper wage', he says, as he relishes his new career in the ironstone mine. His mother initially reacts with horror at the thought – ' "What!" said Mam. "You're not going in that mine!"' – but when, at the age of 11, Ned secures a job as a trapper, his mother concedes. Sniffing at the news, she promises him 'a fine big jam sandwich' to take with him. Ned '...struggles through the first week of work', but becomes accustomed to his environment and eventually becomes a horse driver, encouraged by the camaraderie of fellow miners. In his retrospective at the end of the text, Ned delights his young grandson with stories of his past and boasts of being in charge of the whole stable block of 90 horses at 30 years of age. *Ironstone Valley*, like *The Flither Pickers* and *The Herring Girls*, perceives working life as a necessity that can, and must, be borne, and although Tomlinson's texts may sometimes present an optimistic vision of long-ago England, she offers a further perspective on working children. Independent and frequently assertive, they are hardly victims but, rather, economic assets who willingly contribute to the smooth running of family life.

The past and the present

Family life, as Tomlinson portrays it, is entirely absent from the world of Creep, the protagonist of Jill Paton Walsh's *A Chance Child* (1978). Described as 'part fantasy, part historical documentary' by Carpenter and Prichard (1984), Paton Walsh's novel is an extraordinary indictment of the present which juxtaposes the ill-treatment of a modern-day child against that of child workers in nineteenth century England and chooses to relocate him within the Victorian past. In John Stephens' *Language and Ideology in Children's Fiction* (1992), Paton Walsh is quoted as stating, 'Who cares about facts? We shall not find truth in them. Though we may, if we seek for graver and more philosophical meanings, be able to forge truth from them.' *A Chance Child* incorporates actual historical documents but also strives to achieve objective observations of images from the past. It does so in order to locate 'graver...meanings' that expose preconceptions about 'the bad old days'. And it applies the latter term not merely to the past, but to the present day.

Creep, introduced as 'a ragged and shivering child...its thin arms hugged around its ribs', might be the archetype of a Victorian waif, but is the unwanted issue of a present-day liaison between his married mother and a lover – 'well, he had a different dad, while ours was away din't he', explains Pauline. Creep is half-brother to

Christopher and Pauline, who maintain his survival behind 'the black triangular door of the cupboard under the stairs'. Although Creep *has* been seen by a neighbour, his existence is doubted: 'none of your neighbours ever saw a brother', says a welfare worker to the children. Creep's birth certificate is finally found. Denied a proper name – 'Even his name isn't a real one...Just swearing' says Christopher – Creep chooses to 'go back' down a canal and finds his identity among other, ill-treated children of the previous century. His nineteenth century existence is verified by the library records and by the preserved autobiography that Christopher finds. It reveals a respectable, successful life that would undoubtedly have been denied to Creep in his twentieth century 'past'.

The suggestion that a child worker of nineteenth century industrial England might have achieved a more successful life than a twentieth or twenty-first century child is, of course, relative; Creep is abused and consequently cannot be deemed 'the norm'. But the other main characters in Paton Walsh's story – Blackie and Tom – appear similarly successful within their working world, demonstrating a freedom of choice and independence that allows their movement from job to job and offers them a certain satisfaction. Tom decides to return to mining in a new pit and tells Blackie, 'it ain't that bad down there'. Blackie, abused by her former chain-maker boss and deformed by fire, takes Creep's advice to remain at the mill because 'that Ann thou work'st for is kind enough'. Desperate for a conventional future with 'a house down by the riverbank...and little ones', contemporary perspective might deem Blackie a pitiful creature, but she is far from helpless. Worldly-wise, she demonstrates a maturity that would, today, be perceived as beyond her years, although, within her time, she is simply a survivor who, like many others, must necessarily take care of herself.

For a child of today to take care of herself may be an anathema to current thinking, but this contrast between past and present is highly significant. While the children of the working-class societies depicted in historical children's novels are often independent and self-supporting, modern children – although better fed, homed and educated – are essentially denied the sense of independence and maturity granted to their fictional equivalents. There is, admittedly, no true parity between the two; one is fiction and the other fact. Nevertheless, the comparison is striking and invites speculation about the very nature of childhood itself. To portray working children of the past solely as pitiable victims and to accept only the modern construct of 'proper' childhood, is both to reject the past and sacrifice the potential for a redefinition of the child as an individual capable of sustaining herself. To challenge the contemporary cult of childhood, albeit implicitly, is to provoke debate.

Elaine Moss (1989) asserts that our present and future are shaped by our past; it would seem all the more essential that the child reader of historical fiction is presented with wide-ranging possibilities of the past, rather than limited assumptions rooted in the present day. Judgements about the future can have little value if they are founded on contemporary bias; an author who attempts a broader perspective must surely offer greater scope for insight into the past – and thus perhaps the present and future – than one who appears to draw primarily on cultural expectations. And because historical fiction for children is, by nature, a flexible medium through which all aspects of history can be explored and all possibilities examined, it has long been, and remains, a valuable route to the past. It can never be truly possible to reproduce, with certainty, the experiences of working children of earlier centuries or comprehend their way of life. But a genuine authorial desire to probe beyond the given 'truths' of history may, at the very least, provide the potential for a reader's greater understanding of the past.

Notes

1. In her study of London life from 1870 to 1914, Davin suggests that the phrase 'child labour' carries 'a heavy negative load' and prefers to use the less loaded term 'children's work'.
2. For an exploration of 'the agency, activism, and heroism' of working children see Susan Campbell Bartoletti (1999) 'The power of work and wages: working toward historicity in children's fiction', *Children's Literature Association Quarterly* **24**(3), 112–17.
3. A recent example is David Almond's *Kit's Wilderness*. Although not a traditional historical novel, Almond's story emphasises the interrelatedness of past and present through Kit's experiences with the long dead child miners of his hometown. Almond, D. (1999) *Kit's Wilderness*. London: Hodder.
4. Joan Aiken's *Midnight is a Place* (1974) also addresses this issue. Protagonist Lucas Bell's essay, 'Why Industry is a Good Thing', prompts him to write, 'Industry is a good thing because it is better to work in a carpet factory than to be out in the rain with nothing to eat.' But Lucas also wonders if this is true. Aiken, J. (1974) *Midnight is a Place*. London: Hodder.

References

Aiken, J. (1996) 'Interpreting the past: reflections of an Historical Novelist', in Egoff, S. *et al.* (eds) *Only Connect: Readings on children's literature*, 3rd edn., 62–73. Oxford: Oxford University Press.

Burgess, M. (1998) *The Copper Treasure*. London: A & C Black.

Carpenter, H. and Prichard M. (1984) *The Oxford Companion to Children's Literature*, London: Oxford University Press.

Cody, D. (1987) 'Child Labor', The Victorian Web. Internet. (Accessed November 2000) http:// landow.stg. brown.edu/victorian.history/hist8.html

Cookson, C. (1970) *The Nipper*. Harmondsworth: Penguin.

Cookson, C. (1974) *Our John Willie*. London. Macdonal and Janes.

Davin, A. (1996) *Growing up Poor: Home, school and street in London 1870-1914*. London: Rivers Oram Press.

Garfield, L. (1976–78) *Apprentices*, (series of books). London: Heinemann.

Kilner, G. (1979) *Joe Burkinshaw's Progress*. London: Methuen.

Lively, P. (1975) *Boy Without a Name*. London: William Heinemann.

Lovett, M. (1972) *Jonathan*. London: Faber & Faber.

Moss, E. (1989) 'The historical imagination', *Signal* **60**, 143–55.

Paton Walsh, J. (1978) *A Chance Child*. London: Macmillan.

Price, S. (1975) *Twopence a Tub*. London: Faber.

Rahn, S. (1991) 'An evolving past: the story of historical fiction and nonfiction for children', *The Lion and the Unicorn* **15**(1), 1–26.

Stephens, J. (1992) *Language and Ideology in Children's Fiction*. Harlow: Longman.

Tomlinson, T. (1987) *The Flither Pickers*. Hebden Bridge: Littlewood Press.

Tomlinson, T. (1991) *The Rope Carrier*. London: Julia MacRae.

Tomlinson, T. (1994) *The Herring Girls*. London: Julia MacRae.

Tomlinson, T. (1998) *Ironstone Valley*. London: A & C Black.

Chapter 8

Passage to America: migration and change

Fiona M. Collins

The question of migrating from one country to another has engaged the imagination of many a writer. Migration as a topic offers writers a human experience of fundamental importance, a wide range of eras and all the drama and emotional turmoil of a journey, involving loss, hardship and the unknown but also hope, challenge and the excitement of the new. Fiona Collins considers four novels which cover migration to America, and she points up how, while the novels may share broad similarities in structuring (reflecting, as they do, the characters' early difficult situations, leaving, travelling, arriving, adjusting), they develop particularity with their differing eras, emphases, preoccupations, ideas and messages.

> The act of migration concerns people and places, but it also concerns time.
>
> (White 1995)

Throughout the ages, people have moved or migrated from one region to another and from one country to another. Migration is not only an event of the past but an experience that still continues today. People have always migrated. They move countries for a variety of reasons. A great many are metaphorically and even literally pushed from their homeland through political and religious persecution, war, famine, hunger and poverty. They are lured to their new homeland by the chance of a better life, financial security and perhaps the thought of living under a more liberal regime. When migrants reach their new land, they have different experiences according to whether they are alone or in a group, how they are received and their ability to assimilate.

Writers of historical fiction have been drawn to this area of human experience because it is rich in drama and emotion. They want their stories to give the young reader an understanding of the hardships and fears that moving from place to place involves, as well as reflecting the sense of loss that is intrinsic in leaving one's homeland, the challenges which occur during the journey and the adjustments that have to be made on arrival. It is not surprising that the act of migration, covering as it does so great a length of time, so many feelings and so many different places, has been explored in so many children's books.

In this chapter I am going to discuss children's books which deal with migration from Europe to America from the seventeenth century to the beginning of the twentieth century. These stories all include, though with differing emphases, the migrants' reasons for leaving their homeland, the voyage and the first part of their new lives in America. While this narrowing of focus inevitably excludes valuable texts and by no means tells the complete story of migration, it enables me to focus on four very important and significant books from British, Canadian and Irish writers.

The books I have chosen reflect three different groups of migrants. The first book is *Witch Child* by Celia Rees (2000) set in 1659, between Cromwell's death and the Restoration. It is Mary Newbury's story written as her diary. Mary's grandmother has been hung as a witch and, to protect her from the same fate, Mary's mother sends her, with a group of Puritans, to America. In 1620, the Pilgrim Fathers, who were Puritans, sailed for America and settled in Plymouth. Ten years later a second group of English Puritans, led by John Winthrop, established a colony in Massachusetts Bay, the main port being Salem. This is where Rees sends Mary and her fellow Puritan travellers in *Witch Child*. The Puritans were seeking a new life for themselves that would enable them to follow their religion freely. The story is about Mary's new life and the persecution she experiences from the Puritans.

Between 1830 and 1860 many Europeans migrated to America from Europe, including Irish migrants fleeing from the ravishes of the famine (Payant and Rose 1999). Most migrants experienced a warm welcome to their new country but the Irish experienced overt prejudice. The next two books deal with this period. *Bound for America*, set in 1847, by Elizabeth Lutzeier (2000), is a sequel to her earlier story *The Coldest Winter* (1991). The story follows a family from Ireland to North America. It focuses on Eamonn, the oldest son, and describes his fortunes and misfortunes on arriving in America. The second Irish story is *Wildflower Girl*, written by Marita Conlon-McKenna (1991). The story is the second in a trilogy and tells of 13-year-old Peggy's search for a new life in America. It begins in 1850, after the family's experiences of the famine, and is a story of Peggy's life as a maid in Boston.

From 1880–1920 a further wave of migration occurred. These were people from southern and eastern Europe. They dressed differently and had different religions from the American Protestant majority and they also spoke different languages. They were leaving Europe because of religious persecution and economic hardship and on entering North America they were met with strict migration laws and many who were ill were returned to their countries of origin and those who remained did not always find a welcome. *Days of Terror*, by Barbara Smucker (1979), is set during the later years of this period and gives a vivid description of the lives of a large farming community of German speaking Mennonites and their reasons for fleeing the Ukraine after the Russian revolution. As the title implies, the families are terrorised over a period of time. They did not speak Russian and lived in their own communities. Their beliefs also made them different, 'for almost 400 years our people have held to the Bible teachings of peace and non-resistance...Our forefathers suffered for the right not to bear arms' (Smucker 1979). The story tells of their plight and their final escape, as a group, to Canada.

Even though these stories are set in different periods, each author has followed a similar format and pattern. I intend to discuss each text according to this pattern. Within the stories, the journeys are significant as they are about discovery, times of hardship and misfortunes for the child travellers who have to deal with crises and uncertainty along the way. Peter Hollindale argues that such a journey can be seen as 'a life-event and metaphor'. He adds, 'When children go on a journey – any journey, whether in life or fictions – the complexities of childness are highlighted, especially if the children are unaccompanied by adults, above all, if they are alone' (Hollindale 2001).

However, although these stories have similarities in overall shape, they do differ in form, content and characters' experiences as well as the period in which they are set. All of the books give a broad view of why the migrants leave their homeland, whether voluntarily or not. In *Witch Child*, Mary Newbury leaves her home because she is in fear of her life due to the witch-hunts practised at the time. By contrast, both the Irish stories make indirect reference to the famine in relation to reasons for leaving. In addition, we are told that Eamonn's family, in *Bound for America*, is migrating because of their father's death from the fever and the family's eviction from their home by the landlord. Peggy, in *Wildflower Girl*, set just after the worst years of the famine, leaves because prospects are better in America.

Of all the books discussed, *Days of Terror* (Smucker 1979) gives the deepest insight into the reasons for leaving. The story focuses on the Neufeld family, and in particular on Peter, who is the second son. At the beginning of the story, the reader is told that this family of successful farmers is living within a Mennonite community in the Ukraine. With the outbreak of World War I, problems begin for the Mennonites, as they are seen to be enemies of Russia, as they are German speaking. From this period, the whole community is affected by the fighting linked to the Revolution and the famine and typhus which accompanies it. The story tells of the family's gradual realisation of the horror of their situation and the understanding that, 'There is no longer hope for our Mennonite people in Russia.' Peter's father sums up the situation for his son. 'Our homes and barns are in ruins, our land is taken from us, many of our churches are closed, and our schools will soon teach against religion...and now our young men are fighting as soldiers.' Smucker tells how Otto Neufeld, the oldest son, joins the Self Defence Force, which is set up in order to protect the Mennonite community. This Force is opposed to the community's belief of pacifism and non-resistance. Because of this and linked with the effects of war, famine, illness and ideological change, the community is forced to leave their adopted homeland. They migrate, as a community to Canada, with the help and support of other Mennonite communities in both Europe and North America.

The voyage

As stated before, the stories all devote attention to the voyage across the Atlantic. Although the books are set over a period of 250 years, the experiences that the travellers have during this journey are very similar. The authors show that this is a significant period for the child traveller, whether travelling alone or with the family. Through the journey, the child, filled with thoughts and fears of leaving home and of new found responsibilities, has to grow up quickly. However none of the authors leaves the lone child traveller without adult assistance and both Mary Newbury, in 1659, and Peggy O'Driscoll, in 1850, are taken under the wing of a surrogate mother, in the form of Martha for Mary and Mrs Molloy for Peggy.

The narratives all reflect how difficult the beginning of the journey is for the travellers as they realise that they will be unlikely to see their homeland again. The texts set in the nineteenth and twentieth centuries also show how the migrants are checked for age and illness before they board the boat. In *Wildflower Girl* Peggy, leaving Ireland in 1850, is questioned in detail about her age and Nell Molloy supports her by saying that she is a distant relative. When the Neufeld family (*Days of Terror*) come to embark, in 1920, the official does not allow the young daughter and aunt to travel as 'the little girl has measles' and it was felt that the aunt did not look well enough to travel. Smucker brings the trauma of the leaving into sharp focus by the family being separated on departure. 'The parting came so suddenly that the emptiness was like the sudden disappearance of a falling star' (Smucker 1979).

In all the stories, the voyage can be seen as a metaphor, and microcosm, of life. Throughout the voyage, whether it is three months as in *Witch Child* or nine days on a steam ship as in *Days of Terror*, thoughts and hopes for the new life are explored and discussed by all. And as the voyage continues, symbols of life and death are ever present. However, on each voyage, each individual author explores how her characters deal with the voyage in different ways.

The voyage for Mary and the Puritans in 1659 is traumatic as the small sailing ship is at the mercy of the sea and the weather for such a length of time. Mary tells the reader of the times when the ship is becalmed, when 'there is not a breath of wind' and when there are storms, and the wind 'screams in the rigging, howling like a living thing' (*Witch Child*). She describes in her diary how the Puritans' strong belief helps them cope with the trauma. One entry in the diary relates how, after ten weeks at sea, Elias Cornwell, the Puritan leader, calls for a day of fasting and prayer, to pray for God's forgiveness so that He would show them the way to their new land. 'We stood, hands clasped, heads bowed, and Elias Cornwell's deep preaching voice swept over us, calling on God's Providence, asking for His forgiveness, begging for deliverance' (Rees 2000).

By contrast, the beginning of the voyage in *Bound for America* gives a general feeling that this is a great adventure – for all. Parties are given and people celebrate the beginning of their new lives. 'They danced under the stars until the whistle blew at twelve o'clock.' The feeling is that this would be a new beginning for the migrants and all had great hopes for their new lives. 'Everyone knew that in America all of the people were treated the same, rich or poor' (Lutzeier 2000). Here Lutzeier shows the naïvety of the migrants and puts later horrors of the voyage into sharp relief.

The description of the living conditions in the pre-twentieth century ships reflects the horrors that the migrants experienced, 'packed as tight as the cattle in the hold and likely to smell as rank' (*Witch Child*). The seasickness and illness made the cabins smell worse. Steerage class was a 'wide gloomy area where small narrow bunks were crowded together' (*Wildflower Girl*). Each author describes how, as the voyage continues, so the smells become worse and everyone feels cooped up like birds in a cage (*Wildflower Girl*). The only relief for the passengers is to go up on to the deck, when the weather is fine, to get some fresh air and to get away from the sickness below.

The books, all, interestingly, written by female authors, tell of female experiences during the voyage and through this readers begin to understand women's role during a particular period, whether it is the seventeenth century or the nineteenth century. The skills and knowledge that women used through the generations are explored in relation to childbirth, health care, cooking and sewing. Mary shows, in *Witch Child*, that she can deliver a baby and sew and that she has knowledge of herbs. In *Wildflower Girl*, Peggy looks after young children and cares for ill or dying passengers.

In all of the stories, seasickness prevails until the migrants find their sea legs. Frequently, a storm occurs and with this, disaster strikes, often a death. In *Wildflower Girl*, a sailor is swept overboard and two passengers, a baby and an old man, drown by slipping under the water in the hold. Both are buried at sea. 'Horrified, Peggy clenched her eyes shut as the two bundles were tossed overboard.' The storms often spoilt the food as the ships' holds leak. Water barrels smash against the sides when they are not tied down securely enough, resulting in further crises as food and water are then rationed.

Death is ever present on the voyages. On the Irish boats, death not only occurs through the storms but also from cabin fever. Passengers are constantly worried that they are going to catch it. 'Mammy waited until they were up on deck. "She'll be gone before morning," she said, "and soon we'll all be gone"' (*Bound for America*). The cramped sleeping quarters mean that the fever is quickly passed from one person to another. 'Peggy looked over at Mrs Molloy. She looked sick, and one of the younger children lay beside her, ill now with cabin fever because of the stuffy conditions' (*Wildflower Girl*). Not only did the passengers have cabin fever but also typhoid. In *Bound for America*, the ship is not allowed to dock at Boston and has to sail on to Quebec as it is classed as a 'plague ship'. When the ship arrives in Canada, the passengers are put into quarantine on Grosse Island. Here over 5,000 Irish migrants died in 1847 without ever reaching their true destination. Of the two books, centred on the Irish Diaspora, Elizabeth Lutzeier, in *Bound for America*, paints the more horrific picture of the voyage, quarantine and conditions that the famine victims had to endure when they reached Canada. On the voyage in *Days of Terror*, the typhus fever is also present; however in this story, Barbara Smucker (1979) takes a more optimistic narrative line and 'after a few days they felt somewhat better'.

In each of these four stories the author has tried to show how the voyage both challenges and changes the young migrants. It acts as a bridge between their old lives and the new life they will make for themselves in North America.

Arrival and assimilation

In this last section of the chapter, I explore the migrants' stories in their new land and how the individual authors shape their characters' new lives to reflect the contemporary ideologies of those authors, thereby developing a unique narrative line. Two of the stories, *Witch Child* and *Bound for America*, show how the characters, Mary Newbury in 1659 and Eamonn in 1848, experience persecution and discrimination. By contrast, optimism and hope of assimilation into the new country are reflected in the other two titles. However:

> Once migrants entered America they all had the similar experience of feeling like an alien, of an uprooted stranger in a strange land and of being thrown into the melting pot of America. The new migrant would have to pick up the ways of the native-born, and eventually, but perhaps not until the second generation, join the throng of assimilated Americans.   (Payant and Rose 1999)

Puritan migration – seventeenth century

The Puritans in *Witch Child* enter a country that has been colonised 39 years previously by the Pilgrim Fathers. The migrants arrive with livestock and fowl to make a living from the land. On reaching Salem, Mary realises the harshness of her new life. 'The good folk of Salem show us how life will be. This is no land of milk and honey. Their faces show a history of work and hardship' (Rees 2000). While in Salem, the Puritans see Native American Indians for the first time and the Indians' clothes and appearances shock them. Some of the young Puritan girls refer to the Indians as 'savages' and mutter that they could have killed them. However, from this initial viewing, Rees entwines an interesting post-colonial theme. She is looking at the situation with twentieth century eyes, informed by later awareness. The Puritans need the Indians to lead them to find the Reverend Johnson and his followers, who had left England years before. Mary writes in her diary that the Indians 'are at home in the forest. If they feel threats about them, they do not show it...In the morning, when they break camp, they leave no sign that they have ever been there.' As we read the diary, we feel that Mary, as an outsider, has an understanding of and respect for the Indians, which her fellow travellers do not develop.

In the new settlement life is hard. Houses need to be built, crops to be sown and herbs to be found. Mary, with a fine knowledge of herbs, passed on to her by her grandmother, picks herbs for Jonah, the apothecary. During one of her visits to the forest, one of the Indians, Jaybird, leaves her soap leaves, as he has seen her washing in a forest pool. It is also Jaybird who saves Jonah's life. Jonah had been erecting a house and a log falls on his foot, breaking it. The foot blackens and he develops a fever. Although Martha puts a simple poultice of herbs on the foot this does no good. It is only when Jaybird leaves herbs and powders, with instructions for use, that Jonah's life is saved. Martha, Mary's surrogate mother, says that the cure was a miracle and that 'We are all God's children. They are better Christians, than some I could name, despite their heathen ways.' Through this episode Rees gives a post-colonial perspective. She conveys the knowledge and awareness that the Native

Americans have about their own land, as well as their willingness to help the new comers. As McGillis (1999) argues, 'Post-colonial narratives – whether fictional or critical – open space for the reader to see and hear peoples from a variety of back-grounds and practices.'

Rees also makes a comment, through the narrative, on the Puritan migrants and the way that their prejudices and beliefs travel with them to America. Strong beliefs die hard, especially when migrants continue to live within the same community. Rees shows this bigotry through the Reverend Johnson's distrust of Mary. Initially he dislikes her because he does not understand her. To him, she is too independent and too head strong. The Reverend does not like the fact that she wanders in the woods alone. After church one Sunday, he asks her if she is obedient and after her reply he states: ' "Rebellion is as the sin of witchcraft," so it is written in the Book of Samuel.' Later he believes that Mary has been involved in the deaths of his wife and child and accuses her of being a witch – echoes of *The Crucible* by Arthur Miller (1968). Mary writes in her diary, of the Reverend, 'He is a shrewd man, but his belief in spells and witchcraft warps his perceptions away from mere human sense into something else' (*Witch Child*). The story ends with Mary being identified by a witch finder, who comes to the settlement. Mary is forced to run away or suffer the same punishment as her grandmother. Martha, who aims to follow Mary, writes at the end of Mary's diary that they hope to go to places where 'folk are freer to follow their own conscience, which is one of the reasons we crossed over the ocean in the first place'. In this extract we see a longing for liberal thought and a wish as new migrants to be accepted more into the culture of their adopted homeland.

Irish migration – nineteenth century

As Keenan (1997) states, within post famine stories, America became 'a place of refuge, a place where prosperity can be experienced, a place where new stories can begin'. *Bound for America* and *Wildflower Girl* relate the hardships that the Irish migrant has to endure on arrival. Through the two central characters of Eamonn and Peggy, the reader sees the difficulties experienced in finding work and being accepted. Both Eamonn and Peggy are literate, bright young people eager to make a new life in America but they both encounter difficulties to some degree.

Of the two, Eamonn's story is the more political in symbolising the Irish migrants' experiences. Eamonn leaves Quebec, where his boat docks, and makes his way alone to Boston to search for his aunt. Unable to find her, he seeks work in the city but every-where he looks he sees the notice, 'No Irish need apply' (*Bound for America*). Through Eamonn's experiences, Lutzeier shows what it is like to be discriminated against as an unwanted migrant, but she also shows his tenacity in looking for a job. However, it is only when a policeman tells Eamonn of a mill owned by an Irish man that he finds a job. Later in the story, when all the mills in Massachusetts are on strike in order to stop the use of child labour, Eamonn reflects on the importance of soli-darity: 'This was America. No one could treat one of them badly without having to face up to all of them.' Lutzeier shows the initial hardships that the new Irish migrants faced and the contradictions that surrounded them. The difficulty linked to such an ideo-logical position, in relation to unions and striking, is highlighted through Eamonn's thought patterns as he tries to explain to himself why people stop working when money is needed so badly. As Mr Brady says to Eamonn, 'This is America. We shouldn't have to choose between letting our children starve to death because we have no money to buy food and letting them get killed by machines. This is America, Eamonn.'

By contrast, Conlon-McKenna (1991) presents a different view of the life for the young Irish migrant worker during this period. Peggy, arriving alone in 1850, seeks work as a maid. She is adamant that she does not want to work in a factory. Unlike Eamonn, Peggy does not face extreme hardships. Her story is one of optimism. Her first position is difficult, but that is short lived, and she finds a suitable job, as a maid, with a wealthy family outside Boston. The work is hard but not exhausting. She does experience prejudice in the family but it is mild in comparison with Eamonn's experiences and the prejudice is only from the spoilt daughter of the house. The daughter makes comments such as 'those Irish' and Peggy is called 'Bridget' deliberately. The daughter also accuses her of being a thief. But Peggy is a strong character and stands up for herself.

Conlon-McKenna (in a talk given at the Irish club in London on 15 March 2000) defended her optimistic portrayal of Peggy by saying that she did not want her to be portrayed as a victim; too many Irish have been portrayed in this way. She emerges as an independent young woman making her way in a new country. Throughout the story, various characters become role models and these open up her eyes to new opportunities. Mrs Madden, the housekeeper, says to her:

> 'You know Peggy you're very bright. Not that many in service can read and write, and obviously you're good with numbers too. I've spotted you scanning my row of figures. Things are tough at the moment, but hard work, so they say, never killed anyone. Keep on working and I'm sure you'll go places. You've got brains and spirit and a good nature.'   (Conlon-McKenna 1991)

Wildflower Girl ends with a Thanksgiving dinner and Conlon-McKenna stated that the reason for this is that, 'I thought Thanksgiving because it's celebrating the immigrant...I wanted to recognise that Irish immigrants were as much a part of the culture as the much earlier pilgrims and that Peggy was a pilgrim herself' (Smith 1997). The book reflects the story of a new Irish American making her way in her adopted country and the trilogy ends with Peggy travelling with her husband to the West to make a new life.

Keenan (1997) argues that 'being true to the past means being true to a time when moral and social sensibilities were different from today's and that to sanitise the past is to do an injustice and to condescend to the present'. Looking back at these two Irish texts, one might be tempted to ask which story actually gives the truer account of the Irish experience. Conlon-McKenna's reluctance to make Peggy a victim could be seen as sanitising the past. However it is important to remember that different people will undoubtedly have met with very different experiences. The mills and factories did employ Irish workers in great numbers and working conditions were very poor but that is not to say that individual young women, like Peggy, did not have less harsh experiences and make a success of their new lives.

Mennonite migration – twentieth century

For the migrating Mennonites, and in particular for the Neufeld family, in *Days of Terror* (Smucker 1979), the arrival in Canada is cushioned by being looked after by other members of their community. Jobs are found for them and Smucker describes how they are all housed with other Mennonite families. However the Neufelds do not speak English and the language that the Canadian Mennonites speak is different from the German that the Russian Mennonites speak.

'They gathered round the newly arrived Russian Mennonites, speaking English words and a strange German they call "Pennsylvania Dutch"' (Smucker 1979). Smucker does not explore this further but prefers to focus more on the welcome that the family is given: '"How can they be so good to us?" Mother spoke with awe. "We are complete strangers to them."' The family is reunited with their little daughter and Otto, who had joined the Self Defence Force in Russia, and thus voluntarily (though temporarily) alienated himself from the family. At the end of the story, the family travels to the Prairies to meet their friends and family and start a new life as farmers once again but in a new country. Peter reflects that this is like a dream, after all the days of terror that the family had experienced. At the end of the story, there is a feeling that this time the Mennonites will assimilate, learn the language and become Canadians and not stay outsiders as they had done in the Ukraine.

In each of the four books the author has shown the arrival in a different manner even if, as with *Bound for America* and *Wildflower Girl*, they are set in the same period. As shown previously, each stage, of the migration process, can be viewed both in a positive and negative light. The stories reflect the different experiences of the child traveller and, although they are similar in the way they are patterned, they do all reflect a uniqueness of human experience. In the same way the authors' contemporary ideologies help shape and represent the historical material. However, no one story is able to give a complete picture of migration because every migrant's story is different. These four books do, in different ways, explore some of the issues which are ever present when writing about the ways in which humans have struggled and survived as they have moved from place to place in the world.

References

Conlon-McKenna, M. (1991) *Wildflower Girl*. London: Puffin.

Hollindale, P. (2001) 'Odysseys: the childness of journeying children', *Signal* **94**, 29–44.

Keenan, C. (1997) 'Reflecting a new confidence: Irish historical fiction for children', *The Lion and the Unicorn* **21**, 369–78.

Lutzeier, E. (1991) *The Coldest Winter*. Oxford: Oxford University Press.

Lutzeier, E. (2000) *Bound for America*. Oxford: Oxford University Press.

McGillis, R. (1999) *Voices of the Other Children's Literature and the Postcolonial Context*. New York: Garland.

Miller, A. (1968) *The Crucible*. Penguin: Harmondsworth.

Payant, K. and Rose T. (eds) (1999) *The Immigrant Experience in North American Literature: Carving out a niche*. Westport CT: Greenwood.

Rees C. (2000) *Witch Child*. London: Bloomsbury.

Smith, L. (1997) 'Interview with Marita Conlon-McKenna', *The Lion and the Unicorn* **21**, 379–86.

Smucker, B. (1979) *Days of Terror*. London: Puffin.

White, P. (1995) 'Geography, literature and migration' in King, R. *et al.* (eds) *Writing Across the Worlds: Literature and migration*. London: Routledge.

Section 2
Writing about the narrative past

Chapter 9
Waking quests

Julian Atterton

Julian Atterton roams over several issues in this chapter which is both personally and theoretically revealing. His childhood games of battles and intrigues, early immersion in Sutcliff, Treece, Trease and the all-important role of location are all seen as part of his personal make-up as an historical novelist. He shares with us the process of being critically edited and read, and reflects on the heady charms of addictive research as he tries to capture the essence of a time and a place. He discusses the importance of keeping a story moving despite the need to inform and he shows how such issues as courage and heroism are properly problematised.

I've always envied those novelists who coolly assess the literary possibilities of a theme, its niche in the market and how to pitch their style accordingly, and then write a blockbuster. In my case, ideas have come unbidden, and I can only claim conscious control of what I have tried to make of them.

As a 25-year-old completing a dissertation on the modern novel, I was turning over ideas for a witty contemporary fiction when a stroll along Bamburgh beach changed my life. Looking up at the castle, I remembered how it had once been taken by Urien of Rheged. Next day, gazing at the hill-forts of the Cheviots, I imagined a boy fleeing west when the first English came and settled, and his return with Urien's army on the expedition which came so close to throwing the English back into the sea. This was a story worth a novel, I realised with a gulp, and in the next breath I realised that it could make a story like the Rosemary Sutcliff novels I had loved as a child. If this tale were to be told, it should be told like hers, as a novel for anyone over ten. I found myself writing historical fiction for children because it seemed the only honest aesthetic response to the tale I had in mind.

The few books then available on sixth-century history and archaeology were quickly read, and I wrote *The Last Harper* (1983) in an intuitive imaginative trance of an innocence I may never know again. My role-models were Rosemary Sutcliff and Robert Louis Stevenson, and in an effort to match their high styles, I tried too hard to impress. I was lucky that the story was strong enough to work despite the writer here and there getting in the way. I realised at the end that I had written a sublimated autobiography, for I was that boy who had lost his father at the age of 11, and who wished to be a harper, a teller of the tales of the land.

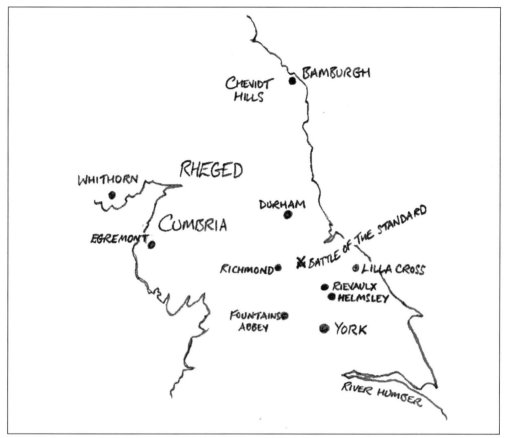

Figure 9.1 Land within the bounds of the ancient kingdom of Northumbria

It was the land itself – Bamburgh and the Cheviots – which had given me *The Last Harper*, and it has been the land which has inspired every novel I have written since (Figure 9.1). The story of Lilla Cross on the North York Moors gave me the idea for *The Fire of the Kings* (1984), and the castles and abbeys I loved as a child inspired the three medieval novels which followed. The first of them, *The Tournament of Fortune* (1985a), is almost a personal pilgrimage. It opens in Richmond Castle on its bluff above the Swale, imagines life as a Cistercian novice in Fountains Abbey, then moves to the city of York with its medieval bustle. A few chapters later, as I came to describe Robert's first glimpse of the white walls of Rievaulx Abbey, tears welled up in my eyes and I said to myself, 'Yes, I wrote this to come to Rievaulx.' I have spent my adult life wandering the schools and libraries of Northumbria as a performing storyteller and creative writing tutor, all the while gazing, reading the past of the land and telling its tales. By Northumbria I mean the land within the bounds of the ancient kingdom, which stretched northwards from the Humber to the Firth of Forth, and west to Cumbria and Whithorn in Galloway.

Each novel, then, has been an imaginative journey through the landscape at one particular moment in its past. The glory of this is that the land itself expands. It was bigger in the past; it took longer to get from place to place, with all sorts of adventure likely on the way. A recognisable geography is transformed by the past into as vast and diverse a world as Tolkien's Middle Earth – or it can be, if the writing succeeds.

The technical problem facing any writer of historical fiction is how completely to paint the backdrop. Descriptions of land, dwellings and clothing create the sense of the moment in time, but no one writing for young readers can afford to overload the text with information. The story must move, and keep moving, and I've been haunted by the number of children who tell me they find Rosemary Sutcliff hard to read because 'there is so much description'. They're too polite to tell me what they think of me but I've been as guilty of overloading the text as anyone.

I've been fortunate in this respect to have worked with editors like Julia MacRae and Delia Huddy. They suggested cutting a page from the second chapter of *The Last Harper*, and when I looked I realised that it consisted entirely of characters discussing the political configuration of the north in the sixth century in a rush of unpronounceable names, giving information the reader does not at this point need to know. The ideal technique is to save information until the moment when it becomes dramatically urgent, and it is most important to get this right in the opening chapters, where a reader must be hooked and carried away. This goes against what I suspect is the natural impulse of any writer beginning a historical novel and trying to conjure from zero a whole world, which is to describe everything in detail to make it real. I still do this, but have learnt how on my second draft to cut all the reader can do without.

Beyond style, there remains a question of ambition. I do not believe there is anything wrong in a text challenging a reader, and I particularly enjoy complicated plots. I cannot help wanting my stories to be as complicated as I can make them, and though the aim of my second and third drafts is to get everything as clear as possible, I'm then worn out and need an editor to read the story and tell me where I really am impossible to follow. My longest and most complex novel is *Knights of the Sacred Blade* (1989). It tells the story of a band of companions on a three-year quest which takes them the length and breadth of twelfth-century Northumbria, and I could not resist having the people they meet tell them stories about each place they come to. Julia MacRae threw up her hands, and we went through these 'asides' with a vengeance and lopped off 20 pages. Even so, *Knights of the Sacred Blade* remains my most demanding novel. Editing is not always subtraction. In the sequel, *Knights of the Lost Domain* (1991), Julia and Delia felt I'd rushed at one point in the narrative, and the result was an extra chapter.

Apart from the 'Knights' duet, each novel has been a separate journey. I don't feel I have a favourite period, but all my novels so far have been set in the thousand years between the fall of Rome and the late Middle Ages. A lot can change in a thousand years, and the sixth century of *The Last Harper* is an utterly different world from the fourteenth-century late medieval mayhem of *The Tournament of Fortune*. Ideas come unbidden, and each journey is a journey in pursuit.

You can, of course, travel to the past and use it any way you like. I could have filled *The Last Harper* with Dark Age magicians and spells, and woven it into a Tolkienesque fantasy. I could have invented a historical period I would have loved to see but which only exists in fiction, as does Joan Aiken imagining an England in which the Stuarts still ruled. Instead, weaned as I was on Rosemary Sutcliff, Henry Treece and Geoffrey Trease, I went for what I hoped was realism. I wanted a faithful portrait of people as they were at that moment in time, and this has been my aim ever since, though part of the fun has been discovering that each different century had its own idea of what was real.

My second novel, *The Fire of the Kings*, set out to be a straight saga-telling of the life of Edwin, the remarkable man who brought Christianity to Northumbria. One of my sources was *The Anglo-Saxon Chronicle*, which by its own format gave me a perfect method of compiling information. I put together my own chronicle of the first half of the seventh century, slotting the stories told by Bede into their relevant years, and by the time this was finished, I was ready to start writing. I have used this method with every novel since, and as the more recent the century, the more is known, it can be a quite an adventure. I spent six months researching *Knights of the Sacred Blade*, and had to call a halt and start writing or go insane. There are magical moments in that phase of pursuit. One February day in the Dean and Chapter Library in Durham Cathedral, I could read no longer because my hands were frozen, my buttocks numb on the wooden bench, and my nose beginning to snuffle. Here was medieval scholarship indeed. As I rose to flee to the coffee bar, I looked out through the window at the river flowing beneath the citadel, and the twelfth century seemed only yesterday.

On the first of these waking quests, *The Fire of the Kings*, my talisman was a stone tower in the walls of York which had been built by Edwin's masons. I used to stand in its round-arched doorway and daydream my way into Edwin's thoughts. Each age has its own geography of the imagination, its own emotional vocabulary. Conjure it accurately and the characters will speak as they might in life have spoken. If on the other hand you put in their mouths something they could never have thought, let alone said, the result is not just a false note but a weakening in the conjured illusion. Once you have thought your way back into the geography of Edwin's world, you understand perfectly the mythic place that Rome held in his imagination. All around him were the ruins of Roman greatness and law, and no small part of the power of Christianity for him was that it came from Rome. Writing the novel took me even further inside his head. Having lived the terrors of Edwin's youth in exile, I admired him all the more for the way in which, when power at last came into his hands, he used it wisely.

I wanted to tell his life as a saga, a song of deeds, because I felt this was a pattern true to his time, a form he would have recognised. In the event, I was forced to compromise by the complexity of even seventh-century life. Edwin's youthful wanderings were many, and that phase of his life I simplified in the name of art. The gaps in what was known I filled with imagination, but my aim was to be utterly true to what was known. When the story was written, I was surprised to find that the pattern of Edwin's life mirrors the narrative structure of *Beowulf* (Alexander

1973), with Aethelfrith the Grendel our hero who kills to win fame, and Penda the Fire-Drake drawing the aged warrior out to his last battle. On some inner level, I must surely have known this all along, but it left me convinced that realism can only ever be half the story. Stories are recognised and shaped on a deeper level.

On a first reading of any narrative, we pick up clues, we sniff possibilities, we guess at possible outcomes. Any story creates expectations in the reader, and they will either be fulfilled or disappointed. I've been intrigued to learn of moments when I let the reader down. There was no way that harper Gwion was ever going to be able to gaze at Urien's daughter from anything closer than afar, but one neighbour of my mother's cryptic reaction to *The Last Harper* was the comment, 'So he didn't get the girl.' In his eyes, the story failed to deliver what it promised. Another reader told me of his disappointment at the end of *Knights of the Sacred Blade* when Simon finally lifts the lost sword of the ancient kings from where it has lain hidden for centuries – and it promptly snaps at the hilt, sodden with rust. Both these endings seemed the only realistic outcome, but for at least two readers they were a let-down.

I began brooding on how to fulfil expectations of romance and fantasy while telling a realistic story, and my last three novels have played in different ways with the classic story-pattern of the quest-romance. Precisely because it was the most successful literary genre of the Middle Ages, it provides the perfect narrative form for any voyage through those centuries, a shape the characters themselves would have recognised. *The Tournament of Fortune* tells of the famine and fear that followed Bannockburn, nine of the most miserable years in the history of northern England. Robert's quest, and his adventures with the beautiful Marie, act as a thread of light making a dark tale bearable, a romance to balance the chronicle. The novel ends with their wedding bells because, having survived so much, they deserve no less.

My happiest time has been in the twelfth century, riding with Simon de Falaise in *Knights of the Sacred Blade* and *Knights of the Lost Domain.* This was the age when knighthood itself was young, the great abbeys newly-founded, the North still reeling from the smash-and-grab of the Norman Conquest and a melting-pot of English, French, Norse and Scot. Each novel tells both a true story from history and a quest-romance from my deepest day-dreams. As a child I used to long for amazing adventures with wonderful companions, and through Simon de Falaise I have lived them. His quest is my invention, but everywhere he goes is true to how it was, and every tale he is told is true. Driving his quest are the real events through which he moves, culminating in the Battle of the Standard in 1138. This was an age of miracles and wonders, and the true characters are themselves of heroic proportions: King David of the Scots, a wise and beloved man haunted by old ambitions; Walter Espec, the doughty knight recorded as rallying the Yorkshiremen before the Battle of the Standard with a speech invoking King Arthur; Archbishop Thurstan of York, an aged prelate of almost Merlinesque power.

Incredibly, these years also presented me with the perfect villain, a man so widely regarded as evil that when his son was drowned in an accident, Ailred of Rievaulx, one of the sweetest souls in Christendom, remarked that it was clearly God's judgement on the sins of the father. This was William FitzDuncan. Researching his misdeeds, I noted that in 1138 he was attacking Egremont in Cumbria, and by 1140 was lord of it, and this was enough to set me dreaming *Knights of the Lost Domain.*

The adventures of Simon de Falaise come closest in spirit to the games I played as a child with my knights and castle on the sitting-room floor. All my stories have their roots in that dreamworld, and I know now that I am writing for the child reader I was then, who at the age of 12 wrote Rosemary Sutcliff a fan letter. Books are as magical to me now as they were then, a journey to another world. The novels of Rosemary Sutcliff and Henry Treece were my favourite places to go and hide. I could almost say that all that has changed is that nowadays I conjure the other-worlds for myself.

The truth, of course, is that I feel several centuries older than the child I once was. Somewhere along the way, I grew up. I may be propelled by an eternal sense of wonder, but I have an adult sensibility. As a schoolboy, I loved writing fight scenes; as an adult, I find them terrifying. As a child, I believed it was heroic to fearlessly take on all comers, but in *The Fire of the Kings* I felt Edwin heroic precisely because he sought to avoid violence and end the cycle of war, and his ultimate failure had for me the weight of tragedy. This led George English of Radio Newcastle to call me 'a post-Vietnam author'. Another theme here and in the Knights novels is of sentimental education, mistakes made and learnt from, experience as a widening of sensitivity. Simon de Falaise has not only to find the Sacred Blade but also to work out what to make of his desires and how to fight despite his fear, in a white heat of concentration for which he has trained. The poor lad also repeatedly finds himself having to understand both sides of any quarrel, and choose knowing there is sometimes no right or wrong, only loyalty. No one is beyond redemption, not even William FitzDuncan. I am continually impressed by how children ask the deepest questions with a startling directness, and if there is a moral responsibility in writing for children, I believe it is the obligation to be honest, to show life how I feel it to be.

In ending a novel, however, I think a child reader deserves a glimpse of how I feel life should be, with light and darkness in balance, and the imagined world at peace. There will always be stories, like *The Fire of the Kings*, where the truth will not let me have my way, and all I can do is what Osric does on the final page, send the children away to safety before turning to face the end.

Bibliography

Alexander, M. (1973) *Beowulf*. Harmondsworth: Penguin Books.
The Anglo-Saxon Chronicle. Everyman's Library, J. M. Dent.
Atterton, J. (1983) *The Last Harper*. London: Julia MacRae.
Atterton, J. (1984) *The Fire of the Kings*. London: Julia MacRae.
Atterton, J. (1985a) *The Tournament of Fortune*. London: Julia MacRae.
Atterton, J. (1985b) *The Shape-Changer*. London: Julia MacRae.
Atterton, J. (1989) *Knights of the Sacred Blade*. London: Julia MacRae.
Atterton, J. (1991) *Knights of the Lost Domain*. London: Julia MacRae.
Atterton, J. (1995a) *Robin Hood and the Sheriff*. London: Julia MacRae.
Atterton, J. (1995b) *The Outlaw Robin Hood*. London: Julia MacRae.

Chapter 10

'Over the stile and into the past': *Children of Winter* and other historical fiction

Berlie Doherty

Berlie Doherty illuminates for us here how her own memories of childhood, the surroundings where she lives, the memories of other living people, family documents, visits to locations, chance encounters, research in museums, drawings and reading all provide ideas and contexts for her stories. But research must not clog the story which should ideally meet its readers' needs for a certain timeless quality and a secondary world where it is easy to believe in the characters and imagine the setting. To this end, Doherty employs narrative devices such as time-slip and varied narrative voices.

It could be said that every piece of fiction is an historical document, because it sets, in time, the style, manners and philosophy of a period, as well as the physical presence of the characters and their immediate world. Between writing and publication, it is already set in the past. Thus in my most recent novel, *Holly Starcross* (2001), I found myself recording in great detail a meal in a Happy Eater, mentioning the child singer Charlotte Church, mobile phones, e-mail and the Internet, as a way of consciously securing a historical reference and authenticity to a story which in itself is timeless, being about the flow of love between a child and her missing father.

Just as I wanted to secure Holly in the year 2001, so I sought to secure my first book, *How Green You Are!* (1982) and its sequel, *The Making of Fingers Finnigan* (1983), in the mid-1950s. I was not aware at the time that I was writing a piece of social history. I was simply exploring my own childhood as a way of establishing a recognisable setting for my story. I had the idea that if I recreated the familiar territory of my childhood in a way that was vivid and recognisable, then the child reader would feel comfortable there too. So we have children playing out on the beach and in the street for hours on end, cowboys and Indians on the 'telly', and Mrs Marriot's kitchen shop as the place where Bee realises that she has grown away from her best friend Julie, who has recently started to go to the convent grammar school.

It wasn't like a shop, because everything she sold she'd made herself. She'd have things in trays on their table – cakes and bread and ginger biscuits and cough candy – but it was really queer because when you went in you couldn't smell any of the lovely things laid out on the table. All you could smell was boiled fish. They'd three cats. You sometimes got bits of cat fur stuck to your toffee apple.

(How Green You Are!)

The windy open-air swimming pool, the local laundry 'clattering away, wheezing out steam like an old woman who's smoked too much' (Doherty 1982), the ferry across the Mersey, were places I visited in the stories, not from a sense of nostalgia but because I felt at home there, and wanted my readers to feel at home too. I felt if I got the geography right, the stories would emerge naturally. One such was the story/chapter entitled 'Finnigan's Angel and the Saturday Matinee' (Doherty 1983) which, like the 'Weird George' chapter in *How Green You Are!* stood on its own as a Radio 4 short story (entitled *Finnigan's Angel*). Here I'm describing one of the major social events of a child in the mid-1950s.

Saturday morning, every week till we were about twelve, we used to go to the matinee at the picture house on the prom. It was great. When the wind was blowing in really strong from the sea you could taste the grit of sand in your interval ice cream, and when it rained you avoided the back seats or you got dripped on. We always saw the same films five or six times in a year, so it didn't matter that the projector broke down so often; in fact, we looked forward to it happening.

(The Making of Fingers Finnigan)

More than anything else in these two first books I was unconsciously recapturing a sense of community, which had all but disappeared by the time I was writing about it, in the late 1970s and early 1980s.

On good evenings we'd sit on our steps gossiping, doing the veg for tea, and our mums would stand leaning on the doorways with cups of tea in their hands, calling across to each other and waiting for the bread cart to come round. It was driven by an elderly chap called Wallo, and pulled by Peggotty, his horse. Peggotty and my mum got on really well together. If there was any bread left over from the day before Mum would put jam on it and save it for Peggotty, and the horse came to expect this little treat, and though she was pretty slow at getting about she would gallop past the last few houses on the street up to ours, and stamp on the step. If she didn't get what she wanted soon enough she'd come right in, or as far as the cart would let her, snorting and tossing her long head back till she got her slice. I didn't like to be the one who gave it to her, though – I didn't like to feel the slap of her wet mouth across my hand, or to hear the solid chomping of her enormous teeth. Sometimes she'd leave a payment in a big steaming dollop on the pavement outside, and I'd have to shovel it into a bucket and put it into the back yard for Dad to take to his allotment. I didn't mind doing that.   *(The Making of Fingers Finnigan)*

Every chapter in those two first books contains an element of autobiography and moves on to something which is completely made up. I have described this process in my autobiographical chapter in *Something about the Author* (1993a), and when I talk to children about writing, I like to call these two elements 'I Remember' and 'Let's Pretend'. For me they have become the essential ingredients of story writing. But the 'I remembers' are not always my own, and when I came to write *Granny Was A Buffer Girl* (1986), a family novel which spans three generations, I began by looking at the 1920s, when my parents were young. One of the chapters in the book, 'Bridie and Jack', is actually about my Catholic mother and Anglican father's forbidden courtship and secret marriage, and describes the wayward couple roaring off into their future – and my own – on the back of my father's Matchless motor bike. It first appeared on Radio Merseyside as *A Liverpool Love Story*. When I came to write *Granny was a Buffer Girl*, I decided to include that story but to move the setting to Sheffield because I had had the idea of writing about Sheffield buffer girls. Now I had put my mind to writing about a particular city, I was able to pinpoint my locations, such as the Cutlers' Hall and the Rivelin Valley where the grinding mills used to be, and the great, pulsing steel works along the Rother Valley. My favourite research is live, talking to people who have first hand experience of a place or an event, so I contacted retired buffer girls through Radio Sheffield and talked to them about their working conditions in the buffing shops in the 1930s.

> It never occurred to him to look among the buffer girls, even though the sickly sweet metal-and-hot dust smell of their work lay heavy in every room, and the whirr of their machinery wound interminably through the day, and the lusty singing of the girls at their work chimed in every corner. If he had climbed up to the top floor he would have seen the long buffing shop hot and bright with sunlight pouring through the roof windows, and the forty girls standing in their row putting the gleam on all those articles he inspected. They would be holding their faces away from the sand-dust that the wheel sprayed back at them, and from time to time they'd dash with their mugs to the tap in the corner and swill their mouths out, or they'd stretch back their shoulders to ease the ache, or flex the muscles of their feet.   (*Granny Was a Buffer Girl*)

In *The Sailing Ship Tree* (1998), I was looking directly into my father's childhood. He was born in 1902, a twin, the son of the butler of an estate in Liverpool. My father talked frequently about his 'country' childhood, about watching the sailing-ships coming into busy Liverpool Bay, along with steamships and liners, and about playing with the children of the other servants and with the son of a shipping line owner, whom they called Master. Dad and his brother would hang 'like stick insects' from the great trees in the drive, watching the carriages sweeping up to the 'Big House'. Throughout his 94 years, he never lost his respectful attitude towards 'the gentry', touching his cap to anyone whom he regarded as his superior. He wrote anecdotal stories which were never published, and when he died I decided to take the evidence, or clues, which the stories presented about childhood in the first decade of the last century, and use them as a springboard for a novel that was both about my father and about an event that never happened, about his childhood and about childhood itself.

My research took me first to the 'Big House', Bark Hill, in Aigburth, which is now I. M. Marsh College and modernised so not easy to recreate in the imagination. I then went up the road to Sudley, a Victorian house belonging to the Holt's shipping family, bequeathed to the people of Liverpool by Emma Holt as an art gallery. Though smaller than Bark Hill, Sudley remains as it would have looked at the time of my father's childhood, and here I could imagine the lonely young master at his lessons or pacing the long corridors, and the inquisitive maid Tweeny going silently about her tasks. I saw the tiny lodge cottage which replicated the one where my father and his parents and two siblings lived and I saw the massive old trees in the drive, the sailing-ships of my story.

My next visit was to the Merseyside Maritime Museum, where I learned about ships like the *Titanic*, the thronging dockyards, the emigration liners, and the 'mass of humanity labouring...in adverse conditions to keep the ships moving' (Kennerley 1996). I also used for reference a precious diary that my grandfather, whom I never met, wrote in 1896 when he travelled by steamship to Australia, in which he describes the frequent stops for coal, when everyone on board, passengers and crew alike, got covered in coal dust.

I was fascinated equally with the gentry and with the servants, and thus decided to split my narration between the twins, Dorothy and Walter (my aunt and father), the young master George and an invented child servant, Tweeny. I then had first person insight into both the servants' and the masters' lives. Tweeny holds the balance between the two worlds.

> I'm invisible. Nobody sees Tweeny. I have to slip upstairs to do me polishing and melt away in the shadders when the gentry come past. I have to take me orders from Mrs Bains or Joan and keep out of everybody's way while I'm doing me jobs. Everybody's busy, nobody's got time to notice me. Set the tray for the Dowager and run up to her maid with it and disappear quick. Collect the scraps for the cats and disappear quick. Rub the doors and floors till I can see myself in them, but don't let anybody see me. Nobody notices me as long as I do me job. I'm everywhere and I'm nowhere. Nobody sees me and I see everybody.
>
> (*The Sailing Ship Tree*)

But if Tweeny is the all-seeing eye and the device that brings the plot to its head, it was my father's anecdotes and observations that gave me the essential perception of place and time and which set the atmosphere of the piece. No amount of historical documentation can replace personal experience. In many sections like the following extract my father's memories and my imagined enhancements of them are so entwined that I no longer know where one ends and the other begins. It describes a visit to the butler's pantry.

> Pa stood with his back to us, in a green baize apron tied around his waist and the starched cuffs of his shirt pushed above his powdery elbows. He still had his white gloves on though. He was intent on his task of counting out pieces of silver cutlery to put in the big cupboard. There was a fire blazing and a comfy red chair. It was bigger than the room in the cottage where we all had to live and eat. Next to the window a bright-yellow canary bobbed and trilled in its cage. I never knew till then that Pa had a canary. Pa continued to count under his breath until he had all the knives and forks and spoons nestled away in their own felt compartments.

Then he closed the door with its brass knob and locked it. He turned gravely, rolling his sleeves back down with quick jerks of his wrists.

(*The Sailing Ship Tree*)

The first book that I consciously set in the past was *Children of Winter*, which was published in 1985. It is interesting to note that when I mentioned to my editor that I was writing a book set at the time of the Great Plague she said regretfully that children dislike historical fiction and that it would be very hard to sell. I had just started to write it, and it is because of her apprehensiveness that I introduced the 'time-slip' device as a way of drawing the modern child into the past. Things have changed a great deal since then, maybe because of the initiative of using 'real books' in schools and because of the National Curriculum, where for a time *Children of Winter* fell happily into the 'Tudors and Stuarts' category. Whatever the reason, it is apparent from the popularity of this book and of *Street Child* (1993b) in particular that historical fiction is currently fashionable, both in school and out.

Children of Winter is a story of survival, set in Derbyshire at the time of the Great Plague. It is not an attempt to recreate the Eyam story, with which I'm very familiar, as I live only a few miles from the village. That brave history had been beautifully told in Jill Paton Walsh's *A Parcel of Patterns* in 1983. My novel concentrates on a child's distant perception of the horror of the plague, of separation from family, of home making under alien conditions, and of the mutual support of the two sisters and brother. In that sense it could have been a novel about refugees, evacuees, survivors of a war or major natural disaster. The fact that it is set in a particular time and place gives me the colour I need to make my story live, but it is not a documentary of seventeenth century life. The plague hangs as a nightmare between the children's home life and their necessary isolation from it, as when they encounter their mother's friend Maggie Hoggs at the stepping-stones which they have promised never to cross. It is as if she is shrouded in grief, screaming at them from one bank of the river to the other.

> ''Tis well for thee, hiding up there in the hills! I know thee. And why should tha be saved, tell me that, when all mine are dead? Why should the Lord spare thee, and take all mine?'
>
> She flung herself into the river, not waiting till she reached the stepping-stones, and ploughed across it, thigh deep in the murky water and with her long robes flowing like billowing wings around her. She held her arms out to the children as if she would embrace them and drag them all down with her.
>
> (*Children of Winter*)

When the shepherd Clem comes in a state of high fever he brings the horror of the plague to their barn, with his news of the silent, empty street of their village, deserted cottages and smokeless chimneys, bread as stale as stones on the table.

> 'Our Moll was alone in the house, and she was alone because those three children of hers were all dead, and her husband was out digging the ground for a place to put them in. I went to comfort her, and she screamed at me to get away from her, and save myself at least. It was too late for her, she said.'
>
> (*Children of Winter*)

The atmosphere and sense of the historical period in which the story of *Children of Winter* is set is intended to work in the same way as it does in *Daughter of the Sea* (1996). It is a time that is not our own, in which a human drama is played out to its inevitable conclusion. *Daughter of the Sea*, which I call a folk-novel, is set on a remote island (in my head, Papa Stour in the Shetlands, which I visited for the first time after I had completed the first draft of the novel) where men and women perform ancient tasks of domestic farming and fishing and are at the mercy of the elements and of the powerful creatures of the sea.

> The women hone knives on the stone, and their hands will be brown from the sea and from the fish-gut slime. And as they work they talk to each other of things they've always known. That's when the story's told.   (*Daughter of the Sea*)

What I tried to capture here was a sense of the timelessness of folklore and magic. I set it vaguely at the time of the Scottish clearances and dressed the people and their customs accordingly, but it is never intended to be an historical document of that period.

Street Child (1993b), however, was a different matter. Here I was writing about an historically documented figure, Doctor Barnardo, and about a child who is known to have existed, Jim Jarvis. If I chose to write about them I had to make the historical setting authentic and tangible. To write for children about a childhood of destitution and hardship is not an easy task, and in many ways the fact that I was setting the novel in a specific period, the 1860s, enabled me to create a physical world that played as powerful a part as any of the characters, clad in the sombre hues of an uncaring and sometimes grotesque Victorian London. Here, of course, the memories of back street hovels, stinking wharves, workhouses and their gloomy schools and infirmaries, were not my own but those of the people who recorded the period, Barnardo himself, museum archivists, and, most graphically, Charles Dickens. I did not, however, turn to Dickens' novels but to his journals, *All the Year Round* (1859–95), which he both edited and contributed to. It was his astonishing report of carpet-beating being carried out in the infirmary wards of the workhouse, 'carpet-beating (is) carried out as a trade in the infirmary wards, the dust and flue settling upon the sick and dying' that informed the following passage in *Street Child*.

> The air was thick with dust and heavy with a rhythmic thudding sound. Lines had been strung from one end of the ward to the other, and carpets flung across them. Women and big boys with their sleeves rolled up were hitting the carpets with flattened sticks, and at every stroke the dust shivered in the air like clouds of flies. In their beds the sick people gasped and coughed and begged for water, and the old nurse shuffled from patient to patient and moaned with them and told them off in turns.   (*Street Child*)

The history of Jim Jarvis himself was the first in a series of short biographical pamphlets which Barnardo circulated to the wealthy in the hope of raising aware-ness of the plight of destitute boys and contributions towards funding a home for them (Barnardo and Shaw undated). He called Jim 'my first Arab' and in a few para-graphs described how the boy had turned up at his Ragged School and refused to leave. He had been orphaned at five, had run away from the workhouse, been picked up by a coal bargee and had run away from him because of his persistent cruelty, and had joined the street urchins, begging, stealing and sleeping rough. This was all I had to go on, but it was enough to whet my curiosity and set me off on several weeks of research before I began to write anything at all. I loved the research, which is very beguiling, opening up new avenues of investigation at every turn. On a visit to relatives in Kent I came across a converted coal lighter and wrote to its owners. They sent me drawings and details of how a man and a boy would have handled the huge sail and the loading and unloading of 30 tons of coal, how they slept on board, how their lives and work were dominated by the tide. All this was fascinating – I had never even heard of a lighter until then. I could have gone on and on researching the social history of the period, but I had a novel to write.

The challenge for the novelist is to know when to leave the research behind and get on with the story. You have to resist the temptation to pour in all the fascinating details that you've gleaned – it only belongs to the story if it is relevant and helps the reader to walk freely round the location of the drama. In the end there is only one aim in the writing of historical fiction – to create a setting that is so vivid that the child readers can imagine themselves there, can place themselves in another time and understand the universals that transcend the particular.

> Catherine felt her mind turning and turning in the centre of the gale, listening to a sound that seemed to take her away to another time; that seemed to bring memories of calm and comfort down from the great slabs of rock that protected their barn, and the hill, and the valley below, and the blighted village; that would always protect them, ages from now.   (*Children of Winter*)

References

Barnardo, Dr and Shaw, A. P. (undated) *My First Arab* (pamphlet).

Dickens, C. (1859–95) *All the Year Round*, weekly journal. London: Charles Dickens.

Doherty, B. (1982) *How Green You Are!* London: Methuen.

Doherty, B. (1983) *The Making of Fingers Finnigan*. London: Methuen.

Doherty, B. (1985) *Children of Winter*. London: Methuen.

Doherty, B. (1986) *Granny Was a Buffer Girl*. London: Methuen.

Doherty, B. (1993a) 'I remember and let's pretend', in Nakamara, J (ed.) *Something about the Author* volume 16. Detroit: Gale Research Inc.

Doherty, B. (1993b) *Street Child*. London: Hamish Hamilton.

Doherty, B. (1996) *Daughter of the Sea*. London: Hamish Hamilton.

Doherty, B. (1998) *The Sailing Ship Tree*. London: Hamish Hamilton.

Doherty, B. (2001) *Holly Starcross*. London: Hamish Hamilton.

Kennerley, A. (1996) 'Keeping ships moving' in *Room Service: Aspects of life aboard the ocean liner*, papers presented to a research day school. Liverpool: Liverpool University Press and National Museums and Galleries on Merseyside.

Paton Walsh, J. (1983) *A Parcel of Patterns*. London: Kestrel/Viking

Chapter 11

Flesh on the bones

Michael Foreman

War Boy and War Game *are two of the most original and popular illustrated histor-ical books for children. Michael Foreman explains the autobiographical origins of the books and the approaches he used in order to make picture books out of the immense events of world wars. He also indicates how memory is activated, how research is essential but not the whole story, and how convictions power the writing and the motivation to bring such topics to a child audience. This short, moving account has some of the impact of the books themselves.*

When I was a small boy growing up in the War, I thought that was what life was like. I did not know a world without war. I thought war was normal. Our village on the East coast of England was full of soldiers and surrounded by airfields (Figure 11.1). Sailors filled every spare room in every house. The woods hid tanks and heavy guns. The skies were full of butterflies and bombers. The German Luftwaffe made nightly bombing raids and sometimes dive-bombers made daylight raids, interrupting our games of football. We boys played sports, went fishing, stole apples and did all the things which boys have always done, but against a background of war. It seemed normal. It also seemed normal to have no father. My father was already dead, and the fathers of my friends were all away in the war. Every family was a one-parent family.

After the war my teenage years were lived under a nuclear cloud. The Cold War threatened instant and mass destruction. So when I came to do my first book, aged 21, at the height of the Cold War, I was not going to do a book about fairy tale princesses and furry animals. My first book, *The General* (1961), was an anti-war book, as was the second, *The Two Giants* (1967), to be followed by *Moose* (1971), and *War and Peas* (1974). To do books showing the folly of war seemed natural to me. What surprised me was that I could find no other picture books dealing with this subject.

In case you think I was obsessed, I also touched a few other subjects from the kidnapping of Father Christmas, *The Great Sleigh Robbery* (1968), to pollution, *Dinosaurs and all that Rubbish* (1972), to feminism, *All the King's Horses* (1976), and to racism *Panda's Puzzle* (1977). But in all these books I did not use real people. I used a symbolic 'General' and a stereotypical American and a Russian. The 'Two Giants' were 'collaged' from torn paper and represented the Super Powers as did

Figure 11.1 Michael Foreman aged three years

the Bear and Bald Eagle in *Moose*. The resulting books had the appearance of children's books, even if the subject matter was unusual.

It was only when I came to work on *War Boy* (1989), that I used real events and real people. My sons were at the age when they bubbled questions: they were a constant fountain of why and when and what was it like? Especially, what was it like when you were our age? when you were a boy? In answering their questions I found myself unblocking a logjam of memories. And curiously, the earliest memories were the clearest. It was only by reliving the early memories that I was able to grow into the later ones.

When verifying dates and family stories for *War Boy*, I spoke to many relatives. I was struck by the absence of uncles. I had a full complement of ancient aunts, but my uncles had died as very young men in the First World War. So, while working on *War Boy*, I became fascinated by the story of my dead uncles. Their names were on the village War Memorial which I have drawn in *War Boy*. They were farm boys. They could shoot a bounding hare at two hundred yards. They were crack shots.

They became snipers. One day in 1916 the War Office sent my granny the army cap belonging to her son, Billy. There was a bullet hole in it. He had just been killed by a German sniper. Recently, a Gulf War veteran told me, 'Yes, it takes a sniper to kill a sniper.'

War Game (1993) is dedicated to those four uncles who died in the First War. I have used their Christian names for the main characters, but it is not their story. It is based on real events and my uncles played their part in the various scenes depicted, but they were just four lads among millions, and precisely how they died will never be known. I have traced the graves of three of them and, when standing there in Flanders Fields, so similar in their openness to the same sky as the home fields of East Anglia, I felt closer to those fallen young men than I did to their now ancient sisters. I stood on the wall of a cemetery and looked out across the site of the impromptu Christmas football match. Behind me, row upon row of white gravestones stood like a vast crowd of ghosts, and before me it seemed the players had just left the field.

I returned and spent many hours in the archives of the Imperial War Museum, just as I had for *War Boy*. I found first hand accounts of the Christmas truce written by ordinary soldiers, and largely discredited at the time by the Official Reports. There is no doubt that facts are crucial but historical fact is not enough. With the turn of the Millennium, the Great War must truly seem like ancient history to today's children. Historical fact does not bridge that gap. It tells you what happened, but historical fiction can take you there. Just to fill a book with facts would make it an information book, and the artist would be a technical illustrator. There is nothing wrong with that. But if those facts can be made to live, to engage the imagination, perhaps children will feel, as well as understand. Imagination puts flesh on the bones of fact.

Squeezing a subject as big as a world war into a picture book poses obvious problems. I had to take a small view of a vast event. *War Boy* was a small boy's eye view, one boy's experience and memories of a family in a particular moment of history (Figure 11.2). With *War Game*, I limited the period covered from the Declaration of War until the first Christmas. Starting the book with a youthful village football match and ending with the game in No Man's Land gave the book a structure, a circular framework, as well as engaging the interest of present day children through their familiarity with football.

I wanted both books to have the feeling of sketch books which could have been done at the time, visual records of the events. And to add to the immediacy and feeling of reality I used printed ephemera of the period...cigarette cards, aircraft recognition cards, ration books and advertisements. The text would run between the pictures in informal bite-size chunks, like diary entries, easily digested and not stuffed with dates and statistics. *War Boy* was a series of unconnected memories and needed to be illustrated in a variety of techniques, instant line drawings for incidental memories and more detailed full-colour watercolours for the more significant memories.

I have received many more letters from readers of *War Boy* and *War Game* than for any of my other books. Response came from the very young and the very old. I thought *War Boy* would be the remaindered book of all time and of interest only to my family but the reaction was such that I was encouraged to continue the story

Figure 11.2 Memories of a childhood during war

into *After the War was Over* (1995), which begins on the day *War Boy* ends. Subsequently, some schools have produced books of their own with the children interviewing grandparents and elderly uncles and aunts about their wartime memories. Every family has a fund of stories which should not be neglected and forgotten.

When I was a teenager I hated anything to do with war including Remembrance Days and men wearing medals and marching to military bands. The War was too recent, too close. It was, I thought, time to put all that behind us. It seemed to me that war itself was being glorified. But now Remembrance Days move me deeply. Those men who wear the medals are now very old and their stories should be told. Each year this becomes more important. It is important not that we just remember the War but that we remember the causes of war so that we can recognise the symptoms, the poisonous seeds, before they take root.

The future has been given to our children by the old men and women of my parents' generation. We, the generation in between, must ensure that the sacrifices and experiences of that older generation are understood and appreciated by the children of today.

Figure 11.3

References

Foreman, M. and Charter, J. (1961) *The General*. London: Routledge/Dutton.

Foreman, M. (1967) *The Two Giants*. London: Brockhampton/Pantheon.

Foreman, M. (1968) *The Great Sleigh Robbery*. London: Hamish Hamilton/Pantheon.

Foreman, M. (1971) *Moose*. London: Hamish Hamilton/Pantheon.

Foreman, M. (1972) *Dinosaurs and all that Rubbish*. London: Hamish Hamilton/Cromwell.

Foreman, M. (1974) *War and Peas*. London: Hamish Hamilton/Cromwell.

Foreman, M. (1976) *All the King's Horses*. London: Hamish Hamilton/Bradbury.

Foreman, M. (1977) *Panda's Puzzle*. London: Hamish Hamilton/Bradbury.

Foreman, M. (1989) *War Boy*. London: Pavilion Books.

Foreman, M. (1993) *War Game*. London: Pavilion Books.

Foreman, M. (1995) *After the War was Over*. London: Pavilion Books.

Chapter 12

Daddy, or serendipity

Philip Pullman

This reprinted article was first published in Children's Literature in Education *volume 23 number 3, 1992. Philip Pullman charts how his ideas 'come to rest in the part of the mind where stories grow'; the 'Daddy' of the title refers to a poem, on a picture postcard, that he discovered by chance. He explains why he is attracted to the Victorian period, the basis for his historical trilogy, saying that 'there is much more material lying about' including intriguing photographs. He reflects on the questions of authentic sounding dialogue, changed language use, the place of irony in tone, the thorny issue of originality and the inescapable presence of ideology.*

Some years ago, I used to work in a library in the Charing Cross Road, and every lunchtime I'd wander around the little courts and alleys nearby, or go up to Covent Garden, still a real market then; and when I had a shilling or two (it was as long ago as that) in my pocket, I'd go into a shop in Cecil Court and browse through the theatrical memorabilia in search of something that was simultaneously interesting and cheap.

One day I found, in a box of old postcards, a couple that intrigued me. They were a pair: photographs, with the verses of a sentimental poem printed underneath. The poem is called *Daddy*, and it's told in the voice of a little girl whose birthday it is. She and her father are sitting miserably in their poorly furnished room, and they're miserable because Mother has died. 'I wonder if Mother is thinking of us, Because it's my birthday night,' say the last two lines. The first photograph shows a man dressed as a labourer, even to the strings around the legs of his trousers, holding a little girl of eight or nine on his lap. (Those lengths of string tied under the knee are called bowyangs. I found that out recently by accident, and now that I know it, I shall certainly use it. It's another example of research by serendipity.) The second shows him weeping, the little girl tenderly stroking his head, and Mother gazing down from Heaven, dressed in white and surrounded by wisps of cotton wool.

The postcards are undated, but I'd guess they're Edwardian rather than Victorian. There was clearly a flourishing trade in such things: they're published by Bamforth, who are still producing picture postcards, though now of the comic-saucy variety. I kept the pictures on my desk for years, but didn't look very closely at them until, one day, I noticed something I hadn't seen before: how obviously stagey the setting was.

First printed in Children's Literature in Education, vol. 23, No. 3, 1992. Reprinted by permission of Human Sciences Press.

The windows are not real windows, but white sheets with black strips painted on to represent glazing bars; the fireplace is hastily put together out of bricks and planks; and so on. The idea of a photographic studio where they took pictures of invented scenes – a sort of precursor of the movie studio: not movies but stillies, perhaps – seemed such a richly promising setting that I couldn't resist the cheerful improvisatory vigour of it. It came to rest in the part of my mind where stories grow, and many years later the taking of that photograph emerged on page 122 of *The Ruby in the Smoke* (Puffin 1987), by which time the little girl had a name and a history. She didn't stop there. I'm writing about her now, in a book called *The Tin Princess*.

DADDY

Take my head on your shoulder, Daddy,
Turn your face to the west,
It is just the hour when the sky turns gold,
The hour that mother loves best.
The day has been long without you, Daddy,
You've been such a while away,
And now you're as tired of your work Daddy,
As I am tired of play. But I've got you,
And you've got me, so everything seems right,
I wonder if Mother is thinking of us,
Because it is my birthday night.

Why do your big tears fall, Daddy,
Mother's not far away,
I often seem to hear her voice
Falling across my play,
And it sometimes makes me cry, Daddy,
To think that it's none of it true,
Till I fall asleep to dream, Daddy,
Of home and Mother and you,
For I've got you and you've got me,
So everything seems right,
We're all the world to each other, Daddy,
For Mother, dear Mother, once told me so.

I tell that story because it illustrates part of the serendipity of research – if I can dignify what I do to find out about the background of my stories with a name that really implies a procedure more scholarly altogether. There's nothing scholarly about the way I 'research': the material is largely brought to me by luck, and I read what interests me, and stop when I'm bored. I read in order to be able to invent convincingly. And I read material about the time of Queen Victoria not because I've decided to write a novel set in 1872, say: I set a novel then because I'm already fascinated by that period. I could never write a novel set in the time of the Crusades: the period doesn't pull me toward it. The interest comes first.

The Victorian period is easier to research, or serendipitise, than the Middle Ages not only because there's a lot more material lying about but because of the nature of some of that material. In one sense, the Victorians are more real to us than any age before them: the real-ness (I don't quite mean reality) of, say, Dr Johnson or Elizabeth I is of a different kind, as different as painting is from photography. A loose bootlace, a splash of mud on a trouser leg, a clumsily folded shawl – a million details which a painter would have to choose whether or not to include, and then would probably leave out – confirm the real-ness of the subject. And then there are the subjects themselves. Dr Johnson and Elizabeth I were painted because they were eminent; there are far fewer representations of their servants, or men and women in the street. But we're all familiar with the great Victorian photographs of slum children, of fishermen mending their nets, of farmers holding horses. They're easy to come by – the series of Victorian and Edwardian books of photographs, published by Batsford, is widely available – and they're enormously popular.

And there are plenty of original photographs about. Originals are better than reproductions in books; they're often sharper and clearer, but more to the point, they are real. The subject of the photograph might have handled this very piece of card. I have a sense – I wouldn't say that it was remotely connected with anything psychic, but it does induce a subtle thrill – of real connection with the past when I touch them. I'm thinking of two in particular that I own. One shows a young couple who look as if they've just become engaged. It's a studio portrait taken (to judge by their clothes) in about 1870, in either Norwich or Scarborough, because the photographer had studios in both places, according to the florid label on the back. Nothing out of the ordinary so far; but they were an unusual couple to find in Norwich or Scarborough in the latter half of the nineteenth century. Did he come from somewhere else? Did they settle there? Did they have children? What they must have met in the way of prejudice and suspicion can only be imagined. But it *can* be imagined – and that's my point: there's a story in it.

The other photograph shows a murky-looking cemetery, with a newly dug grave covered in flowers. When I show this to primary school children I say, 'Can you see the ghost?' and then point him out: standing behind the grave there's the figure of a man in a cloth cap, his right arm bent, his hand on his heart. It's only vaguely visible, because at some stage during the printing someone has scratched the image very carefully off the negative, and left a man-shaped space. And there's a story in that. Why go to those lengths? What kind of family tensions, hatreds, jealousies… I don't need to go on. There's no shortage of stories begging to be told.

But stories live in language, and that demands research as well, because the further away we go from the present day, the more salient a certain problem becomes. In simple terms it poses itself like this: 'Do I write in present-day English or English of the period?' The Middle Ages, for instance: if the characters are speaking modern English, why are they wearing armour? Or: if they're going on a Crusade, why aren't they speaking Middle English? To write about Crusaders in their kind of English would allow the dialogue to sound authentic, but would grievously restrict the readership. If you want readers, you have to use present-day English; but that can easily sound incongruous. Would a knight in armour be able to say something like 'Come off it'? You'd have to find an equivalent that had the force of the idiom without being too closely anchored in a speech-society that didn't yet exist. (The *parole* of the speaker's utterance would have to match the *langue* of his clothes.) The best you can hope for is a sort of dignified neutrality that reads like a good translation, because a translation is what it would inevitably be. A similar thing is true, incidentally, of science-fiction set in the future, or in distant parts of the universe: everything spoken is a translation from a language that doesn't exist.

(There's a curious parallel here with the phenomenon of period plays on videotape. In the early, unsophisticated days of TV drama, when the classic serial was still in vogue, costume drama was often made on video. Seeing it repeated now produces an odd dislocation: we associate the brightness and immediacy of the video image with 'live' TV like news broadcasts, where we know that what we are seeing is taking place at this very moment in a studio. The subtlety of lighting and the different kind of sharpness – the different *quality* of image – we see on film has an entirely different effect. Film, we know, can't be taking place now: it has had to be processed, developed, and so on; it belongs to the past. So we accept costume drama on film much more readily than on video: the past-ness and the present-ness don't clash.)

So although the language in which I write about Victorian characters can't be Victorian English, it has to work like it. I have to know what's possible. A word like competence, for example: 'Margaret, like Sally, valued competence when she saw it; it was one of the reasons they liked each other' (*The Tiger in the Well*, 1991 p. 270) has undergone a slight semantic shift since the year 1881 in which *The Tiger in the Well* is set. Then, it would have been easier to see it out of the corner of one's eye and half understand the meaning 'sufficient income to live on'. That meaning has retreated a little since then. I've explained more fully elsewhere (*Signal* 60, September 1989) the technique I call *leakage*, whereby I make use of this phenomenon of subliminal 'misreading' by planting a word that can have a different, but reinforcing, meaning. Here is a case in point. The older meaning of *competence* is actually relevant here, since the two characters in this scene have just been discussing how to prevent the theft of Sally's money. The proximity of 'value' reinforces this (I'm not talking about close attention to the text here, but the sort of thing that happens when we read in a hurry, impatient for the story).

But the knot is tighter than this. *Competence* also has a legal meaning: 'capable of being brought forward, admissible; within the jurisdiction of a court.' And again this association is reinforced, because Margaret is talking to a lawyer, and they are discussing the details of a legal case. Furthermore, readers have met that notion already, because when Sally herself is talking to the lawyer on p. 245, he says, 'Extradition would not be competent' and goes on to explain, 'It wouldn't apply,' thus demonstrating his competence...

Do I really expect any reader to be conscious of all that?

No, of course not. But I am. It's a game I play for my own pleasure. And in order to satisfy myself that these connections work, I have to use various dictionaries, notably (of course) the complete *Oxford English Dictionary*, with magnifying glass. I need to be sure that a sense I want to suggest was current in 1881 (or whenever), and no other dictionary will do.

But as well as the semantic aspect of language there's something less easy to describe. I think it's located in the rhythm, though irony comes into it as well. I have in mind a quality I see in three writers who flourished around the end of the last and the beginning of this century: Jerome K. Jerome, W. W. Jacobs, and the unjustly forgotten Australian author Norman Lindsay. The particular note, the special flavour, of the tone of Jerome's *Three Men in a Boat* is one I've enjoyed since I first read it at the age of nine:

> George goes to sleep at a bank from ten to four each day, except Saturdays, when they wake him up and put him outside at two.   (*Three Men in a Boat*, 1889)

You find the same tone in W. W. Jacobs:

> 'Boys!' he said, at last. 'That's the third time this week, and yet if I was to catch one and skin 'im alive I suppose I should get into trouble over it. Even 'is own father and mother would make a fuss, most likely.'   (*Deep Waters*, 1919)

And Norman Lindsay has a touch of it too:

> 'While you do the fighting,' said Bunyip bravely, 'I shall mind the Puddin'.'

'The trouble is,' said Bill, 'that this is a very secret, crafty Puddin', an if you wasn't up to his game he'd be askin' you to look at a spider an then run away while your back is turned.'

'That's right,' said the Puddin', gloomily. 'Take a Puddin's character away. Don't mind his feelings.'

'We don't mind your feelin's, Albert,' said Bill. 'What we minds is your treacherous 'abits.' (*The Magic Pudding*, 1918)

Once it's heard, that tone is unmistakable. If there's anything of that tone in my writing I'd be glad, because its ironic astringency pleases me enormously, and if it has a location in time it's roughly at the period I'm writing about or a little later, so if I get something like it I'm not too far off.

What about originality, though? Aren't I just parroting? Isn't it derivative? We make too much of this quality called originality: I think that we learn by imitation. Everything is an imitation of something else, in a way; and literary theory comes up with nice words like intertextuality to account for it. Writing is about writing as well as about life, and if you sincerely imitate the models that are congenial to you, you can't help but improve your command of the material. The danger comes, I suppose, when you begin to imitate yourself. So I read and imitate the writers I admire, and many of them – by chance – happen to have flourished around the turn of the century. It all reinforces that tone I referred to.

I thought, incidentally, before I'd read any, that I'd find an appropriate tone to imitate in penny dreadfuls: *Boys of England, Deadwood Dick, Jack Harkaway* and the like. I was wrong, because there's no place for irony in tales of that sort. They were written, most of them, in too much of a hurry and far too earnestly. The prose they contain is extremely interesting, but for the light it throws on the authors' and readers' understanding of narrative – and on the various ideologies nakedly on display – rather than for any qualities that are worth imitating.

However, we can't avoid displaying an ideology of some sort, whether veiled or naked, so the best we can do is to be intelligent about it. What I write is art of a sort, I hope; it has to work in terms of story and pattern, but nothing is unmixed, thank God; everything is confused and impure, and there's a sense in which I would have chosen to write about the late nineteenth century even if the other considerations hadn't brought me to it. Because I've got another purpose in mind as well. That was a time when the seeds of the present day were germinating. Feminism, to take an obvious example. I didn't set out to write a trilogy with a female protagonist and give her exciting and interesting things to do: the story chose me. But I was glad to find a medium in which I could show how feminism, for example, didn't spring fully armed from the head of Germaine Greer but was being discussed, and was influencing people, a hundred or more years ago. The drug trade has a past as well; it didn't begin with *Miami Vice*; it's intimately entwined with our economic history. Terrorism – the modern sense of that very word first appeared then, and one of the characters in *The Tiger in the Well* learns it.

And finally, in the same book, I wanted to talk about socialism. It's had a bad press in the past few years; it's been depicted as the dreary source of every kind of repression, misery, and failure. I wanted to show that it has a better history than that, that there was a time when it was the best response of the best people to the conditions around them. I wanted to celebrate a little: to celebrate the efforts of working people to educate themselves: the Workingmen's Literary and Philosophical Institute, in *The Shadow in the North*; the efforts of middle-class philanthropists to alleviate suffering among the poor; the Spitalfields Social Mission in *The Tiger in the Well*. (Here, as in many other places, I owe a great debt to William J. Fishman's *East End 1888* (Duckworth 1988) – a book full of horror and darkness, laid out with enormous learning and lit with a steady, unflinching compassion. Reading and re-reading it is an experience more like life than like research.) So my ideology is educational. I was a teacher for too many years to stop teaching just because I'm no longer paid to do it; and as teachers used to know long before the National Curriculum gave them other things to think about, stories are a pretty good way to teach.

References (books by Philip Pullman)

Pullman, P. (1985) *The Ruby in the Smoke*. Oxford: Oxford University Press.
Pullman, P. (1986) *The Shadow in the Plate*. Oxford: Oxford University Press.
Pullman, P. (1988) *The Shadow in the North*. Harmondsworth: Puffin.
Pullman, P. (1991) *The Tiger in the Well*. London: Viking.

Chapter 13

History and time

Rosemary Sutcliff

This reprinted article is a paper that Rosemary Sutcliff gave at a CLNE (Children's Literature New England) conference, Travellers in Time, *at Cambridge University in the summer of 1989[1]. The paper clearly outlines Sutcliff's thoughts as a writer of historical fiction, the significance of historical fiction in relation to children learning about history (that it 'breathes life' into the subject) and the importance of reflecting continuity between eras for readers. She shares openly, with her audience, her method of working on her books and how, for her, historical fiction is 'a one way trip backwards'. She concludes the paper by discussing the significance of the historical details that bring her books to life for the young reader.*

I suppose we all know that if we go back to the earliest people – lacking all known history, all written records, any kind of calendar, any fixed points to hang memory on – awareness of time must have been so vague that they had very definite need to spill blood into the earth at seed time to bring about the harvest, light great fires at the dark of the year to give strength to the sun and bring life back to the world, because they had no guarantee that without their help any of these things would happen. That would be the state of things until, as a few thousand years went by, wise men took to looking at the skies, and the first calendars – Stonehenge may have been one of them, though not nearly the earliest – came into being. Then of course the whole thing became gradually more formalised and, if not brought under control, at any rate brought to a state where it was possible to think about it, both forward and backward, visualise it and give it symbolic shapes.

According to the theologian O. Culmann in his book *Christ and Time* the symbol of time for primitive Christianity as well as for Biblical Judaism is the upward sloping line, while for Hellenism it is the circle. (In many ancient faiths the snake swallowing its own tail is the symbol of Eternity.)

This belief in the cyclical nature of the Universe was based on the concept of the Great Year, which has two distinct interpretations: on one hand it is simply the period needed for sun, moon and planets to get back to exactly the same relative positions as they had held before, in some specific earlier point in time. On the

[1] Reprinted by permission of David Higham Associates.

other hand it signified the whole life span of the world from its formation to its destruction and rebirth. The two interpretations were combined in late antiquity by the Stoics, who believed that when the heavenly bodies returned at fixed intervals of time to the positions they had held at the beginning of the world, everything would return to being exactly as it was in the beginning, and the entire cycle would repeat itself again in every detail. Nemesius, a fourth-century Bishop of Emasa, put it later:

> Socrates and Plato and each individual man will live again with the same friends and fellow citizens. Every city and village and field will be restored just as it was, and this restoration of the universe takes place not once but over and over again. Indeed to eternity without end.

I think he must have been writing about this as someone else's belief, not as his own, unless of course he was some kind of heretic. Around five hundred years earlier, Virgil said the same thing, but more poetically 'Now is come the last age of the song of Cumae; the great line of the centuries begins anew... a second Typhis shall then arise, and a second Argo to carry heroes; and again shall great Achilles be sent to Troy.'

Which brings us rather nicely to Homer and the historians and storytellers. Though Homer dealt with allegedly historical subjects, his history was of the 'aristocratic' kind, which is in fact hero myth with maybe a seed of history somewhere in the midst of it. It involves no chronology, no real sense of the passage of time. Despite Odysseus's twenty-year absence, neither he nor Penelope seem any older when he finally gets home. Only poor Argos, the dog. The Apple of Discord, which starts the Trojan war, is thrown down among the guests at the wedding feast of Achilles' parents; the judgement of Paris, the abduction of Helen and the outbreak of the war all follow each other without pause, but by the time the black ships sail for troy, Achilles, who according to our ideas of time-lapse can't have been *much* more than a twinkle in his father's eye, is a grown warrior. And to confuse the issue still further, seems, before the end of the ten-year siege, to have sons also of fighting age. (I speak of this from bitter experience, being in the midst of trying to produce a retelling of the Siege of Troy for eight to ten-year-olds.) For Homer it clearly made no difference that year follows year.

By the time of Herodotus and Thucydides, history had ceased to be a matter of isolated episodes covering the lives and deeds of heroes, and began to depend on continuity of events, institutions, laws. The passage of time had become more relevant. But even so, Herodotus still had much of the minstrel about him and can always be relied on to abandon fact in favour of a good story or even a juicy piece of gossip, whereas Thucydides, a perfectionist with a dry historian's mind, aware of the smoky splendors and general vagueness behind him if he looked back, considered that serious history could be concerned only with the present or the most immediate past, because anything beyond that was in the very nature of things thoroughly unreliable.

But to go back to the Christians and the straight ascending line. For the early Christians the Crucifixion was a unique event. It was not subject to repetition, and so for them time had to be linear and not cyclic. This essentially historical view of time with its emphasis on 'Once and for Always' is the very essence of Christianity, and this is brought out clearly in St Paul's Epistle to the Hebrews:

> nor yet that be should offer himself often, as the High Priest entereth into the Holy Place every year with the blood of others, for then must he often have suffered since the foundation of the world. But now once in the end of the world hath he appeared to put away sin by the sacrifice of himself.

The end of the world was not of course quite so near as St Paul and the early Christian Church expected. But for men who believed what was in that Epistle there could be no way but straight ahead; and for us, following that teaching, time has been a straight line leading from way behind us to way in front, ever since.

Nevertheless, one of the greatest historical philosophers in the eighteenth century, Giovanibattista Vico, professor of rhetoric in the University of Naples, believed in historic cycles. He interpreted the concept in a more sophisticated way than previous believers had done. He maintained that certain periods of history had a general basic nature which reappeared in certain other periods, so that it was possible to argue by analogy from one such period to another. He drew a parallel between the barbarism of the Christian early Middle Ages in Western Europe and the barbarism of the Homeric Age, pointing out certain common features, such as rule by a warrior aristocracy, a ballad literature (our own Celtic, Bronze and Iron Ages fit in with that), and he called such periods 'Heroic'. He did not think that history is strictly circular, because new things are always being created, and therefore the whole process must move slowly forward. As R. G. Collingwood puts it: 'Not a circle but a spiral; for history never repeats itself, but comes round in each new phase in a form made different by what has gone before.' The barbarism of the Western Middle Ages is different from that of Homeric Greece through the influence of Christianity, (an influence which doesn't seem to have gentled it much, actually, when one thinks of the brutalities of the Crusades). Vico thought, however, that similar periods tended to reappear in the same order; a Heroic period always followed by what he called a Classical Period, in which thought prevailed over imagination, prose over poetry ... I know this works for Homeric Greece. I'm not so sure about the Middle Ages. I can't find a classical period for them until the eighteenth century, which seems to leave rather a lot between.

Vico also believed that 'man is a being who can only be understood historically'. In other words, knowledge of our past is vital to our understanding of ourselves – which makes him a man after my own heart.

Many years ago, when I was sure of myself as only someone scarcely out of their apprenticeship can be, I was talking to an audience of school teachers in the Midlands that are sodden and unkind, when a County Inspector of Education stood up and asked me what was my justification for writing historical novels, which he clearly considered a bastard form, instead of leaving the job to legitimate historians who knew what they were talking about. I looked him straight in the eye and said: 'Historians and teachers, you and your kind, can produce the bare bones, all in their right order, but still bare bones; I and my kind can breathe life into them. And history is not bare bones alone, it's a living process.' Looking back I'm rather shaken at my hardihood, but I still think I was right.

There are of course two views of history, the Man's-eye view and the God's-eye view. It is because history books for the young must of necessity take the God's eye view that they can so often and so easily become dull; that, and because they so often break their subject up into small static pictures, each as it were separately framed by the reigns of successive monarchs, instead of treating it as a living and continuous process of which we are part, and of which our descendants, always supposing that we have not blown the world up or destroyed the ozone layer by then, will be a part also. It is enormously important that the young should be given this sense of continuity, of their roots behind them. Because to know and really understand something of where we came from, as Giovanibattista Vico would have agreed, can play a big part in helping us to understand and cope with where we are now and where we are going. All of us, in our own particular stretch of history, stand too close up to be able to follow the whole pattern, and we never know-how the story ends, and this is especially true of us today, because we seem to have come to one of Vico's patches which, the last time-round, covered the end of the Roman Empire and, if he was right, then the next stage should be the Dark Ages. You couldn't really call St Dunstan and the glories of Wessex 'The Dark', but the Romans could not know about that. We can hope that we are not going irrevocably into the Dark, but we can't know. We can't know if there is a St Dunstan or a Wessex for us; we are in exactly the same boat as the Romans sixteen or seventeen hundred years ago.

That is why children can surely get a truer picture of the past if something that breathes life into the bare bones is given to them over and above the factual side of history. They need the Man's-eye view as well as the God's-eye view of the past; and that means us, the tellers of tales, the historical novelist. Not, I hasten to say, the dealers in Historical Romance, which is quite another matter.

The young have a strong feeling for the primitive and fundamental things of life. That is why myths and legends certainly not meant for children in the first place have been largely taken over by them. It is one reason why children enjoy Westerns, even in these days of science fiction; one reason, come to that, why I enjoy them too. I used to think that there was something shameful in enjoying Westerns once one was past the age of running around with two fingers stuck out, shouting 'Bang, bang, you're dead!'. But then it dawned on me that they are or were the Hero Myths of the Middle West. They seem to come from an earlier, rougher and more splendid time – Homer might not have scorned them – they have all the elements of Heroic Myth; outsize characters, big basic themes – love and hate, comradeship between men, loyalty and divided loyalty, treachery, revenge for slain kinsfolk, the age-old struggle between light and dark, in which the Hero, standing for light, though sometimes of a rather murky kind, always wins, but sometimes at the cost of his own life; the deep sense of ritual, especially the ritual of death. We all know *High Noon* and all those other walks through empty towns, footsteps echoing in heat-drenched silence, or doom-laden pulse beat of accompanying music as tension mounts; the hands held carefully away from the six-shooter still in its holster, the Goodies wearing white hats and the Baddies black – that bit of ritual almost as rigidly adhered to as the fact that in Pantomime the Demon King always enters from the left of the stage and the Fairy Godmother from the right.

Myths and Legends, Westerns, my sort of historical novel, are all alike in dealing with these big basic themes, though in somewhat different ways. As I said, the instinct for this is strong in children. In most adults it has been pushed down, sometimes only a little way, sometimes almost entirely, into the subconscious. But it's always there, in the same place as the Australian Aboriginal keeps his dream time, in tribal memory and race memory; and it still needs feeding and watering, because without it the soul of man is not quite complete.

So – there is my right to tell my own kind of historical stories. I can't play with time, making intricate patterns of it; I can't handle time-slips; I could never have written *Red Shift* or *A Traveller in Time* or *Tom's Midnight Garden.* For me, writing a historical novel entails a one-way trip backwards into some particular point in time and space, and once there bringing it to life as convincingly as possible. The question then arises 'How is it done?'. I can't do it from the outside, looking backward, only by making the trip myself, and a very lonely trip it can be, and soaking myself in time and place so that I can tell the story from the inside looking out, through the eyes of people who don't know the outcome of the battle being fought at Hastings over the Downs this afternoon. That is what makes a child write and say, 'It makes me feel as though I was there'.

At one time when I was doing quite a lot of talking for schools, I used to start off by saying to my audience, 'Now I want you to shut your eyes and do some strong imagining for me.

'Those of you who want to be a boy: you are a young Roman soldier on sentry duty on Hadrian's Wall. You're marching slowly up and down the rampart walk, keeping a sharp eye open to the north, because it's always from the north that trouble comes. It came last week – cattle raiders. That was your first taste of action, and you have a gash in your sword-arm to show for it; it's half-healed now, and it itches in the way that healing cuts very often do. The mizzle rain blows in your face, and the watch seems a very long one but you're going to a cockfight in the fortress ditch later on tonight, and that cheers you up.

'Those of you who want to be a girl needn't go so far back, only as far as London in the Middle Ages. You're a merchant's daughter, and twelve or thirteen years old, and your father has arranged for you to marry another merchant, maybe ten years older than you are. He has gone abroad on business, and you have just had a letter from him and you're excited and pleased because, although your father chose him for you, you do rather like him. You're reading your letter in a patch of sunlight in a room over the warehouse – people mostly lived over the shop or the business in those days – and there's a clove pink in a Venetian glass on the table, its shadow falling across the page, and outside a man wheeling a handcart piled with cabbages pulls to one side while a company of men-alarms goes jingling by.'

Then after a suitable pause, 'All right, come back to here and now.

'Those two were real people. The soldier was a Syrian by birth, he served many years in Britain, married a British girl and settled down, and we have his name, Barates, on a tombstone. The merchant's daughter was called Catherine, and the letter still exists. It's a nice letter, gentle, humorous, one can almost see the young merchant smiling to himself as he writes it in an inn chamber by candlelight: "Grow up as quickly as you can, so that we can be married. Go to my horse and ask him for three of his years, and I will pay them back to him again from my own, with a horse-cake by way of interest, when I come home." '

That usually got the audience tuned in, and in a state of mind to listen to me without too much shuffling.

I do much the same kind of thing on my own account when finding my way into the book of the moment. But of course in that case there are a good few other things to be dealt with first, because it's no good doing too much soaking oneself in time and place without first making reasonably sure that one has got time and place right – well, as right as one can. And that means research, and a lot of it.

But let me make one thing clear: I never start off with the research; I mean I never decide in cool blood that it would be interesting to set the next book in a particular time and place and then start to read up about it. First has to come the Basic Idea, and it is no good my going in search of the Idea, it has to come looking for me. Sometimes it comes from outside, from something read or seen or experienced, once from a little privately published handbook on the Lake District turned out by a friend in spring cleaning his attic, once from seeing in an Athens museum a dagger with lily flowers inlaid on the blade. Sometimes it comes from inside, like the thought out of nowhere which I had one morning while making toast. 'Yes, but when the Romans were withdrawn from Britain they had been here four hundred years. They had settled and intermarried. Some of them would be virtually British, others would have at the very least a British grandmother. Some of them must have gone willfully missing to remain in Britain when the galleys sailed.' It was a really dazzling thought, and while its further possibilities were dawning on me I burned the toast; but it resulted in *The Lantern Bearers.*

From the Basic Idea springs the theme; not yet the plot. I'm not terribly good at plots anyway, and tend to have themes instead. At this point I buy a large red exercise book – it has to be red, that's a kind of personal ritual of my own – and start on research. First of all the historical background. At this stage I am dealing with the history of facts, or supposed facts. Theme and plot, if any, often develop with the history in a process somewhat like weaving; and by this stage I am beginning to feel my way into time and place and get the feel of it, the smell of it.

There are two kinds of Truth, the Truth of Fact and the Truth of the Spirit; and it is possible to be meticulous about fact and yet catch no atmosphere of the period at all. Sometimes there's a gap in known facts which can only be filled by the Truth of the Spirit. This of course is dangerous because it can become only invention, and the only possible test is 'Does it smell right?'. If it does, then it's probably the best one can do. Into the red exercise book also go details of daily life. What houses do my people live in, what food do they eat, what weapons do they carry, what songs do they sing? How do they make their marriages? How do they bury their dead?

Details of place, too; the actual lie of the land, flora and fauna, weather and atmospherics, marks of human occupation, taking care that nothing from a later period than the story gets in by mistake.

Details of the people of the story, both historical and fictional, who are now beginning to emerge from the background, their looks and characters and previous history, anything and everything that can help to conjure them into real people with back views as well as front ones, not just cardboard cut-outs wearing Olde Worlde costumes.

Some people believe that human beings change fundamentally as time goes by. I don't – or only on the surface. The men of the first Elizabeth's reign thought no shame to cry in public if they felt like it; the men of my youth had been so trained to think it not done that by the time they were sixteen most of them couldn't cry at all except with great pain and difficulty for, say, the death of a wife or a dog. But that doesn't mean that the capacity for grief is any different. I have seen an Etruscan tomb with the figures of a man and a woman lying very calmly on top of it that makes nonsense of the idea that the Ancients did not know love between men and women in the way that we know it. One has to be careful about the samenesses and the differences, all the same.

Usually the book has become urgent and I have started to write it well before the research is finished; and it is at this point that my people and their world really start to develop. All their particulars in the red exercise book are really only blueprint, only theory. I know what somebody looks like; I know that he has blue eyes and speaks with a slight stammer, because I have decreed that he should, nothing to do with him at all. But once the writing starts, he begins to take on a life of his own, and he goes on doing it until the time comes when, if I make him do something out of character, I know it instantly as one knows it of a friend in whose company one has passed a good deal of time. 'I don't believe he would have done that, said that, reacted in that way.' Then I have to set to work to discover how he would in fact have reacted, what choice he would have made. And if that doesn't fit with the story, that's just too bad, adjustments will have to be made. By this stage also of course there is the chance that he will do his own thing when really I wanted him to do something quite different.

By the time the book is finished, I have lived with the characters in it for maybe a year of my time, maybe a year or two or twenty years of theirs, and I feel oddly bereft. But with any luck the Basic Idea of the next book is already with me. If it isn't, I am not at all happy until it arrives, not only for my next supply of bread-and-butter, but also because without a book on the stocks I suffer from a sense of being cut off from some kind of supply line; a sort of loneliness – or rather, aloneness.

At the risk of repeating myself: I spoke a while back of the importance of giving children a sense of continuity in time and history, and some awareness of their roots behind them, to help them understand where they came from and where they are going to. This I think was first given to me by the books my mother read to me when I was a child, and it has mattered deeply and potently to me ever since. And so in the natural way of things I have, over the years, woven a sort of web that here and there runs from one book to another, so that the continuity does not break between book and book. I don't decide on these spider-threads in advance and drag them here and there in any arbitrary way; I simply allow them to grow naturally and surface where they will, and wherever and whenever they surface, I am pleased to see them as one is pleased to see a familiar face one had not particularly expected to see.

Continuity is a very comforting and reassuring thing, in a sense which goes beyond the personal, and far beyond our normal usage of those words – the sense in which the First World War poets must have been aware of it in the certainty that if they were blown up tomorrow Spring would still come back to the places that they loved, and there would, probably, be honey still for tea.

It's the 'Life Goes On' thing.

I hope you won't think that I'm being egocentric and over-pleased with myself if I round all this off by reading you a couple of extracts from my own books at points where the spider's threads surface and which give me pleasure as though I had had nothing to do with spinning them myself.

The first is in *Frontier Wolf* set in the mid-fourth century and centering on a Roman frontier post:

> Just where the track dipped to the paved ford below the pony's watering pool a tall stone stood up, leaning a little, in the wayside grass. Dark, smooth, with somehow the look about it of having passed through fire; the look too of being very old, older than anything else in that countryside. As they trotted by, Gavrus leaned from his saddle and lightly touched the smooth-worn crest in passing; and Alexion, glancing round for another view of the thing, saw the leader of the escort echo the gesture, and the men behind him . . . Another custom of the Pack, he supposed, and clearly one that you did not ask about. Oh well, there'd be time for finding out about such things later. Too much time maybe. So much time that childish things became important because they helped to fill it up a little. A small cold shiver took him between the shoulders, the kind of shiver out of nowhere that makes men laugh and say that a grey goose is flying over their graves.

And then later in the story:

> Alexion, reaching aside by long custom to touch the Lady in passing, felt the stone rain-wet and heart-cold and curiously empty, and knew, though he instantly denied the knowledge in himself, that the Romans would not come back.

The book I have just finished, which is with Bodley Head now, is woven into *The Gododdin*, the seventh century epic of a kamikaze style raid by a company of post-Roman British warriors on a Saxon war host gathering at what is now Catterick Bridge. In the course of training for this raid three of them are holing up in the ruins of the same fort around two hundred and fifty years later, and it seemed obvious that there must be some mention of the stone which Alexion's troopers had called the Lady. So:

> We went down to the burn that ran through its steep gorge below the western rampart, and drank and filled the leather bottle where the water ran clear and deep above the remains of a paved ford. There was an upright stone, I mind, marking the place where an old track from the fort must have entered the water, heading westward; a black stone, dappled with grey and golden lichen. I set my hand on its rounded poll, and got the odd uncanny feel that it was used to the touch of men's hands in passing. But that must have been long and long ago.

One more, drawn from *Knight's Fee*. Early Norman, sited in the Down country near my home; but it concerns also *Warrior Scarlet*, set in the same countryside but in the Bronze Age, and telling the story of a boy with a withered right arm. A few years after writing *Warrior Scarlet*, I came across the mention in an old book of a flint celt that had been dug up on my stretch of the Downs. A tool or weapon shaped something like an axehead to be held in the hand without any haft. They're not uncommon, but this one was special, being shaped for use in the left hand. Obviously it was Drem's, my Bronze Age boy's. It was too late to give it to him in his own book, but I had to get it to him somehow; so I gave it to him in retrospect through *Knight's Fee* which I was writing then.

Two boys, one Norman, one Saxon, up from the valley farm of Dean in the lambing season, to spend a night with the shepherd kind on the High Downs:

They huddled close, for the wind seeped through the hurdles for all the lacing of furze branches. Ship and White Eye and Joyeuse lying nose-on-paws among their feet. Randal sat with his hunched shoulder leaning against Bevis who leaned companionably back, and stared a little sleepily into the fire, where a red hollow like the gaping mouth of a dragon had opened under the crackling thorn branches, and listened to the soft hush of the wind across the thatch. 'And all the time the wind blows over' he thought. 'Ancret's people, and the Saxons, and Harold dead at Hastings over yonder, and now the Normans; and all the while the wind blowing over the Downs, just the same.' Half asleep as he was, he was suddenly aware of the new life in the lambing pens, the constant watchful coming and going of shepherds and dogs and lanterns, as something not just happening now, but reaching back and back, and forward and forward, into the very roots of things that were beyond time.

Something of the same mood must have been upon Lewin also, for when he had brought out the meal bag and tipped barley meal into the birchwood bowl, thrusting away the dogs' soft, expectant muzzles, he rose – but he could not stand upright in the little bothy – rooted in the willow basket hanging from the roof, in which he kept his few personal belongings, and brought out something wrapped in a rag of yellow cloth.

'I'll show you a thing,' he said to Randal, 'sitting here at nights I've had it in my heart to show you, a good while past. Showed it to the young master when he stood no higher than my belt.' And as Randal looked up expectantly from the fire, and Bevis watched with the interest alight in his thin eager face, he unfolded the yellow rag and put into the boy's hand a thing not unlike a double axehead made from flint, mealy grey and tawny with the outer weathering that flint gathers through the years. An axehead, but with no hole to take the haft, nor any flanges for binding it on.

Without quite knowing why he did so, for he was not left handed, Randal put out his left hand for it, and felt his fingers dose over it as something infinitely familiar. But he had never seen such an object before.

'What is it?' he demanded.

'What it is called, I do not know, but with such things it is in my mind that men fought the wolf-kind, and maybe each other, very long ago. I have seen others turned up on the Downs, but never one to equal that one. I found it up on Long Down years ago, and kept it, because it was made for a left-handed man even as I.'

Randal shifted it to his right hand, and found that it was true. One could use it perfectly well with the right hand, but it did not lie there happily, as in the left.

'Left handed, or one handed.' He did not know what made him say that. He leaned forward, looking at it in the light of the fire – and then, maybe because of the strange mood he was in, maybe because he was half asleep, maybe because of that dark thread of the Old Blood that Ancret had recognised, running in his veins, an odd thing happened. Once, in the outer bailey at Arundel, he had watched spell-bound while a wonder-worker who made live pigeons come out of an empty basket, had made a striped pebble picked up from the dirt where the fowls were scratching, grow in his hand without any visible change, into a yellow iris flower. He could see now the shimmering silken fall of the petals, the dark hair-fine intricacy of the veining that sprang from the slender throat, the sheer singing strength of the colour. And as the pebble had become a flower, so the thing he held was suddenly warm as though fresh from the knapper's hand and the outer crust of the centuries all gone like a little dust, leaving the beautiful dark blue flint in all its newness. It was as though the thing flowered between his hands. He had an extraordinary sense of kinship with the unknown man who had first closed his fingers over that strange weapon, who had perhaps seen the wolves leaping about the lambing folds, as he, Randal, had almost seen them for an instant tonight; an extraordinary feeling of oneness with Dean, of some living bond running back through the blue, living flint, making him part of other men and sheep and wolves, and they a part of him.

References

The original article did not include a reference list. We supply here the bibliographical details of Rosemary Sutcliff's novels mentioned in the text.

Sutcliff, R. (1958) *Warrior Scarlet*. Oxford: Oxford University Press.
Sutcliff, R. (1959) *The Lantern Bearers*. Oxford: Oxford University Press.
Sutcliff, R. (1960) *Knight's Fee*. Oxford: Oxford University Press.
Sutcliff, R. (1980) *Frontier Wolf*. Oxford: Oxford University Press.
Sutcliff, R. (1990) *The Shining Company*. London: The Bodley Head.

Section 3
Teaching the narrative past

Chapter 14

Up and Down the City Road: history through dramatic action

Geoff Fox

An encounter with some antique puppets led Geoff Fox to write a play which he set in 1851. He records here the experience of writing and producing the play in a middle school. With a melodramatic plot reminiscent of the Victorian music-hall, and a cast of Mayhew's 'poor', the play clearly challenged but also captivated performers and audience alike. Geoff Fox's account is followed by his reflections on the many advantages of such work, not only in terms of historical understanding and experience of speaking the period language but also in terms of increased confidence and other less predictable benefits.

Origins

'You might like to take a look at what's on the table in the front room,' suggested my friend.

It didn't look particularly exciting – a black wooden box, about the size of a child's coffin.

'Lift the lid.'

And there they were – a richly-costumed set of 'Punch and Judy' puppets, from the quarrelsome couple themselves to Jack Ketch the Hangman, The Beadle, the Crocodile – all of them.

There was a letter in the box, written by the niece of Mr E. J. Shears, Punchman and Undertaker. It mentioned that Mr Shears had carved the puppets himself and performed on the streets of London in the mid-nineteenth century; in fact, his fame was such that he had been summoned to play before Queen Victoria and her family at the Palace.

My friend owned a successful firm which produced small ceramic figures – bears and cats getting up to mischief, modelled with wit and attention to fine detail. Now he was considering launching a series of the Punch and Judy characters and wanted me to write the text of a picture book to be sold alongside them; he was interested in a story that would explain how Mr Shears came to perform for the royals.

That book never happened. Some marketing problem cropped up, but by then the story had arrived.

The story-line

Some years later, the story became a play, *Up and Down the City Road*, performed by the Year Seven and Eight Drama Club at St Osmund's Middle School, Dorchester, in March 2001.[1] An outline of the plot will provide a context for the ensuing account of its evolution, the rehearsal process and some discussion of what the cast learned from the experience.

The story is set in London in 1851, and the audience enters the drama studio to be greeted by hustling street entertainers (including Ernie Shears, the Punchman, at work in his splendidly decorated booth) and clamouring hawkers of biscuits, pot-pourri, lemon sherbert, aniseed balls and clementines. At a piercing whistle, the audience (by now seated and in blackout) discovers the cast frozen in a series of menacing, violent images across a set spanning some 20 metres. Three beams flicker across the contorted figures, picking out faces set in grimaces of malevolence or fear. Then, from the tableaux, comes a repeated chant rising from whisper to threatening shout:

> Punch and Judy
> Fought for a pie:
> Punch gave Judy
> A knock in the eye.
>
> Says Punch to Judy,
> 'Will you have any more?'
> Says Judy to Punch,
> 'My eye is sore.'

The story which unfolds is that of the kidnapping of Sally Shears, the popular daughter of the Punchman. We meet Sally singing and dancing to the delight of the spectators at Ernie's booth. While Ernie and his 'bottler', Long Tom, are packing up for the night, Sally disappears. Ernie and Tom search desperately among their friends: the Great Sallemantro the sword and snake swallower, Pedro the penny profilist, Sarah the 'blind' violinist ('Sorry Ernie, couldn't quite see you there in the dark'), a couple of young street reciters, and Silly Billy, 'your favourite comedian', whose tired jokes delivered from the top of an old cabin trunk draw only catcalls from his listeners. All swear they have not seen Sally, but as Ernie leaves Billy, we realise that the comedian, desperate for money to buy medicine for his dying wife, is the kidnapper, and that little Sally is a captive in the cabin trunk.

The story now divides into parallel plots. Ernie enlists the aid of Sniffy and his 'Ferrets', a private army of mudlarks and crossing-sweepers whom we find searching for pickings along the Thames tideline. Mr Jack Black, Rat and Mole Destroyer to Her Majesty, Mr Jeremy Tiffin, also holder of a royal appointment as the Queen's Bug Destroyer, and the formidable Chief Inspector Shacklock join the hunt.

Meanwhile, in the other strand of the plot, Billy sells Sally's dress to Nellie, a second-hand clothes dealer, *almost* sells her hair to Old Ruth the wig-maker, and finally arranges to sell Sally herself to King Atlas, the brutal leader of a troupe of acrobats. Atlas needs her for 'topping out the pyramids and the dancing inbetweentimes', since Little Joanie, Sally's predecessor, has been injured. Girls with broken legs are no use to Atlas, who refuses to pass any money over to Billy until he sees for himself what Sally can do.

Hunters and hunted come together at Greenwich Fair on Easter Monday, when all London gathers to enjoy the delights of such performers as the illusionist, Signor Sivori and his amazing Bambini Sivori. With the help of a garrulous costermonger's wife, Ernie and his friends track Atlas down to Cap'n Ralph's 'Ratting for the Sportsman', where Butcher the bull-terrier is pitted against the freshest sewer rats in London ('plucked this morning from Shadwell Stair by the bravest flusherman in London Town'). It is in the ratting ring that the action reaches its bloodthirsty and wildly melodramatic climax.

At last, Ernie and Sally reunited, Mr Tiffin can tell Ernie what he's been longing to tell him for most of the play. During an expedition to the Palace to remove a bug from Princess Charlotte's regal four-poster, Tiffin has been asked if he knows of a good Punch and Judy man to entertain at the birthday party of one of the little highnesses. Ernie, Long Tom and Sally play before Queen Victoria who, on this occasion, pronounces herself 'most amused'. Song and celebration conclude the play.

This outline gives no account of the music, the chanted rhymes culled from the period and the use of subdued lighting which accompanied the action; but these elements were essential in creating a sense of period, as well as an edge of excitement, throughout the play.

Finding the story

The story was not long in coming. I went straight to Henry Mayhew's *London Labour and the London Poor* (1861–2) where I remembered there was a section on a Punchman. In 1849 the *Morning Chronicle* decided to offer its readers a wide-ranging survey of the nation's poor, and Mayhew's work as the paper's Metropolitan Correspondent was to be matched by contributions from investigators in other parts of the country.[2] Mayhew was determined to maintain scientific objectivity in his work: for example, his original scheme included the preparation of extensive statistical data concerning different trades. As the project developed, however, it was his interviews with individuals – from the blind street-seller of tailors' needles to a French hurdy-gurdy player – which were most popular with his readers.

After disagreements with the *Chronicle*, Mayhew began to publish his work independently in weekly parts. Eventually, in 1861–2, he produced the four-volume work for which he is best remembered, *London Labour and the London Poor*.

Mayhew is often compared to his contemporary, Charles Dickens. Both worked in early adult life as journalists and spent time exploring the London streets. Both had a keen eye – and ear – for the bizarre, the comic and the pathetic, but where

Mayhew is usually concerned to allow his subjects to speak for themselves, Dickens' characters are shaped by their author's fictional ends. For my purposes, Mayhew's self-effacement allowed a direct contact with actual men and women of the time. Dickens proved influential in other ways through his evocation of Greenwich Fair and his account of his visit to the London underworld with the fearsome Inspector Field (Vallance 1966).

I began with Mayhew's Punchman. Since I wanted to develop a wider sense of life on the streets where Ernie Shears worked, I read most of the character portraits in Peter Quennell's three volumes of extracts from *London Labour and the London Poor* (1950, 1951a, b). Either directly, or as fusions of two or three portraits, some 20 of the play's 40 characters owe their origins to Mayhew, and his description of 'A Night at the Ratting' also made fruitful if macabre reading.

I read numerous accounts of Victorian entertainments, working and living conditions, crime and detection. In a book-fair (improbably, in a suburb of Montreal), I found a linen-backed street map of London in 1851, ('three shillings and sixpence plain, five shillings hand-coloured') incorporating a circle centred on Charing Cross, marking the four mile radius limit for cab fares at 6d a mile. I already knew Gustave Doré's atmospheric illustrations for London (Jerrold and Doré 1872), accompanying the text by Blanchard Jerrold, Mayhew's brother-in-law. Eventually, the Doré compositions found their way onto our set in a series of beautifully executed images on off-white drapes hung against the studio's blackout curtains.

It seems extraordinary that Mayhew's work is not, to my knowledge, extensively used in schools, despite the prominence given to the Victorians in the National Curriculum. The factual information is fascinating, but it is the narrative energy of the anecdotes and the detailed observation of character which would give children a sense of life among the poor of London. The language may need some mediation, but teachers willing to undertake role-plays based on Mayhew's interviews could leave an indelible memory among their pupils.

The school

There could hardly have been a more favourable context for the project. The staff includes three exceptional drama teachers who have themselves written and published plays. A drama club attended by over 50 Year Seven and Eight pupils meets every Friday after school and a club for younger pupils meets earlier in the week. The clubs attract girls and boys from a wide spectrum of academic abilities, and that range was reflected in our cast. Drama is timetabled for all pupils in a good facility (a surplus Post Office hut bought for £1.00 and, rather more expensively, transformed into a spacious studio). There is equally impressive music and art, and both departments gave the play generous practical support.

The school expects excellence in the classroom and on the sports field. There is a strong programme of extra-curricular activities, trips abroad and visits to residential centres. All of this places heavy demands upon staff and students alike but many of the teachers found time and energy to contribute to our project in some way – baking dozens of tasty biscuits for the hawkers, making the Punch and Judy booth, and producing a superb period programme decorated with Victorian advertisements and an illustration of a Punchman and his stall. The office manager looked after the tickets each evening, took orders for photographs and took care of much else besides. Victorian artefacts were expertly displayed close to the studio. Almost all of the staff came to see the play; some of them, and several parents, came twice.

Sue Cottam, one of the drama teachers, has the kind of shrewd entrepreneurial eye which Arts people have had to develop in a post-lottery world. After filling in forms and undergoing an interview, we were awarded £2,650 towards the funding of the project by Age Concern, who offered Millennial Awards for schemes in which someone over 55 (myself) worked alongside young people.

The two drama teachers who were working on the play generously welcomed me as a co-director.

Rehearsals and performances

Our performance week was fixed for late March. Workshops before Christmas explored the street songs and the harsh nature of life among the London underclass at the time. We had a visit from 'Professor' Higgins, a professional Punch and Judy man of some 50 years' experience who presented a Victorian version of Punch and Judy, and then talked about the traditions of the genre. Questions inevitably focused on the swazzle – how Punch's voice was created, the dangers of swallowing one's swazzle and the consequent remedial strategies ('Eat lots of porridge and keep looking'). Finally Professor Higgins performed the kind of show he gives six times daily on Weymouth beach every summer, full of rumbustious audience participation ('He's behind you!').

All three of us wanted to do more to develop the children's feeling for the period. I wondered whether I might offer several short sessions in role as some of Mayhew's characters, telling them about life on the streets, much as Mayhew's original subjects had talked to him. The value of such work partly rests in the questions children ask, and I knew that information communicated through this means often proves more memorable than conventional text-based approaches. I hoped we could use slides of the Doré illustrations to give the cast a sense of the poverty and danger of daily life alongside the resilience of the people and their spirit of community.

In the event, there simply was no time for such work. Lunch-times were crowded and staff needed a break. Teachers know well that the National Curriculum, with its attendant monitoring and assessment and its emphasis upon literacy and numeracy, allows little time for the reflective planning, and attention to dramatic and logistical detail which underpin a production. The very purposefulness of the school in every way meant that drama staff were reluctant to ask their colleagues to sacrifice lesson time for extra work on the play; though, as performance week approached, I was able to work during the school day on a number of occasions with two or three of the main characters.

As it was, the scale of the numerous large crowd scenes (in the Red Lion Pub, at Greenwich Fair, around the Ratting Ring) meant that we gave over every Friday after-school session and several other rehearsals to working with all 50 children –

the musicians, the technical crew and the two girls handling the props. There was no avoiding this, but it meant that progress was slow. We reached the final Thursday before performance week with the last two scenes untouched. Plays are traditionally 'never going to be ready' four or five days before they open, but on this occasion we were genuinely behind schedule. Three hours on the Saturday and a whole day in the studio out of lessons on the Monday helped, but we were hardly overconfident about the Tuesday afternoon opening performance to the Year Fives.

St Osmund's believes that every child in the school (which runs from Year Five to Year Eight) should see the school production. So, from Tuesday to Friday, afternoon performances were given to each year group with audiences numbering between 150 and 190. On the Wednesday to Saturday evenings, our audience comprised around 90 staff, parents, relatives, friends and siblings – safety regulations precluded larger numbers.

There was, we hoped, humour to be found in both the dialogue and the action in the play but our past experience suggested that school audiences were likely to be fairly muted in their responses during the performance. Children's interest tends to be focused on narrative. The Year Fives watched in well-bred silence, but applauded enthusiastically at the end. There were 20 minutes or so of school left after they had got back to their classrooms, and Sue asked her colleagues if they would let the audience write reactions to the play, or even letters to cast members since the school operates a 'friends' system which pairs older and younger pupils. We were excited, and relieved, by the whole-hearted responses and, as always, surprised by the details the young children focused upon. Some actors received fan letters from their young 'friends'; the only compliment I ever received myself was that I reminded someone of their grandmother's partner.

The other school performances went well, despite the inevitable slight slump on Day Two, once the adrenalin-charged first show was out of the system. Performing to your peers at the age of 11 or 12 is far from easy when overt enthusiasm is deeply uncool, so I much admired the cast's disciplined performances to Years Seven and Eight. In the end, they won these audiences over into genuine interest and even manifest chuckles.

By the time they reached these year groups, the actors' confidence had been transformed by the reception they received from the evening audiences. Parents know how to manage these things and a couple of infectious laughs and splutters of applause at the end of some early scenes swiftly helped the cast across a threshold into self-belief and enjoyment.

Learning

For directors of school productions, the satisfactions often lie in watching a performer come to 'own' a character; or, more accurately, in watching a character come to own a performer. Some children began, with instinctive judgement, to take their characters into areas which had never been suggested to them in rehearsal. Very often, this was evident in body language: Jack Black's flick of a pointing thumb over the shoulder when telling an anecdote, Cap'n Ralph's animated salesmanship as he drummed up trade for his ratting ring, the crazed glances of Silly Billy struggling to explain his crime. Such moves are often unconscious – it's the character at work rather than the actor. There were shifts of rhythm in a line as an actor found a new emphasis. Not all the children managed this, of course; and some of those who did were not the ones we had expected. Because we are teachers, there was a satisfaction in reactions such as a parent telling us, with some emotion, that she'd never thought she'd see her child 'do anything like that'.

With this chapter in mind, I had planned to talk with several groups of children before and after performance week, focusing upon what they had learned about the Victorians through the play. It was not just the demands of the play which prevented the implementation of my plan. I hesitated to ask my co-directors if they could organise interviews for me. They and their colleagues were just too busy. We would finish a rehearsal at 5.30 p.m. or later, and they would be off to their classrooms for an hour or two to set up the next day's work or even to conduct interviews with parents.

In the end, I managed short tape recordings with a dozen of the cast in odd moments. Much of their factual learning related to the lives of the Victorian under-class on the streets. (Their work on the Victorians in lessons, I later learned, had concentrated upon the emerging middle classes and work on politicians and the royal family.) They hadn't known of mudlarks and crossing-sweepers, of the colourful street-entertainers, of the edge of danger and violence beneath the middle-class Victorian values, of the dirt and the poverty ('They were really unhygienic about things, weren't they?'). They were struck by the costumes they were wearing, and the lack of jewellery. (All but one of the girls in my class have their ears pierced.) They liked the sense of community between the street people and their respect for the Queen. They'd learned how someone like Silly Billy, whose wife was dying through malnutrition, had no safety net of state provision beneath him. And they'd learned about Queen Victoria being Not Amused.

Factual learning slips into wider areas. Some of this was a matter of 'by indirection find direction out', a setting of a distant culture alongside their own. They were very impressed by the fact that most of the people they were playing had actually lived 150 years ago; that Mr Tiffin really had found a bug in the bed of Princess Charlotte ('Wow! It's really weird to think of it like that.'); that Ernie Shears had played before the Queen; that the original Silly Billy had told Mayhew the two feeble jokes he told in the play. (On the Saturday, the loyal parents laughed heartily and insisted on clapping Billy's efforts.)

Then there was the language. Because Mayhew was so concerned to give his characters their own voices, it was possible to echo the speech of the nineteenth century characters in the text of the play. Several of the children spoke of 'feeling the language'. The fusion of actor and character depends heavily upon finding an idiom; many of the cast loved attempting the cockney accent, but they also savoured the taste of the vocabulary and syntax on their tongues.

Several pupils talked about their sense of 'actually being there'. They compared the experience to what is possible in the classroom, even in a school as well-staffed and well-resourced as St Osmund's. ('I like *doing* it rather than just reading or seeing it on TV' and 'Sometimes, it feels as if you're actually real when you're in the middle of the fair or somewhere.') Others spoke of a basic satisfaction that they could stand in front of almost two hundred people and simply speak audibly in our version of cockney or in a parodied upper-class drawl. For some, this had taken considerable courage; for all, it was serious work ('I never thought how hard it would be. I'd go home and say to Mum, "I can't stand all these practices – we have to work so hard, and I thought it would just be fun." But it's great. It's really worth it.')

These reactions, and many other evidences of personal growth, may seem to fall outside the scope of this book, but this kind of learning is interlocked with learning about history, which cannot happen in a vacuum. Learning only thrives in an enabling context and depends upon the interplay of the learner's intellect and emotion.

In the 1960s, I taught in a direct grant boys' grammar school which, like St Osmund's, had a reputation for excellence. A feature writer for *Punch* spent a week in the school, gathering material for an article. 'Never have I seen an institution where activity is valued so highly at the expense of reflection,' she wrote. That seemed to me a desperate indictment. In the 1960s my school *chose* to be that kind of community; the pressures now are largely externally imposed, as every teacher knows. The price is high, if it means the exclusion of the kind of committed learning which needs time.

Reflective time is not readily available in schools. There's nothing new in this recognition – someone makes the point in the *Times Educational Supplement* (TES) almost every week[3] but it may be worth listing some of the kinds of learning which a drama project can generate, if only as a reminder of what we are losing when the relentless search for Level 4s drains staff and pupils of energy and time so that sustained artistic experience for children is excluded.

The learning which such a project generates is idiosyncratic. It depends on where you start from: your experience, your knowledge, your personality, your place in the social group and even your family. What is learned cannot be predicted and is not measurable. What you learn might be in all or any of these areas:

- factual information
- historical empathy
- an awakening of curiosity in the past
- vocal skills
- physical confidence
- technical skills with lights, costumes or props
- musical skills
- social confidence
- self-discipline and, perhaps, selflessness

and many, many other elements, all within a context of commitment and creative activity with others. You might learn that it is fine to be enthusiastic and to show it. You might share the excitement of 'cracking' a scene. You might learn from working with adults who are pushing themselves hard – sometimes getting it wrong, or being frustrated and irritated, no longer shielded by the 'teacher' role, but just other people doing their best.

There is much anecdotal evidence that this kind of experience *sticks* and, as it were, re-emerges at a later date. You cannot possibly foresee when an individual will make a connection, complete a pattern, years down a road begun with the play. For one, a concern about the lives of socially deprived people may have taken root. Another might have experienced the excitement of 'touching' a mind from long ago – Mayhew's or their character's – and want to do so again.

The historical data and the dramatic text of *Up and Down the City Road* were, I hope, carefully researched and crafted. We might guess at what children might learn and hope that it might prove to have a lasting impact; but in the end, what was learned could not be anticipated, or reduced to aims and objectives. However unfashionable acts of well-grounded faith as a basis for action may be in contemporary education, they remain territory which is too important to surrender.

Notes

1. The play was initially accepted for publication, subject to minor changes, by a major publisher when I first wrote it. I was reluctant to make the suggested changes, and put the manuscript on one side. When I got round to revising the play, the new editor at the publishers liked it very much as a piece of drama but said she now wanted only 'Issue' plays. Would I write a play about racism, dyslexia, child abuse, drug abuse, bullying, learning disorders or eating difficulties? This, she said, was what teachers wanted. I hope – and believe – she's wrong.

2. For a full account of Mayhew's life and work, see Anne Humpherys, *Travels into the Poor Man's Country*.

3. The day after I wrote this sentence, an article in the *TES* (entitled '3Rs stifle other subjects') reported: 'Inspectors are investigating claims that many primary-aged children are no longer being taught history and geography because schools are concentrating on the basics to meet ministers' targets' (*TES*, 30.03.2001).

References

Humpherys, A. (1977) *Travels into the Poor Man's Country*. Georgia: University of Georgia Press.

Jerrold, B. and Doré, G. (1872) *London: A pilgrimage*. London: Grant and Company.

Mayhew, H. (1861-2) *London Labour and the London Poor*. Reprint (1967). London: Frank Cass.

Quennell, P. (ed.) (1950) *London's Underworld*. London: William Kimber.

Quennell, P. (ed.) (1951a) *Mayhew's Characters*. London: William Kimber.

Quennell, P. (ed.) (1951b) *Mayhew's London*. London: William Kimber.

Vallance, R. (ed.) (1966) *Dickens' London*. London: The Folio Society.

Chapter 15

Stimulating the historical imagination: working with primary age children on books about the plague

Andrea Fellows

Year 4 and Year 6 children worked on two books set, in Derbyshire, in 1665, at the time of the Great Plague. Children of Winter, *by Berlie Doherty, is referred to by Berlie Doherty herself in her chapter in this book; the other book was Jill Paton Walsh's* A Parcel of Patterns. *Andrea Fellows discusses the challenges that these texts give to young readers and shows how she uses drama and supported writing activities to help the children appreciate the particular merits of these historical stories. Examples of children's work are shared with us to illustrate the various ways in which children become involved in the books.*

Year 4 children come into the school hall. A large space has been marked out to form a barn-sized area. The children walk through it, experiencing, in their mind's eye, the size and space. I ask them to use all their senses, to smell the air, to feel the walls, the floor beneath their feet, to taste the damp air, to listen to the creaking of the joists and the rush of the wind around the doorframe. I ask the children to imagine things in the barn in the present day, for example, the fertiliser bags, the bits of tractor, the plastic sweet wrappings left by previous visitors. Then, as the atmosphere takes hold, I encourage the children to explore their findings. They imagine and play the parts of characters that may have visited the barn recently: shepherds and walkers sheltering from bad weather, grumbling farmers commenting on hard times or robbers stashing their loot while on the run from the police. As small groups of children role-play their characters in the barn space, the rest of the class sit around the walls of the barn, like witnesses to time as it passes.

Over several sessions, the children re-create the barn and its visitors and we travel back through different centuries, with stops along the way to illustrate the chronology of the time periods covered. The imagined detritus, left in the barn over the years, diminishes as certain objects and materials are removed as the years roll back. The children explore how and when to take different items out of the space. I set the children the task of finding the voices of people from different times, who might have visited the barn and echo them from the sides of the barn space. The children take it in turns to walk through the deserted barn and listen to the mixture of echoes, from different times up to the present, as supplied by the rest of the class who take the part of invisible ghosts whispering into the barn space. Gradually, we get to know the barn and its inhabitants and claim the territory as our own.

This example of work was inspired by *Children of Winter* (1985) by Berlie Doherty. This story, about the effects of an outbreak of the plague on a family in a remote part of Derbyshire, has an important feature in its setting, in the form of a remote, old barn in the countryside. The book begins in the present when the twentieth century family in the story shelters from the rain in the barn. The children in the family are then transported back through time to survive a winter in the peaks, away from the plague, while their mother and father remain in their village. The barn thus acts as a time portal. In this way I take the children back through time, in the manner described above, in order that they better understand the story.

In the National Literacy Strategy, the suggested year for studying historical fiction is Year 4. However, any narrative work at any stage in Key Stage 2 could be focused on an historical fiction text. As so many historical novels are also good adventure stories, it can be doubly interesting for children, though the more demanding historical texts do tend to require a higher reading ability, some historical background and an ability to deal with contentious issues. Some children in Years 3 and 4 may not be ready to tackle the more complex historical narratives without support. It is important to prepare the way for such books with discussion, role-play, artifacts and, above all, to give time, in order to settle back into a different era.

An historical narrative text such as *Children of Winter* offers a class of mixed ability children many entry points into reading and writing. The time-slip story provides less confident readers and writers with a degree of support by setting the story in the present as well as in the plague era in the sixteenth century in an isolated village in Derbyshire. Readers are able to fix the characters of the modern-day children in the story before the historical detail takes over. A map of the geographical area of the story on the inside cover of the book encourages children to visualise description in the text. In their turn, children find themselves providing their readers with maps to bring their own stories to life.

I have found that a book such as *Children of Winter* gives children models of many of the skills they need to develop as writers. The detail of character portrayal and setting, the plot shape and the feeling for the space between a time in history, which is long gone, and contemporary time, are worked out clearly here so that children reflect some of these features in their own writing. Some of the oral work we did directly contributed to the children's increased awareness of anachronisms in their own thinking and writing; I really felt they were absorbing the differences between the past and the present.

We also considered the kind of language used to express ideas in different historical eras. Once the space and time has been established, the children role-play parts of the story and explore ideas and language through play. We made recordings of this dialogue and of the views expressed by the characters in the role-play and also asked the characters how they felt about the situations that they were in. Sections of the story were then played out as alternatives and the children explored what they thought would happen next. A feeling not only for language but also for the logical structuring of a story started to develop.

Some may argue that there is no time for such activities within a set literacy session. However, I feel that there is a need for such activities, not only for those children who cannot originate ideas for writing with ease but also for those able to extend and develop their own ideas, given time and opportunity. The empathy with character and the appreciation of the interaction of character and place cannot always be created for children just through reading as, for some children, reading may not be a very active process and writing may be a chore. Role-play and making stories around the book can bring literacy alive for such children.

Jill Paton Walsh writes about the same historical era and similar issues of a village community enduring the onslaught of plague in *A Parcel of Patterns* (1983). This is a complex book that might be read with children after *Children of Winter*. It is useful to have two books, which can be contrasted, about the same subject, as there are then opportunities for extension and differentiation. Paton Walsh is skilful at telling her story through authentic-sounding language and weaving her compelling tale around what we know to be a true story. Even though it makes demands on the primary aged child, with support from the teacher, and imaginative entry points, it can be a most rewarding experience for children to move back in time to this dramatic event.

I developed the following activities with Year 6 children over a period of one week. Examples of their work are included here as illustrations of the way in which children responded to these approaches. The examples are first draft pieces and show work in progress.

The young girl Mall, who narrates the story, gossips, reflects and explains the background. The children need to hear the passage read aloud more than once so that they can tune into the voice and the language. I asked the children, working in pairs, to highlight any sections or phrases in the book that they did not understand. This encouraged discussion straight away and allowed the children to interact directly with the text. Difficulties were then addressed through a round robin question/answer session. A good dictionary is a useful resource to have in the classroom for this type of activity as more obscure words can be traced quickly and the teacher can model the process of researching words and their derivatives.

Throughout the literacy strategy, there is an expectation that children build up the use of a reading journal. A journal for notes and preferences about texts can be used for this work as it demonstrates to children ways to tackle a text and how a journal can help a reader break into a text. For example, an extract from a Year 6 child's notes on *A Parcel of Patterns* included a list of things to check (Figure 15.1). The teacher can comment on these first notes and discuss the use of language with the writer. This exercise serves to demonstrate to children that language has evolved over time and is an important indicator of the historical time period under focus. Children slowly acquire an ear for words that have changed their meanings over time. They become aware of the appropriate language to give authenticity to the writing. On a basic level, children can respond to this by noticing the *absence* of modern sayings such as 'Okay' and 'Bye' which tend to dominate children's own writing!

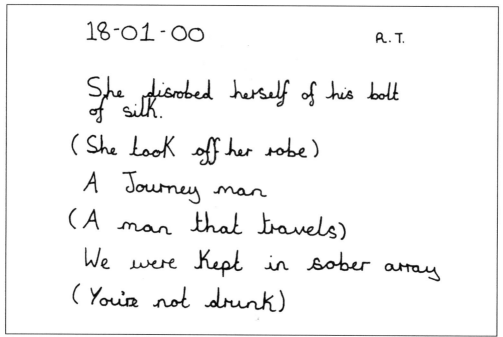

18-01-00   R. T.

She disrobed herself of his bolt
of silk.
(She took off her robe)
A Journey man
(A man that travels)
We were kept in sober array
(You're not drunk)

Figure 15.1 List of things to check arising from *A Parcel of Patterns*

It is also worth, at this initial stage, asking the children to make a note of their initial reaction to the book. It can be quite alarming to be faced with a text that is written in a voice from hundreds of years ago and a character who talks of 'slickensides', 'apparel' and 'raiment'. Children need to be able to express their feelings about this and understand that initial impressions can change. They also need to know that some texts need time to warm up and that they should expect to persevere! 'Toleration of uncertainty' is a skill to develop.

Different activities help children to break into this text. One activity involves taking the character of the narrator and trying to write in the same style. A group of Year 6 writers set about the task of writing examples of Mall's gossip. In her voice, they talked about what people were saying in the village about the various events. They began to appreciate how the author weaves together character, scene-setting and the giving of key information about the story to come.

Figure 15.2 is one example of a Year 6 boy's independent writing for this activity. This child shows a good awareness of the need to show that speech was different at that time in history compared with the present and he has made a good attempt to give a period feel to the voice of Mall. He is aware of the way in which the author is telling the story through the character of Mall and that Mall is speaking retrospectively. He adopts a similar approach. In this extract, London seems to be a very far off and alien place. The sense of places being far distant shows a feeling for a different time period. The bluebell simile picks up the dominance of the natural world and echoes the reference to the similes used, by the author, to describe the character of

17·1·00

The Parcel of Patterns

Mrs Cooper says the fault lies with the Hunts family who came from Cambridge but they say it be George Vicars, I say tis George Vicars and his parcel of patterns. If it had never been made! Tis said a rat was in the box but many say it were the messenger. I found afterwards Derby was stricken with the plague also and the plague was taken thither by a Lord and Lady all the way from London! Rumours are about, in more numbers than bluebells in spring, even to the extent of saying London is destroyed, this is how strange the rumours are Tis said that in London it is thought that foreigners have poisoned the water and are causing the plague, 'tis also said the Londoners are attacking them.

Figure 15.2 'Gossiping' about the cause of the plague

Catherine Momphesson: 'as fresh as a Lent Lily' and 'as slender as a slip of willow'. In all, this child's work shows a competence that allows him to respond to a challenge with confidence and reveals a strong link between comprehension and composition.

Other children meanwhile, who were less confident writers, researched the role of the author to help them to come to terms with the historical aspect of the narrative. For example, one group listed the questions the author would have to ask before starting the work. They needed to ask themselves, 'What would the author need to know about?' This allowed the children to ask questions about the text and the background history, without necessarily knowing the answers. The resulting spidergram or set of questions was then shared with the rest of the class. Highlighting the text is also useful as it encourages the children to return to the text and draw examples from it.

A Year 6 girl raised the points shown in Figure 15.3. All these points arose from the reading of three pages at the beginning of the book and discussions as a class and in small groups. Putting the task in this form allowed the child to raise the point of detail without having to know the background information for herself. There is a vast range of material represented by this list and further activities could be developed. The children could gather references to the geography of the area as the story progresses, and reflect on the role of the landscape in determining the outcome of the story. Different children could pursue different subjects such as symptoms of plague or beliefs about how it occurs or burial arrangements.

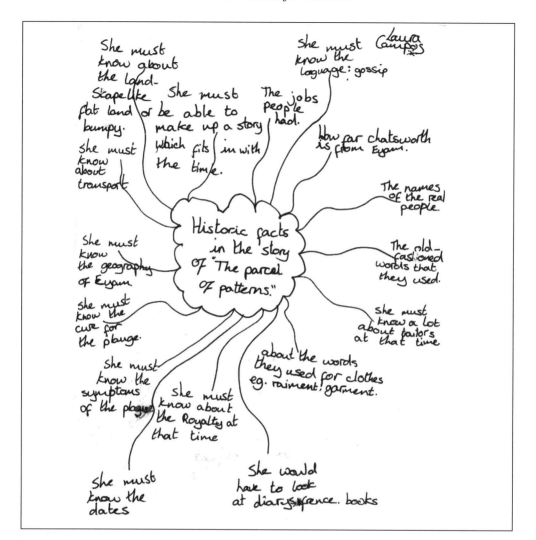

She must know about the land-Scape like flat land or bumpy.

She must know about transport

She must know the geography of Eyam

She must know the cure for the plague.

She must know the symptoms of the plague

She must know about the Royalty at that time

She must know the dates

She must or be able to make up a story which fits in with the time.

She must know about the Royalty at that time

about the words they used for clothes eg. raiment! garment.

She would have to look at diar¬yshfrence. books

She must know the language: gossip   Laura Campos

The jobs people had.

How far chatsworth is from Eyam.

Historic facts in the story of "The parcel of patterns."

The names of the real people.

The old-fashioned words that they used.

She must know a lot about tailors at that time

Figure 15.3 What the author would need to know before starting work

The next step is to see that the author needs to pass this information on to the reader as the story progresses. Children can be encouraged to thread information about time and place through their own work in a similar way and thus avoid big chunks of description. For instance, having a character ask questions, in his or her ignorance, of an another, enables a writer, through the other character's voice, to pass on information to the equally ignorant reader.

A different approach may be to look at the section of the text that compares Eyam, the village where the story is set, with the neighbouring village of Middleton. This demonstrates the way in which a setting can be incorporated naturally into a text. For children to get their bearings, they can use the information to draw a sketch map. Looking at an Ordnance Survey map enables them to compare the fiction with the fact. Translating the text into a picture encourages the children to examine the text very closely. Ultimately, this sort of work helps children incorporate information about settings into their own writing.

Work on character can also be drawn from this short section of the book. Mall, as narrator, writing in the first person with hindsight, withholds direct information about herself but lets slip bits and pieces about her life and her family as she chatters about the village and its inhabitants. The style of writing that reflects the somewhat disjointed stream of observations, is challenging and may best be done through guided reading and discussion. Children could tackle the question of character development through simply listing the characters mentioned and assigning to them a status: important characters or bit parts. This list can then be checked as the text is read to see if the status of the characters changes.

The character of Mall can be tackled by noting the facts that can be discerned in the text and using direct quotation from the text. Children like to challenge each other with information about text and be asked, 'How do you know?' They must then produce their evidence from the text.

One Year 6 boy wrote the points shown in Figure 15.4 about Mall.

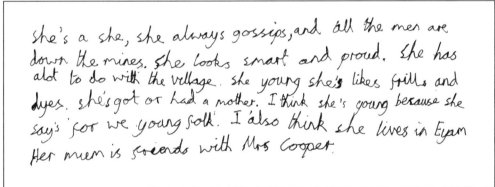

She's a she, she always gossips, and all the men are down the mines. She looks smart and proud. She has alot to do with the village. She young she's likes frills and dyes. She's got or had a mother. I think she's young because she say's 'for we young folk'. I also think she lives in Eyam. Her mum is friends with Mrs Cooper.

Figure 15.4 Character notes about Mall by Year 6 boy

This response is based on a close reading of the text. There was some confusion early on about the gender of Mall as the children assumed her name was a male name. It is interesting that many of the children identified her style of talking as distinctly female! This notion can be explored through discussion in the whole class or in small groups.

Figure 15.5 shows what a Year 6 girl wrote about Mall. There are a couple of points here which need clarifying and the child had to go back to the text to realise that the mother of the two children mentioned was not Mall. The reference to the work in Eyam while the parliament is in London is a misreading of the text that needs to be explained in terms of the change in religious practices during the period of the Commonwealth and Protectorate and after the restoration of the monarchy. In spite of these misunderstandings, the child has picked up information about the

Holly   17.1.00

I think that it is a Female because boys don't normally like to listen to people talking

She is intrested in the gossip I think she's bright because she's Jumping from one place to another. eg. There was work enough in Eyam for a tailor's needle While the parliament was in london.

She is always talking about two things at the same time.

I think she's about twenty because it says she had born two children.

She loves where she lives. eg. she never stopped talking about it.

I think she was bright and she knew what was going on in the village.

Figure 15.5 Character notes about Mall by Year 6 girl

personality of Mall and there is evidence of attempts to infer from the text and move beyond the more simple and obvious facts about the character.

The opening of *A Parcel of Patterns* is an interesting example for demonstrating narrative structure as the narrator hints at the outcomes in the story and is obviously writing with hindsight. From the first line, 'A parcel of patterns brought the Plague to Eyam', through to 'I heard later that the Plague was at Derby at the time when it reached us' and 'The parcel, had it never been sent for, Eyam had known never its dreadful fame' create anticipation in the reader and ambition perhaps in the writer to experiment with such narrative devices in his or her own writing. One way into this, is to suggest that the children try to write the plan for the first section in the book. They will then see that the story has been planned well ahead in order that the author can include such detail at such an early stage and change the order of events to move away from a typically linear story-line. When working on planning for their own writing, children can be encouraged to use their linear plan to try and enter the story at a different place and then fill in the details in a slightly different order. The opening of this book can be compared to other story openings so that the children can see the variety of models available to them.

There are many different approaches that can be taken to introduce narrative texts, and specifically historical fiction texts to children. However, the reading that takes place in the classroom should be first and foremost enjoyable and fulfilling for the child reader. Too much of the sort of activity outlined above may serve to put children off as they may come to associate reading with doing chores! The potential danger with current strategies to deliver the curriculum is that the time for immersing children in good quality texts is limited, meaning that children do not have leisure to interact with whole texts, particularly those texts with more challenge. This deprives them of an appreciation of how a full narrative can work. At some point in the term, the class teacher should make time to read a complete text to a class, a text that they come to love and remember as a positive experience, preferably as an extra to the literacy hours in the week.

The purpose of the discussion above is to show reading good quality texts enables the teacher to demonstrate to children what is possible, while supporting and scaffolding their own attempts to become competent readers and writers. When teaching literacy skills to children, reading and writing should not be disassociated from each other but seen as parts of the same whole. Teachers must assume that children who read well can write well and that those who have not yet reached a position of confidence and independence in reading and writing can still appreciate texts and compose, with support. A good resource will provide opportunities for the teacher to develop that support while providing equally good opportunities for challenging the able child. A good historical fiction text is ideal for that purpose and offers children, who may not encounter it in any other form, a glimpse of another language, another time and another world.

References

Doherty, B. (1985) *Children of Winter.* London: Methuen.
Paton Walsh, J. (1983) *A Parcel of Patterns.* London: Kestrel/Viking.

Chapter 16

Getting under the skin: the EACH Project

Alun Hicks and Dave Martin

Alun Hicks and Dave Martin treat us here to a detailed account of their reading, research and writing project with Dorsetshire pupils that brought together the two curriculum areas of English and history. Marrying the excitement of the story with sound historical detail is essential if a title is to earn its keep in a crowded curriculum. From the initial stimulus of the carefully chosen readings, children in this project were imaginatively supported in deconstructing the novels, researching themselves and then writing short historical extracts. In the process, the pupils grew both as writers and as historians.

Introduction

Extract 1

When animal droppings and garbage and spoiled straw are piled up in a great heap, the rotting and moiling give forth heat. Usually no one gets close enough to notice because of the stench. But the girl noticed and, on that frosty night, burrowed deep into the warm, rotting mulch, heedless of the smell. In any event, the dung heap probably smelled little worse than everything else in her life – the food scraps scavenged from kitchen yards, the stables and sties she slept in when she could, and her own unwashed, unnourished, unloved and unlovely body.

(Cushman 1995b)

Extract 2

The boy came stumbling down between the two big outfields of the village, on his way back from taking Gyrth the shepherd his supper. It was October, and soon Gyrth would be bringing the sheep down from the summer pasture; but at this time of year, when the rams were running with the ewes, he stayed up on the Downs with the flock whole days and nights together. It had rained in the early morning, and the steep rutted chalk of the driftway was slippery, so that anybody would have to go carefully; but the boy, Lovel, had to go more carefully than most, because he was built crooked, with a hunched shoulder and a twisted leg that made him walk lop-sided like a bird with a broken wing. His bony face under the thatch of dusty dark hair was quick and eager and wanted to be friendly; but nobody had ever bothered to notice his face; unless perhaps it was his grandmother, and she had died a week ago.   (Sutcliff 1970)

These two story openings do not immediately reveal themselves as historical fiction for children. There are no dates, no references to gladiators, lords, ladies, knights or other exotic characters that immediately betray the time when the stories are set. But these story openings do offer a view of an exotic world and hints of unfamiliar characters, setting and events. In the first, an orphaned girl, hungry and cold, burrows into pile of manure for warmth. In the second, an orphaned, disabled boy journeys alone in dangerous terrain.

One of the potential appeals of historical fiction, for children at least, is apparent. It shares with the child reader experiences far more extreme and challenging than she/he is likely to experience in contemporary, daily life. No wonder that more than 50 years after the end of the Second World War those six years between 1939 and 1945 still provide source material for an extraordinary range and number of narratives. One could argue that the essential appeal of historical fiction comes down to that sense of 'gosh, what must it have been like to live in those times?'. But for historical fiction to make a significant impact on the school curriculum it needs to offer the teacher something as well. The teacher needs to be convinced of more than the appeal of a 'good' story, whether good means 'well told' or a story set in 'interesting times'. In a very pressurised curriculum, at upper primary and lower secondary level, the teacher needs to know and demonstrate that the fiction chosen will 'fit in' with other curriculum demands. For historical fiction to flourish in schools collaboration between primary coordinators and between teachers of English and teachers of history is important. That collaboration is most important at the theoretical level: it is vital that the significance of story is fully absorbed by historians and the significance of history by teachers of English. Practical collaboration on delivering the curriculum is also desirable, but not always possible to achieve.

When collaboration is possible, its success will depend to a large extent on agreement between history and English teachers about what historical fiction is for. The English teacher might well feel that Joan Aiken's vivid stories of an imagined or alternative past provide the exotic element that children find appealing. The history teacher, quite reasonably, is likely to demand a story set in a context that actually existed even if events, on a domestic scale at least, are invented.

Although the historical novel needs curricular relevance before it is likely to be used in schools, it must first survive as a story with characters that behave with emotional and psychological consistency: to be a 'good' story is not enough, but it is a prerequisite. In a poor novel, good history won't hold the reader, but in a good story, history can be brought to life. Of course the history teacher will be concerned with historical consistency and accuracy, but to mine an historical novel for what it can teach about the past is to guarantee its failure in an aesthetic and curricular sense. And while no history teacher will want pupils to learn 'bad' history from historical novels, to play 'count the anachronisms' is likely to be an arid experience for teacher and pupil.

As an adult reader, which of the above story openings would you wish to pursue? As a teacher, which opening do you suspect that your pupils would go for? We are agreed that we want to know more about Extract 1. And reading it aloud in class would have pupils hooked immediately. One can imagine their groans of disgust as they react to the description of the foul-smelling mess that the girl crawls into. The description is vivid, cinematic almost, with adjectives and nouns piled on top of each other: rotting, moiling, unwashed, garbage, animal droppings, mulch, dung heap. The language is essentially simple (e.g. piled up in a great heap). Even the unfamiliar 'moiling' takes on an obvious sense next to 'rotting'. There is no need for dictionaries here. Yet the play on 'un', describing the girl's lack of cleanliness, food, love and beauty demands that the reader pay attention to the language. Above all, this opening has one strong idea to hang on to.

The second extract in terms of the vocabulary used is as accessible as the first: 'driftway' is the only word that might raise pupil eyebrows. Outwardly at least the syntax in this extract is demanding. Consider also the detail in this opening compared to the first extract. In Extract 1 we need to remember that the central character was a girl who lived an impoverished life. In Extract 2 we have three characters introduced, one of whom is dead by the end of the paragraph, as well as significant temporal and geographical contextual detail. The author of the first extract convinces the reader of the reality of the character's experience and uses language powerfully and sensuously to support the emotional impact. The second author uses language poetically or metaphorically ('made him walk lop-sided like a bird with a broken wing') to create a different sort of narrative.

In the end, the point is not which story is 'better' but what impression the writers make on their readers. Karen Cushman convinces us that, first and foremost, she has a story to tell and through that story, a history will be revealed. We would argue that Rosemary Sutcliff gives the impression of a skilled writer whose aim is to use historical fiction to teach about the past. However the essential point is that regardless of our response as individual adult readers, as teachers we make textual choices with children in mind. We have found, based on evidence of talking to children and of borrowing records from school libraries that Karen Cushman is borrowed while Rosemary Sutcliff remains on the shelf.

Origins of the EACH Project

The 'EACH' (English and/combined with history) Project was set up in October 1993 to explore this potential for the use of historical fiction in the teaching of English and history. In its pilot phase the project involved Year 7 pupils (aged 11 to 12), and their teachers from Wareham Middle School and advisory staff from Dorset Education Professional Development Services. The project's curriculum framework was designed to occupy one school term (see Figure 16.1).

Week	English		History	
1	Start reader – *A Little Lower than the Angels* Pupils keep log: Questions What happens next		Historical question/context What was life like in the Middle Ages?	
2		Types of story/genre e.g. science fiction	The events of 1066 – causation Battle of Hastings – historical sources Domesday Book – Norman/feudal England	
3	Reactions to story Shared perceptions	Black Death – context?	Village life	
4	Reading groups of four begin study of second text Theme – religion, superstition and medicine		Examine/analyse historical texts Begin research groups (on a question) in pairs	
5	Pupils keep log…maps, illustrations, covers, literary devices, time			Chronology framework
6	Character diary/profile		Begin class reference book (double page spreads)	
7				
8	Drawing together of all texts		Complete class reference book	
9	Pupils write and illustrate their own historical fiction – in pairs Questions to consider – setting, location and time, mode of narration, characters (names), are real people involved, purpose, passage of time, plot..			
10				
11				
12	Completion of historical fiction which will constitute an answer to the question – What was life like in the Middle Ages?			

Figure 16.1 The project outline

In the first stage lasting eight weeks pupils read the novel *A Little Lower than the Angels* by Geraldine McCaughrean (1987) as their class reader in English lessons. (Gabriel, a stonemason's apprentice, runs away from his cruel master to join a group of travelling players. They journey across Medieval Britain performing in towns and villages. Eventually they use the miracle plays they perform to convince their audiences that Gabriel has miraculous healing powers. Gabriel himself views the events of the story with naïveté, unable to tell hero from villain, good from bad.) In order to make this story accessible to all pupils a range of strategies was used such as hot seating characters and inviting children to produce a key image and chapter summaries so that they could stay in touch with the narrative.

One group of pupils, in an English lesson, compiled a number of questions they wanted to ask the author Geraldine McCaughrean. For example,

- 'Did you think of the plot before you started writing, or did it just come to you?'
- 'How much of the story is based upon fact?'
- 'Did you base the characters on anyone you know?'
- 'Where did you find the information on medieval history?'
- 'Why did you make Garvey and the mason evil characters?'

These or comparable questions were also ones that pupils needed to consider for themselves for their own writing. They reflect the overlap between the two subject disciplines. In this particular instance the chance to pose these questions to the author Geraldine McCaughrean and to read her very full reply were powerful, motivating forces.

The purpose of all of the above was to bring to the attention of the pupils some of the more prominent characteristics of historical fiction. The pupils then had the opportunity to read a further range of historical fiction set in the period. These supporting texts were chosen to give a range of styles: swashbuckling, comic, and heroic.

At the same time, in history, pupils studied the Medieval Realms History Study unit, Britain 1066–1500. In twos and threes they also undertook research into an aspect of medieval life. Their task was to produce a double page spread, on which they answered valid historical questions, such as: What role did woman play in medicine? or What food did the poor eat? These pages built into a class textbook. Posing a question was essential to their success here. The question provided them with a clear purpose, a set of criteria against which they could either select or reject information, and a definable end point. The class textbook formed a quarry from which pupils could mine ideas to support their story writing.

The pupils' story writing occupied the final four weeks of the term. Working in the same research twos and threes, they wrote their own historical fiction set in the medieval period. The pupils were by now equipped with two essentials, some understanding of the main characteristics of how historical fiction works and some knowledge of medieval life. As their stories developed they used their research and referred to other book resources for additional detail. The end result was a class anthology of medieval stories.

There were a number of conclusions to be drawn from this first phase of the project. Firstly, and not surprisingly, the choice of novel was key. As argued earlier, it was important that at the core of the project was a good story that was historically accurate and accessible to the pupils. This disqualified any novels which were historically accurate yet dull, where it was felt that the writer was trying to teach history rather than tell us a story. As Geoffrey Trease (1964) writes: 'Research must be thorough, but it must also be thoroughly absorbed by the author. It must be integrated in character and action; it must not show obviously in explanatory passages which the reader will instinctively skip.' *A Little Lower than the Angels* was the best choice at the time. Although quite challenging, where the teacher demonstrated enthusiasm and skill, there was no difficulty in engaging the pupils. However, since 1993 a number of children's novels have been published which are set in the medieval period and which would offer alternative choices. Most popular with young readers are those by Henrietta Branford and Karen Cushman.

Reading the novel gave the pupils an insight into how historical fiction worked. Other titles were available to support the 'core' text, but only the higher attaining pupils made use of these. Indeed, not every pupil completed *A Little Lower than the Angels*, but appropriately chosen narrative extracts meant that every pupil had a common, rich reading experience on which to build. And the best pupil stories had clearly borrowed ideas and techniques from the published authors. Above all, the collection of stories produced by the class (14 stories in total) contained within them a variety of story-writing features that could, in discussion, be reflected back to the pupils by the teacher. In their readings to each other pupils discovered how:

- Some pupils concentrated on a sense of place, time and occasion:
  It was a lovely sunny day on 11 September, 1666. This was the day at the end of the harvest when all the serfs got together and had a feast.
- Others, boys mainly, were more concerned with action:
  We are fighting knights and we fight until we surrender.
- Subtle writers tried to hold the reader with hints of future plot development:
  She thought about the fact they didn't know how it felt to be safe. Suddenly her thoughts were disturbed by the sound of screaming.
  They were deep in conversation about how they couldn't pay their taxes when William suddenly saw a light in the woods.
- Those concerned with historical authenticity reassured the reader through establishing the credentials of the storyteller:
  I trained as a novice monk in Bindon Abbey… Because I am educated I am able to write down what we experienced
  or through convincing social detail:
  With him were his wife and her lady in waiting, Robin his squire, and about ten other servants.
- Endings proved to be particularly fruitful because, in their stories, the young writers revealed a great deal about their preoccupations, understandings and misunderstandings. Several of the stories close the narrative with the humble being elevated, reflecting their view of the feudal system.
  They were going to live happily in a castle somewhere with Lightening, Rufus's horse. The King made Rufus a knight. Every prayer had come true and most of all, Georgy was gone forever.

Interestingly this is a similar conclusion to that found in *Knight's Fee* (Sutcliff 1960) where Randal, a former kennel boy, is knighted after the battle of Tinchebrai. Just as with some more famous storytellers, child writers also feel the need to resolve loose ends:

Finally everyone got home. James became a priest at the church next to Edward's castle. Esme became a potion maker to cure the sick in the village. Thomas married Esme after his wife sadly died of the plague, and of course, Edward married Lydia.

Pupils valued the time spent studying the medieval period and, as they became more confident in their own knowledge and understanding, they developed the confidence to write in an unfamiliar setting. For this confidence to develop, two important sources of support were available. Suitable history resources for pupil research were essential in developing knowledge and understanding: pupils could feel confident that the historical settings of their stories were broadly accurate. And paired writing activities meant that each pupil felt supported when making difficult narrative choices. Indeed, it was through these pairings that lower attaining pupils were able to complete a significant and challenging piece of work.

Reading Rosemary Sutcliff

The project then moved on to look at other areas of the past. First was the Roman period where the focus naturally turned to the Roman novels of Rosemary Sutcliff. As suggested earlier, her books represent a challenging read but offer significant rewards for those who persevere: 'Her major books have combined compelling narrative power with the exploration of important and absorbing themes' (Townsend 1990). This comment exemplifies the sort of admiration that librarians and writers for children commonly declare for Rosemary Sutcliff. Her books are to be found on the shelves of most school libraries yet are seldom borrowed. Why is this?

As part of the developing EACH Project, we decided to explore the reactions of secondary school pupils to Rosemary Sutcliff's stories. We had certain expectations. We expected to find some adolescent boredom with 'outdated' times, and perhaps a little irritation with rather wordy prose descriptions. We did not anticipate the very real difficulties that several readers had in getting into the stories in the first place.

This 'research' was low-key. We 'borrowed' 16 Year 7 and Year 8 volunteer pupils from two Dorset schools. We met them in two groups of eight and briefly introduced them to some notions of 'reader response' (when readers read they might anticipate, think back, make pictures, be confused, think of other stories, relate to their own lives, empathise, sympathise or make judgements). Equipped with some ideas for thinking about stories plus a tape-recorder and tape each, all pupils went off with a copy of a Rosemary Sutcliff novel and a sense that these stories would offer excitement and adventure. We selected four as having the greatest potential, *The Eagle of the Ninth* (1954), *The Silver Branch* (1957), *The Lantern Bearers* (1959) and *The Mark of the Horse Lord* (1965). The pupils left us with a promise to their chosen story and an intention to return in three weeks with the book read and comments recorded.

From those tapes we learned that when the pupils did respond positively they almost always talked admiringly of Rosemary Sutcliff's ability to describe a scene so that you could picture what it was like to be there, whether 'there' was the gladiators' arena or a perfume shop. Our young readers could feel the sand beneath their feet and smell the perfume in their nostrils. This sense of period and of empathising with historical people is something that well-written historical fiction manages to achieve. Nigel, reading *The Mark of the Horse Lord*, could imagine the 'dust and sand floating in the air', could feel that he was a part of the story, 'we're all sitting round'. Clive talked about the 'atmosphere' and 'tension', 'you're right in there'. Other positive responses tended to occur when readers took from their story something related to their own experience: Chloe enjoyed the chariot race in *The Eagle of the Ninth* because it contained reference to ponies!

However, many readers gave up before the end. Quite simply, the various difficulties presented by the stories meant that all bar one reader seemed unable to grasp the narrative thread:

- physical location was made doubly difficult by the way the characters moved around Roman Britain and by the sheer difficulty of mentally mapping such settlements as Rutupiae or Isca Dumnorium;
- few readers seemed to have any sense of time passing (historical time or story time);
- few readers seemed to have any real grasp of character relationships;
- even the most able and enthusiastic readers confessed to difficulty with the vocabulary;
- several readers felt that their inability to say names aloud (of people and places) was a significant obstacle to making progress in the story (despite the fact that they were not required to read the story on to tape);
- some girl readers simply resisted the maleness of these stories about honour and fighting.

In short, the difficulties manifested themselves on two levels: unfamiliarity and difficulty with words and names, and unfamiliarity with the Roman society so culturally different from our own. Some of these difficulties are those facing any teacher who chooses to teach a difficult but 'worthwhile' text. Our investigation involved a 'worst-case scenario' – a child alone, reading an historical novel disconnected from a study of the period. The teacher can use the sharing of a novel allied with sympathetic teaching strategies to 'get across' an outwardly difficult story. The teacher of English working with the teacher of history can do much to bridge those cultural and knowledge gaps that make such stories inaccessible.

The Renaissance

The EACH Project was now developing along two lines: research into pupil response to historical fiction along with a broadening of the historical periods and range of stories used. In All Saints Comprehensive School in Weymouth in 1995 work began on the Renaissance period. The history department, working on their own, introduced the reading and writing of historical fiction to all their Year 8 pupils (aged 12–13). It was decided that the pupil stories should be based on the city of Florence during the 1580s, a logical choice given its historical importance as a city-state and the availability of resource material. In the first six weeks of the term, using a range of textbook and Internet resources pupils studied the buildings and people of Renaissance Florence.

The remaining six weeks were then devoted to the pupils' Renaissance stories. To begin, pupils considered how Renaissance Italy had already been depicted in histor-ical fiction. There was little historical fiction written for pupils set in this period so a few extracts from adult authors were chosen, selected for their accessibility. For example, one excellent passage from *The Spring of the Ram* by Dorothy Dunnett (1987) describes a journey across Florence by a group of characters at the height of the Medicis' rule. It provides a vivid description of the streets, buildings and people. Although some of the vocabulary is difficult, the addition of a short glossary enabled teachers to make good use of this as the introductory piece. This was followed by a passage from *Axe for an Abbot* by Elizabeth Eyre (1995) that describes the effects of a summer storm on one of the poorer quarters of Florence.

We then gave the pupils a 'story recipe' to help them plan their narratives and set realistic parameters for their work. It was intended to act as a 'creative constraint'. The aim was for pupils to craft a short story or part of a story rather than a full-blown novel. The intention was to avoid pupils being too ambitious initially and then becoming disappointed when they were unable to realise their plans. Such constraints as 'you must include a thunder storm' and 'you must keep your story time to 48 hours' and 'restrict the number of characters you use to three' helped the pupils to keep their stories manageable.

All the pupils successfully completed their own stories. Many fell into one of two categories: romance (girl meets boy) and crime. Animal stories also featured: Renaissance horse stories were popular in one group! Pleasingly, there were also spy stories (from pupils aware of the rivalry that existed between Renaissance city-states), disaster stories (the River Arno burst its banks with devastating consequences on a large number of occasions), and escape adventure stories based on the Medici family.

Many pupils found the story recipes to be very helpful. Horses, dogs and cats were easily the most popular choices of animal, but an ermine, a ferret, some rats, a snake and a hawk also occurred. Wildly destructive electrical storms were commonplace. These requirements served to stimulate pupil imaginations. Virtually everyone managed to keep their stories within the confines of Florence. The most common weaknesses were a lack of an obvious plot, or a plot that developed promisingly, but then ran out of steam. Interestingly, virtually no one had difficulty writing their story opening:

> *It was a hot, sticky June day and Maria Medici sat gently sewing her tapestry. A cool breeze came in the cracks in the door and slowly around her soft, bare ankles. She shivered as the air slipped through each toe and cooled her delicate, porcelain like feet . . .*

Simple plots tended to work best: Boy has dog. Boy loses dog. Boy is upset and looks for dog with a friend. Boy finds dog and everyone is happy. More sophisticated plots dealing with, for example, political intrigue also made for a good read, but quite often pupils tied themselves (and the reader) in knots by including too many twists and nuances. Widespread use was made of dialogue to the extent that two pupils even attempted to write their conversations in Italian, luckily with English translations provided.

A good sense of place pervaded many stories. Often it was the little details that created that air of historical credibility. Here a pupil refers to the extremes of Renaissance society:

> *As he rode up the streets, he could not help but notice the poor beggars . . . then looming up in front of him he saw the richly ornate building that was the Pazzi residence. He saw the contrast.*

This Renaissance fiction project proved to be a great success and a lot of fun. It had a very positive motivating effect on the Year 8 pupils. Pupils enjoyed working on a single project and appreciated the creative challenges that the story writing provided. In fact, as the project progressed, classes were settling themselves down to their work without the need for any major prompts from the teachers. The majority of pupils felt a sense of achievement in their writing and the anthologies proved to be a major draw in the school library. From the historical point of view pupils acquired a rather better understanding of Renaissance Italy than they had previously done. The story format allowed individuals to delve into all sorts of areas that would have been closed to them, and helped them develop really quite sophisticated representations of Renaissance society.[1]

Implications of the EACH Project

If the argument that historical fiction has value in the school curriculum is accepted, then some important lessons should already be apparent. It cannot be said too often that what matters most is the quality of the story or the story extract chosen. And, as far as is possible, the integrity of the story must be maintained. Those health warnings aside, some other, less obvious lessons need to be drawn out.

For the teacher of English, these issues relate mainly to genre, to the problematising of story writing, and to the role of story 'scaffolding'. There might be a temptation to treat historical fiction as an identifiable literary genre and use the genre as a model for writing. (Pinning down historical fiction as a genre would be an interesting project in itself.) However, the evidence from the project suggests that from historical fiction writing can emerge spy stories, escape stories, crime stories, not to mention westerns, science fiction (time travel) and war. In this context, the teacher has to be prepared to see historical fiction as a starting point for genre study rather than just another genre.

Some might regard it as bizarre or even perverse to set out to make writing for children problematic. Yet it is the apparent ease of making up stories that often leads to disappointing narratives; children's own stories though sometimes delightful, are also capable of being plot-driven, lacking characterisation and setting, and highly derivative. Setting the writing in the past is constraining, but also, we would argue, liberating. Children who are forced to acknowledge that, for example, they don't know how characters in a given historical period might have behaved are also forced to find out. The consequent research can lead to the production of well-drawn characters and very convincing settings. And to make something problematic is not to take away all support. A wide range of scaffolding devices (including story recipes) benefits all pupils, but especially the least able.

For some readers, this approach to reading and writing stories may still smack of too much structure, may imply some obstacle to children's creativity. The evidence from the children's writing we have accumulated suggests the opposite. Working in the context of historical fiction tends to produce writing of a better quality than one would normally expect.

For the teacher of history these issues relate to the key elements of the subject. The story writing gives a purpose to the pupils' research. They are finding out about the past in order to make their settings, characters and plot authentic. This increased motivation allied to the increased time devoted to this type of work can lead to better quality pupil enquiry on a much wider range of features of the past. They are less likely to have a superficial view. The resulting stories reflect pupils' deeper understanding of past societies and the experiences and range of ideas, beliefs and attitudes of the men, women and children in them.

It is also an opportunity for the teacher of history to explore historical fiction as a deliberate interpretation of the past. This is one of the more difficult areas of history to cover but arguably a key one. Much of the average adult's knowledge of history comes from the fictional narratives provided by film, television and historical fiction. In this context deconstructing historical fiction helps pupils to appreciate how such narratives are made, the story decisions that are taken and the effect such decisions have upon what version of the past is portrayed.

The third advantage for the teacher of history is the challenge that the story presents pupils with. Pupils need to work hard on developing their ability to organise and communicate their historical ideas effectively. They have to select, organise and deploy relevant information to produce a well-structured narrative.

Note

1   The lessons of the Rosemary Sutcliff research and of the Renaissance story writing have been brought together in a new publication which returns to the Roman period. *Write Your Own Roman Story* (Brooke *et al.* 2001) is aimed at Year 7 pupils. This takes a step-by-step approach to the writing of historical fiction. Pupils are given the device of a story recipe to work within and a wide range of historical source material to draw upon for their writing. Using a range of extracts taken from published authors, pupils develop their understanding of the prominent characteristics of historical fiction. This aspect is highly structured to model story openings and resolutions, character and setting descriptions, first person and third person narration and the use of dialogue. It includes help on how to

construct a plot by first devising a problem and then working out how the characters deal with the conflicts that arise. At each point, for example in establishing
setting or character, pupils practise their writing technique. Some of these characters and settings can be incorporated into their final stories but they can stand
alone as successful pieces of writing. The pupils still keep creative control, they
decide which characters to use and where to place their story, but there is very
structured support throughout.

In the longer term, the EACH Project plans to continue to develop the twin
strands of research into pupil response to historical fiction along with a broadening of the historical periods and range of stories used. In order to disseminate
these ideas and to invite involvement from others, the project runs a web site
http://www.dorset-cc.gov.uk/educate/each/each1.htm devoted to the use of
historical fiction in the classroom. This site contains a mix of teacher ideas and
discussion, pupil fiction, reviews of historical fiction and pointers to other useful
sources of information for teachers, and it continues to develop.

Bibliography

Branford, H. (1997) *Fire, Bed and Bone.* London: Walker Books.

Brooke, B. *et al.* (2001) *Write Your Own Roman Story.* London: John Murray.

Cushman, K. (1995a) *Catherine, Called Birdy.* New York: Clarion Books.

Cushman, K. (1995b) *The Midwife's Apprentice.* New York: Clarion Books.

Dunnett, D. (1987) *The Spring of the Ram.* London: Penguin.

Eyre, E. (1995) *Axe for an Abbot.* London: Headline Book Publishing.

McCaughrean, G. (1987) *A Little Lower than the Angels.* Oxford: Oxford University
    Press.

Sutcliff, R. (1954) *The Eagle of the Ninth.* Oxford: Oxford University Press.

Sutcliff, R. (1957) *The Silver Branch.* Oxford: Oxford University Press.

Sutcliff, R. (1959) *The Lantern Bearers.* Oxford: Oxford University Press.

Sutcliff, R. (1960) *Knight's Fee.* Oxford: Oxford University Press.

Sutcliff, R. (1965) *The Mark of the Horse Lord.* Oxford: Oxford University Press.

Sutcliff, R. (1970) *The Witch's Brat.* Oxford: Oxford University Press.

Townsend, J. R. (1990) *Written for Children.* London: The Bodley Head.

Trease, G. (1964) *Tales Out of School.* London: Heinemann.

Chapter 17

Slavery and the Underground Railroad: working with students

Liz Laycock

In this chapter Liz Laycock discusses how slavery is written about in children's books. She begins with Uncle Tom's Cabin *and identifies how this is a book of its time. She then introduces the reader to a range of picture books and novels, exploring how the representation of slavery changes over time. The second part of the chapter describes how working with such books helps students to investigate, through drama, discussion and research, issues such as human rights, oppression and globalisation. In these ways, the students learn about the history of slavery and how it is portrayed in children's books.*

Children's historical fiction and historical picture books are dismissed by some historians as trivial and inaccurate representations of facts. In the past 'story' and 'history' were the same (indeed, in French the word 'histoire' still has both meanings); oral stories carried and transmitted all of people's past, their origins, the battles, the cultural mores, the celebration of identity. The story made it easy to remember information about the past. As Anna Davin (1978) asserts, stories 'can convey a range of different knowledge (events, names, relationships, chronological sequence, material background, beliefs and opinions, and so on) and a framework for storing it so, even when complex, they are likely to be understood and remembered'. Historical fiction is likely to engage the imagination and promote reflection in ways which simple knowledge of facts is unlikely to do. This is perhaps especially so on a topic such as slavery, far removed from children's lived experience.

'Knowing about the past…isn't quite the same as understanding and feeling about it' (Aiken 1985). Some children and many young adults may 'know' about elements of the history of slavery. Often they can relate the historical facts about the slave trade, the economic context, the laws, the details of abolitionists and the process of abolition both in Britain and in America and they will unanimously declare opposition to this evil practice. There have been some published first-hand accounts accessible to young readers, notably Julius Lester's collection in *To be a Slave* (Lester and Feelings 1968), but the real 'understanding and feeling' is generally more powerfully developed through fictional narratives. The authors of fiction about slaves and slavery intend their readers to feel something of the reality of life for the slaves as well as to understand the views and motivation of those who opposed the trade. The ideology of authors writing on this subject is almost always 'explicit' – that is, the 'social, political or moral beliefs of the individual writer' are fairly obvious. They are trying 'to change imaginative awareness in line with contemporary social criticism' (Hollindale 1988).

Any consideration of the literature which succeeds in doing this must start with Harriet Beecher-Stowe's *Uncle Tom's Cabin* (1852). This book is not a historical novel because it was written while these events were happening and it was not written for children, but it is important because it was written during the time of slavery, drawing on the writer's first-hand experience of the reality of a society which accepted and approved of slave ownership. Beecher-Stowe was a committed Christian and her intention was to demonstrate that, despite the approval of most churchmen at the time, slavery was an evil and unchristian, albeit legal, trade. Through her creation of Uncle Tom, the wholly good Christian slave tortured and murdered by a slave owner, she presents a stark contrast to Legree the slave owner, embodiment of evil. Modern critics and many black readers are offended by the portrayal of Tom as a passive victim, looking up to and respecting his earlier, better owners and succumbing to the cruel Legree. However, his acceptance of his condition and the suffering he endures is the result of his deeply held Christian belief and the Christian ethic he lives by, and the description of his death has deliberate parallels with the death of Jesus. Tom quotes directly from moments of the Passion as he welcomes death – 'Into thy hands I commend my spirit', 'I forgive ye with all my soul' (Beecher-Stowe 1852). Beecher-Stowe, as narrator, makes this link explicit, 'Oh, my country! These things are done under the shadow of thy laws! O, Christ! Thy church sees them almost in silence! But of old there was One whose suffering changed an instrument of torture, degradation and shame, into a symbol of glory, honour and immortal life.' More than a hundred years after it was written, and despite the author's often unsubtle didacticism, this book still communicates powerfully with the reader.

A much more recent book, *The Slave Dancer* by Paula Fox (1973), has also caused much controversy because of the perspective it seems to present of the slaves as passive victims. But, as Pat Pinsent (1997) writes:

Sometimes what appears to be a defeatist ending may reflect the author's implicit ideology just as much as truth to the facts or to art; critics of *The Slave Dancer* might have been happier if the slaves had risen against the evil crew, whether or not such a revolt had been successful, but it would have been a different book from the one Fox wrote. It may be that her implicit and unacknowledged desire was rather to implicate white readers in the guilt of the slave trade than to display to black readers the passivity of their forebears.

Hollindale (1988) says, 'If the fictional world is fully imagined and realised, it may carry its ideological burden more covertly, showing things as they are but trusting to literary organisation rather than explicitly didactic guidelines to achieve a moral effect' (p. 11). *The Slave Dancer* was highly praised in literary terms when it first appeared, winning the Newbery Medal in 1974. The white central character, kidnapped and enslaved himself on board the slave trading ship, required to play his fife during the voyage for the slave cargo 'dancing', is as helpless as the imprisoned slaves. His fury against them is a symptom of his anger about his own situation, not a condemnation of them. The book, set in 1840, is a powerful indictment of the transportation of slaves, without ever being didactic. The story is told by Jessie, the kidnapped boy, who knew nothing of slavery until he was forced on board this ship, so readers are discovering what 'the middle passage' is all about, as he encounters this evil. By the end, when he has survived, he says:

> I was back in my life, but I was not the same. When I passed a black man, I often turned to look at him, trying to see in his walk the man he had once been before he'd been driven through the dangerous heaving surf to a long boat, toppled into it, chained, brought to a waiting ship all narrowed and stripped for speed, carried through storms, and the bitter brightness of sun-filled days to a place where, if he had survived, he would be sold like cloth.   (Fox 1973)

Through this harrowing experience, Jessie has grown and developed.

In both of these novels the ideology of the author inevitably informs the stance adopted. In the case of Beecher-Stowe, this ideology runs contrary to the beliefs of the majority at the time and sets out to persuade readers of her views. Her novel is an undisguised condemnation of all that slavery involves, represented by both the benign, well-meaning St Clare and the vicious Legree; it is a prime example of what Robert Sutherland (1985) defines as ' the politics of attack'. Fox's book, too, sets out to 'attack' the inhuman transportation of slaves, though, in this case, she is reflecting the changed views of the wider society, even if, in the eyes of some critics, she presents the slaves as powerless and passive. All events are seen through the eyes of the first-person narrator, Jessie, so the reader's responses must be governed to some extent by his emotions and his growing knowledge and understanding.

A recent book, *A Picture of Freedom. The Diary of Clotee, a Slave Girl* (1997) by Patricia McKissack is also written as a first-person narrative, but this time the story is told from the slave's perspective. Clotee has learned to read and write from observing the lessons her mistress teaches daily to her son. Clotee's task was to fan them; as she says:

> It may seem like a silly job. But I don't mind one bit, 'cause while William is learnin', so am I. Standin' there fannin' – up and down, up and down – I come to know my ABCs and the sounds the letters make. I teached myself how to read those words. ... It scares me to know what I know sometimes. Slaves aine s'posed to know how to read and write, but I do.   (McKissack 1997)

The diary is written in a way which conveys Clotee's growing knowledge, vocabulary and understanding of 'Freedom'. The slaves' conditions on this Virginia Plantation are considerably better than those for slaves in the South, the place they all fear most. Some of the events echo those portrayed by Harriet Beecher-Stowe in *Uncle Tom's Cabin* but the slaves are much less passive. Though some, especially Missy, are content to suck up to the white masters (for their own ends), Clotee, Spicy, Hince and Rufus are all prepared to resist and fight for freedom. In this the book reflects our contemporary understanding that resistance was always present. Clotee reports Mas' Henley's belief that his slaves are happy when she says:

> Hince doesn't want to leave Belmont, his only home. You abolitionists don't understand and you never will. Our slaves love us. They run away when you people come down here exciting them about freedom – freedom to do what? They are like children, unable to do for themselves.

She adds, 'They let Mas' Henley rattle on, fooling himself into b'lieving we slaves was happy to be slaves' (McKissack 1997). Mr. Harms, the abolitionist tutor, is a Southerner opposed to slavery whose influence on the young William is crucial to aiding the escaping slaves, but the initiative and the clever plans come from the slaves themselves. This book, published in 1997, demonstrates how extensively thinking about the experience of slaves and slavery has changed.

A similar view is reflected in *Nightjohn* by Gary Paulsen (1993). Again this is first-person narrative by Sarny, a slave girl, believed by the white owners to be stupid. It is powerfully written in modified dialect with vivid, raw description of the physical environment. Nightjohn, the newly arrived slave, can read and wants to teach others because 'They have to read and write. We all have to read and write so we can write about this – what they doing to us. It has to be written' (Paulsen 1993). He had escaped North to freedom, but came back so he could teach reading, and got caught again. Sarny is willing to take the risk of learning, even though she knows the penalties. There is realistic portrayal of the cruelty meted out to slaves; the whippings, attacks by dogs, dismemberment (Nightjohn's toes, because he confesses to teaching Sarny) and death are constantly with the slaves here. Soon after his toes are removed Nightjohn runs and Sarny believes he will never return but he does and Sarny and a few others from other plantations come at night to his 'pit school' to continue to learn to read. The narrative structure of this story leaves the ending open; there is no conclusion, no optimistic ending. Sarny and others remain slaves and Nightjohn comes to teach. But the reader, like the slaves, knows that there is likely to be more trouble ahead and that the battle for freedom will go on.

One of the earliest historical novels for children about slavery, *Brady* (1960), is by the well-respected historical novelist Jean Fritz. This story takes place just before the Civil War in a region (near to Washington) where opinion is fiercely divided on the subject of slavery. Brady, the central character, is embarrassed by his preacher father's strong anti-slavery stance. He has to face up to and reflect upon the issues when events force him to take responsibility for the escaped slave boy his father is hiding. The issues and the impact of a moral stance against slavery are vividly portrayed and the characterisation of Brady is very strong. As he wrestles with the issues, so the reader's thinking is carried forward. The narration is in the third person but with powerful glimpses into Brady's growing understanding and responsibility. The story moves on at a rapid pace and the setting and the historical detail are convincing, presenting the dilemmas faced by those opposed to slavery. Unlike most of the stories about slavery, this one is told from the perspective of the white (albeit anti-slavery) viewpoint, rather than that of the slaves involved.

The best-known escape route for slaves was called 'the Underground Railroad'. It was not a real railroad, but a secret network of courageous people, both black and white, who helped escaped slaves. Railway terminology was used to describe the guides (conductors), the safe houses (stations), and the fugitive slaves (passengers). It is this context which Barbara Smucker draws on in her immensely powerful novel *Underground to Canada* (1978). This book has the characteristics of the best kind of historical fiction – a strong narrative and an accurate evocation of the past. Readers are carried along by an exciting, well-paced journey story; the main characters Julilly and Liza are strongly drawn individuals but are able to represent the many who made similar journeys on the Underground Railroad. Characterisation in this book is skilfully used to engage the reader; empathy with the two girls is created early on through glimpses into their thinking, their responses to events and to one another. The main white characters, Sims, the overseer and Mr Alexander Ross, the ornithologist, are embodiments of the evil white man and the good, abolitionist white man; their physical appearances are made to reflect their natures. Sims is 'fat, red-faced', with 'small, cruel eyes' and 'yellow, uneven teeth', given to sweating, while Ross is a 'portly' and 'big chested' man, whose eyes 'crinkled with good humour', or became 'merry when he laughed'. The trials of the journey, the setbacks, the physical hardship and the fear of the fugitives are vividly portrayed, as are the generous and courageous 'conductors' who risk their own safety to help them on the way.

Alexander Ross, the ornithologist, was a principled Canadian abolitionist and his presence in this story represents the many times he aided escaped slaves – in five years he was instrumental in the escape of over 30 slaves, all the while pursuing ornithological work and building his reputation as a serious scientist. The other real historical figure shown in *Underground to Canada* is Levi Coffin, a Quaker leader, business man and abolitionist. He and his wife, Catherine, are known to have aided more than 3,000 slaves in flight and he gained the title of 'President of the Underground Railroad', though this was not, of course, a formal organisation. Real people who were leading figures in aiding the slaves and championing abolition, people like Harriet Tubman, Frederick Douglass, Peg Leg Joe, are often the subjects of historical books, including picture books.

Picture books

These picture books can represent vividly, incidents from history, the character of the hero, the physical environment and the place in a past time. The best of these make skilful use of the picture book form so that text and pictures work together not only to convey the story, but also to illustrate the meaning of slavery for younger readers. There is a growing number of historical picture books dealing with the subject of slavery. One of the earliest, *Thee Hannah* (de Angeli 1940) demonstrates the Quakers' stance on abolition in the context of a story which deals more broadly with what it means to be a Quaker. The story of Hannah's involvement with an escaped slave woman, which is the climax of the book, was a true one, told to the author by her 90-year-old friend (Hannah in the story) and is recounted in a matter of fact way, without sentimentality or even comment on slavery or those who helped escaped slaves. Its simplicity reflects the honesty and openness of the Quaker participants in events, who act unquestioningly to do what is right.

Of the recently published historical picture books one of the most successful is *Barefoot* (Duncan Edwards and Cole 1997). It is a beautifully illustrated story of a nameless fugitive slave running through woodland pursued by catchers. He is able to interpret the noises of the woods and it is as though the wood animals are helping him by guiding him to water, berries, a place to sleep and helping him avoid capture. He eventually finds the safe house with the quilt displayed thanks to the fireflies lighting the path. The text is simple but the atmosphere of fear in the night is perfectly conveyed through the dark illustration which focuses largely on ground level.

Frederick Douglass: The Last Day of Slavery (Miller and Cedric 1995) is an account of Douglass' early years in slavery and of the fight with the slave breaker Covey, which precipitated his escape. Douglass was born into slavery in 1817. In 1838 he escaped to the North and, because he was one of very few slaves who had learned to read and write, he was able to write and publish, starting in 1845, first-hand accounts of the reality of life as a slave. He became a well-known speaker in the anti-slavery movement, continuing to write and struggle for the freedom of enslaved people until his death in 1895. This book presents a powerful telling of events in Douglass' early life; the text conveys simply and effectively Douglass' thoughts and feelings but it is the illustration which communicates so strongly the context and the cruelty of life in slavery as well as Douglass' courage and dreams. Cedric's dark line drawings with colour wash perfectly reflect and extend Miller's text.

Follow the Drinking Gourd (Winter 1988) takes the words of the slave song and demonstrates their significance. It is believed that the song was taught to the slaves by one 'Peg Leg Joe', a conductor on the Underground Railroad. The song contains very explicit instructions for escape from the Kentucky/Ohio area; escapees followed the pointer to the North Star in the constellation known as 'the big dipper' or 'the drinking gourd'. All escaping slaves knew they had to go North and that this constellation, wherever they started from, pointed to the North Star and the direction they wanted. On this route, according to the song, were hidden signs guiding them to the Ohio River, where they were to be ferried across by Peg Leg Joe, who then set them on the trail of safe houses (railroad stations/conductors) going North to Canada. The book gives the four verses which are still known and shows the meaning of each, as a group of slaves follows the signs. It is believed that there were more verses (Tobin and Dobard 1999) which have been lost because memories faded. The illustration in this book, vibrant paintings which have a folk art style, do not attempt realistic portrayal of landscape, but capture the atmosphere of escape and pursuit most effectively.

Picture book creators have only begun to deal with subjects related to slavery in any substantial way in the late 1980s and 1990s and all are published in America. The timing of these reflects, perhaps, the growing awareness of Americans, black and white, of the history of slavery and concern that children should be informed of the truth about it. Harriet Tubman is the subject of several picture books: *Aunt*

Harriet's Underground Railroad in the Sky (Ringold 1992); *Journey to Freedom* (Wright and Griffith 1994); *Minty* (Schroeder and Pinkney 1996). The first of these is a curious and complex book. The 'flying' children, the real train in the sky, Aunt Harriet as the conductor and the new born baby 'Freedom' are all allegorical, but the account of the reality of slave life and the stations Cassie sees on the escape route are accurate representations of the places and people. The book is a difficult mixture for young readers and requires discussion and considerable re-reading. Ringold's illustration is strong; the black/white contrast comes over clearly, especially through the white faces 'spying' on scenes throughout the book. In work with students (see below) this proved a useful starting point for drama activities exploring the daily life on a plantation and for introducing knowledge about the Underground Railroad and Harriet Tubman and her role as a 'conductor' to safety of escapees.

The picture books contribute an important dimension to reflection on the history of slavery. The information added by the illustration offers the young reader 'the exciting and stimulating liberation of finding out for himself' (Lively 1981). Penelope Lively argues that, 'to stimulate historical curiosity you have to persuade people – of any age – of the reality of the past, which is far more difficult or subtle than telling them how things were done then'. That reality is created in the novels, but is further imagined and developed in the picture book form. Picture books provide a graphic representation of some of the facts about the Underground Railroad escape route. This was the starting point for our work with students.

Working with students

Our intention in selecting the theme of slavery for working with students was to demonstrate the power of children's historical fiction and to introduce the work of some American writers whose work was unfamiliar to the students. We used drama teaching methodology at the students' own level in order to demonstrate its potential as a way of developing responses to historical fiction. As the work proceeded the topic led to related exploration in other curriculum areas and stimulated discussion of wider, contemporary issues relating to slavery.

Student preparation for the first session included reading a short biography of Harriet Tubman and some of the children's literature dealing with slavery. Following initial discussion to set the context and to establish what knowledge students already had, we read aloud extracts from *Underground to Canada* (Smucker 1978) and *Aunt Harriet's Underground Railroad in the Sky* (Ringold 1992). These enabled the tutors leading the session to set up initial role building around life on the plantation and students worked practically, with tutors in role as overseer, plantation owners, visiting preacher, potential purchaser of slaves. Students worked in role as slaves in different contexts – in the house, in the fields, in cabins at night, at a prayer meeting. This organisation enabled tutors working in role to pose problems and edge different slave groups into consideration of issues relating to escape, trust, collective responsibility, as well as the hopes and fears of individuals. Our use of teacher in role, hot-seating, freeze-frame, mime, tableaux and writing in role enabled students to gain some insight into the life of a slave on the plantation, as well as demonstrating the potential of this approach for exploring literature more widely. We introduced some of the songs associated with slavery, especially 'Let my People Go'.

Following the drama activity, students began to explore some of the strands which had been touched on. The first need was to find out more about the geography of the United States from the slave states in the South to the Northern states bordering on Canada, as well as about the historical context of pre-Civil War America. They needed maps to contextualise the escape routes, the distances and the terrain involved. The realisation that there was strong opposition to slavery from many white Americans led to investigation into the part that various groups, especially the Quakers, had played in aiding fugitives. Similarly, it became apparent that most slaves were not passive victims, waiting for help from sympathetic whites, but that many were leaders in the abolition movement and that, for them, learning to read and write was crucial in telling about the reality.

Students discovered the ingenuity and skill of the slaves in secretly passing on information and this led to further investigation of the music rooted in slavery. One student, herself a singer in a modern Gospel choir, researched the meaning of 'The Drinking Gourd' song and, aided by Jeanette Winter's picture book, provided a full translation of the text. This, in turn, led to further research into slave songs (later termed Spirituals) and the hidden messages they contained. The idea of escape and advice about when to leave was encoded in songs sung under the noses of owners – no wonder they tried to ban both singing and drumming! 'Steal Away' contains direction on the best time to run, 'Canaan' and 'the Promised Land' were references to the North (and later, after the Fugitive Slave Law in 1850, to Canada), 'the Gospel train' became code for the Underground Railroad. In an allusion to 'Go down Moses', Harriet Tubman was dubbed 'the Moses of her people'; she loved the songs and used them to signal whether or not it was safe for fugitives to move from place to place.

A fascinating recent book, *Hidden in Plain View* (Tobin and Dobard 1999) explains many of the means of communication and especially that embedded in the quilts, which was another strand followed by students. Patchwork quilt patterns offered further guidance to escaping slaves and some of the mysteries of these are uncovered by the authors of this book. One of the historical picture books, *Sweet Clara and the Freedom Quilt* (Hopkinson and Ransome 1993) deals very explicitly with this link, providing the perfect medium to develop understanding of quilting. The story shows the use made of signs and messages hidden in the quilts made by slaves. Clara maps the plantation on which she works as well as the wider area, drawing on information from slaves who have travelled beyond the boundaries. She uses her eyes and ears to find out distances, landmarks, routes through swamp, which are all incorporated into her 'map'. She makes use of the simplest of the quilting patterns – nine-patch, alternated with plain block – using different colours of fabric to represent fields of crops and stitches to show paths and landmarks. In this respect the back of the quilt was as important as the front and one illustration shows Clara working on the back, as the driver slave tells her how far a neighbouring plantation is. By the time it is finished she has memorised the layout of the land and is able to leave the quilt for others to use as a mnemonic device in later escapes. A student who had looked at the history of quilts in her work in art shared some of what she knew about the names and meanings of the patterns, leading others to follow this strand.

An important part of the follow-up work led into consideration of contemporary issues relating to human rights, oppression, the role of economics and globalisation in exploitation and coerced labour in many parts of the world. In this respect, a recent book *Disposable People* by Kevin Bales (1999) provided crucial information. A reviewer of the book, Richard Pierre Claude, said, 'while the general public is convinced slavery is a historical phenomenon of the ancient past, or perhaps found in small pockets in faraway places, it is actually a widespread tragedy found world-wide and on a large scale' (quoted on book jacket). The study of children's literature about slavery in the past certainly sensitised students to these contemporary issues and much valuable discussion was informed by new understanding and feeling about the past.

Moving on

The most recently published historical novel about slavery is perhaps a sign that the subject is becoming more important in Britain. The Scottish writer Frances Hendry's book, *Chains* (2000), has an unusual structure. Because slavery was not confined to black/white or Africa/America, Hendry has created four interlocking strands which weave together. The book is set at the end of the eighteenth century and her aim is to 'show a few of the forms slavery took at that time, expressing the beliefs and opinions of the time in the words which people of the time would have used' (Hendry 2000). She has created imaginary characters but the action is rooted in factual background. There are four, strongly drawn, central characters: Juliet, a determined young woman who disguises herself as her brother in order to take his place on a merchant (slaving) ship sailing out of Liverpool; Hassan, the grandson of an Arab merchant from Djenne on the Niger river, who accompanies his father, Uzum, 'along the great river' to trade with white men; Gbodi, from the village of Loko near the modern Mali-Niger border, who is captured by slavers from another tribe; Dand, son of a poor Scottish farmer from East Mirren, near Aberdeen, who is kidnapped to be sold as a 'servant' in the West Indies.

The paths of these four cross as each encounters danger and death but each survives. Hassan starts as a master but becomes a slave; Dand starts as a slave but gains his freedom; Gbodi remains enslaved but with determination to do all in her power to undermine and destroy her masters. Juliet, despite her apparent connivance and acceptance of pro-slavery views earlier in the book, emerges firmly convinced that slavery is wrong – 'People owning people – it's abominably wrong!' – and determined to 'work to help change the laws, to stop it'. This work for children acknowledges to some extent the part Britain played in the slave trade in the eighteenth century, although, as Errol Lloyd, the respected author and artist, argues in a recent review article (2001), the views expressed do not reflect or present anti-slavery arguments. The pro-slavery arguments, presented strongly by the white slavers, are not explicitly opposed; it is left to readers, faced with the horror of slavery, to draw their own conclusions. Nevertheless, this book does at least acknowledge the blood on British hands – perhaps this will be the start of an increased awareness of and willingness to reflect on the issue in a British context.

Bibliography

Aiken, J. (1985) 'Interpreting the past', *Children's Literature in Education* **16**(2), 67–83.

Bales, K. (1999) *Disposable People. New slavery in the global economy.* Berkeley: University of California Press.

Beecher-Stowe, H. (1852) *Uncle Tom's Cabin.* London: Dent (Everyman).

Bial, R. (1995) *The Underground Railroad.* Boston: Houghton Miflin.

Davin, A. (1978) 'Historical novels for children', in Grugeon, E. and Walden P. (eds) *Literature and Learning*, 72–84. London: Ward Lock Educational in association with Open University Press.

de Angeli, M. (1940) *Thee, Hannah.* Scotdale, Pennsylvania: Herald Press.

Duncan Edwards, P. and Cole, H. (1997) *Barefoot.* New York: Harper Collins.

Elbert, S. (ed.) (1997) *Louisa May Alcott. On race, sex and slavery.* Boston: Northeastern University Press.

Ferris, J. and K. Ritz (1988) *Go Free or Die.* (Harriet Tubman), Minneapolis: Carolrhoda Books Inc.

Fox, P. (1973) *The Slave Dancer.* London: Macmillan Education.

Fritz, J. (1960) *Brady.* Harmondsworth: Puffin.

Hendry, F. M. (2000) *Chains.* Oxford: Oxford University Press.

Hollindale, P. (1988) *Ideology and the Children's Book.* Stroud: Thimble Press.

Hopkinson, D. and Ransome, J. (1993) *Sweet Clara and the Freedom Quilt.* New York: Alfred A. Knopf.

Johnson, D. (1993) *Now Let Me Fly.* New York: Simon & Schuster.

Lester, J. (1972) *Long Journey Home.* Harmondsworth: Puffin.

Lester, J. and Feelings T. (1968) *To be a Slave.* Harmondsworth: Puffin.

Lively, P. (1981) 'Bones in the sand', *The Horn Book Magazine* **LVII**(6), 641–51.

Lloyd, E. (2001) 'Whose history? The Atlantic slave trade', *Books for Keeps* **127**, 12–13.

McKissack, P. C. (1997) *A Picture of Freedom. The Diary of Clotee, a Slave Girl.* New York: Scholastic Inc.

Miller, W. and Cedric, L. (1995) *Frederick Douglass: The Last Day of Slavery.* New York: Lee and Low Books Inc.

Monjo, F. N. and Brenner F. (1970) *The Drinking Gourd.* New York: Harper Collins.

Paulsen, G. (1993) *Nightjohn.* New York: Bantam Doubleday Dell Inc.

Pinkney, A. D. and Pinkney, B. (1994) *Dear Benjamin Banneker.* San Diego: Harcourt Brace & Company.

Pinsent, P. (1997) *Children's Literature and the Politics of Equality.* London: David Fulton Publishers.

Ringold, F. (1992) *Aunt Harriet's Underground Railroad in the Sky*. New York: Crown Publishers Inc.

Schroeder, A. and Pinkney, J. (1996) *Minty*. New York: Dial Books.

Smucker, B. (1978) *Underground to Canada*. Harmondsworth: Puffin.

Stein, C. R. (1997) *The Underground Railroad*. Connecticut: Children's Press.

Sterling, D. (1954) *Freedom Train. The Story of Harriet Tubman*. New York: Scholastic Inc.

Sutherland, R. (1985) 'Hidden persuaders: political ideologies in literature for children', *Children's Literature in Education* **16**(3), 143–57.

Tobin, J. L. and Dobard, R. G. (1999) *Hidden in Plain View. The secret story of quilts and the Underground Railroad*. New York: Doubleday.

Turner, A. and Himler, R. (1987) *Nettie's Trip South*. New York: Simon & Schuster.

Winter, J. (1988) *Follow the Drinking Gourd*. New York: Alfred A. Knopf.

Wright, C. C. and Griffith, G. (1994) *Journey to Freedom*. New York: Holiday House.

Yates, E. and Unwin, N. C (1950) *Amos Fortune Free Man*. Harmondsworth: Puffin.

Acknowledgements

I am indebted to David Montgomerie at University of Surrey Roehampton for planning and leading the drama workshops with students.

I thank, also, Ellen Rossiter, a former student who willingly shared with me her extensive collection of books on this subject.

Bibliography

Aiken, J. (1996) 'Interpreting the Past: Reflections of an Historical Novelist', in Egoff, S. *et al.* (eds) *Only Connect*, third edition, Toronto: Oxford University Press.

Bawden, N. (1976) A Dead Pig and My Father, in Fox, G. *et al.* (eds) *Writers, Critics and Children*, London: Heinemann.

Bawden, N. (1994) *In My Own Time*, London: Virago.

Blishen, E. (1975) (ed.) *The Thorny Paradise: Writers on Writing for Children*, Harmondsworth: Kestrel.

Burton, H. (1977) The author as historical novelist: one of the elite, in Meek, M., Warlow, A. and Barton, G. (eds) *The Cool Web: The Pattern of Children's Reading*, London: The Bodley Head.

Butts, D. (1992) The Adventure Story, in Butts, D. (ed.) *Stories and Society: Children's Literature in its Social Context*, London: Macmillan.

Cam, H. (1961) *Historical Novels*, London: Historical Association.

Carpenter, H. and Prichard, M. (eds) (1984) *The Oxford Companion to Children's Literature*, Oxford: Oxford University Press.

CLNE (1990) Travellers in Time: past, present and to come.' Proceedings of the summer institute at Newnham College, Cambridge. Cambridge: Children's Literature New England/Green Bay (no stated editor).

Cox, K. and Hughes, P. (1998) History and Children's Fiction, in Hoodless, P. (1998) *History and English in the Primary School: Exploiting the Links*, London: Routledge.

Davin, A. (1978) Historical Novels for Children, in Grugeon, E. and Walden, P. (eds) *Literature and Learning*, London: Ward Lock Educational in association with The Open University Press.

Dixon, B. (1982) *Now Read On: Recommended Fiction for Young People*, London: Pluto Press.

Eyre, F. (1971) *British Children's Books in the Twentieth Century*, London: Longman.

Fisher, J. (1994) *An Index of Historical Fiction for Children and Young People*, Aldershot: Scholar Press.

Fisher, J. (1996) 'Historical Fiction', in Hunt, P. (ed.) *International Companion Encyclopaedia of Children's Literature*, London: Routledge.

Fox, C. (2001) Conflicting Fictions in Meek, M. (ed.) *Children's Literature and National Identity*, Stoke on Trent: Trentham Books.

Graham, J. (2000) 'Venturesome Ways: Historical Fiction and the Novels of Henrietta Branford', in Cliff Hodges, G., Drummond, M. J. and Styles, M. (eds) *Tales, Tellers and Texts*, London: Cassell.

Hollindale, P. (1979) *Choosing Books for Children*, London: Elek.

Hollindale, P. (1988) *Ideology and the Children's Book*, Stroud: Thimble Press.

Hollindale, P. (1990) The Darkening of the Green, *Signal* **61**, January 1990.

Hollindale, P. (1991) 'Lucy Boston, Storyteller', *Signal* **64**, January 1991.

Hollindale, P. (1997) *Signs of Childness in Children's Books*, Stroud: Thimble Press.

Hollindale, P. (1997) Children of Eyam: The Dramatization of History, *Children's Literature in Education*, **28**(4).

Hunt, P. (1994) *An Introduction to Children's Literature*, Oxford: Oxford University Press.

Hunt, P. (1995) *Children's Literature: an Illustrated History,* Oxford: Oxford University Press.

Hunt, P. (2001) *Children's Literature*, Oxford: Blackwell.

Inglis, F. (1975) *Ideology and Imagination*, Cambridge: Cambridge University Press.

Inglis, F. (1981) *The Promise of Happiness*, Cambridge: Cambridge University Press.

Jobe, R. (1993) *Cultural Connections*, Markam, Ontario: Pembroke Publishers.

John, T. (1989) Children's Historical Fiction and a Sense of the Past, in *The Children's Bookroom: Reading and the Use of Books*, Stoke-on-Trent: Trentham Books.

King, C. (1988) 'The Historical Novel: An Under-Used Resource', *Teaching History,* April 1988.

Lathey, G. (1999) *The Impossible Legacy Identity and Purpose in Autobiographical Children's Literature set in the Third Reich and the Second World War*, Berne: Peter Lang.

Lathey, G. (1999) Other Sides of the Story: War in Translated Children's Fiction, *Signal* **88**, January 1999.

Leeson, R. (1976) The spirit of what age? The interpretation of history from a radical standpoint, *Children's Literature in Education* 23, 1976.

Leeson, R. (1985) *Reading and Righting*, London: Collins.

Little, V. and John, T. (1986) *Historical Fiction in the Classroom*, London: Historical Association.

Lively, P. (1994) *Oleander, Jacaranda: A Childhood Perceived*, London: Penguin.

Meek, M., Barton G. and Warlow, A. (eds) (1973) *The Cool Web*. London: The Bodley Head.

Meek, M. (1960) *Geoffrey Trease*, London: Bodley Head Monograph.

Meek, M. (ed.) (2001) *Children's Literature and National Identity*, Stoke on Trent: Trentham Books.

Moss, E. (1989) The Historical Imagination, *Signal* **60**, January 1989.

Paton Walsh, P. (1972) History is Fiction, *Horn Book Magazine* February 1972.

Pinsent, P. (1997) *Children's Literature and the Politics of Equality*, London: David Fulton Publishers.

Rahn, S. (1991) An Evolving Past: The Story of Historical Fiction and Non-Fiction for Children, *The Lion and the Unicorn* **15**(1).

Rustin, M. and Rustin, M. (1987) *Narratives of Love and Loss: Studies in Modern Children's Literature*, London: Verso.

Self, D. (1991) The Lost Asset? The Historical Novel in the Classroom, *Children's Literature in Education* **22**(1).

Silvey, A. (ed.) (1995) *Children's Books and their Creators,* New York: Houghton Mifflin Company.

Sutcliff, R. (1960) *Kipling*, London: Bodley Head Monograph.

Stephens, J. (1992) *Language and Ideology in Children's Fiction*, London: Longman.

Sutherland, R. (1985) Hidden Persuaders: Political Ideologies in Literature for Children, *Children's Literature in Education* **16**(3).

Sutherland, Z. and Arbuthnot, M. H. (1991, eighth edition) *Children and Books*, New York: Harper Collins.

Tomlinson, C. (ed.) (1998) *Children's Books from Other Countries,* Lanham, Maryland: Scarecrow Press, Inc.

Townsend, J. R. (1965, first edition, revised five times, last edition 1990) *Written for Children*, Harmondsworth: Penguin.

Townsend, J. R. (1979) *A Sounding of Storytellers*, London: Kestrel.

Trease, G. (1949) *Tales out of School*, London: Heinemann.

Trease, G. (1995) The Historical Novelist at Work, in Fox, G. (ed.) *Celebrating Children's Literature in Education*, London: Hodder and Stoughton.

Index

Author Index

Ahlberg, A. 55
Ahlberg, J. 55
Aiken, J. 20, 21, 32–41, 65, 71, 87, 139, 150
Almond, D. 71
Arbuthnot, M. H. 22
Arnold, G. 6
Atkinson, D. 21
Atterton, J. vii, 84–89

Bakhtin, M. 38, 39
Bales, K. 158
Ballantyne, R. M. 6
Banks, M. R. 12
Barnardo, Dr. 95
Bartoletti, S. C. 71
Bawden, N. 16
Beecher-Stowe, H. 151, 152
Bell, L. 71
Boston, L. 43, 45–48, 49
Bowman, A. 3
Branford, H. 14, 18, 143
Briggs, R. 56
Brighton, C. 56–58
Brink, C. R. 15
Brooke, B. 148
Brown, R. 60
Bulwer-Lytton, E. 3
Burgess, M. 68
Burridge, J. 34, 35
Burton, H. 16, 17
Butts, D. vii, 2, 5, 43

Cam, H. 23
Carpenter, H. 34, 69
Carter, P. 13
Cedric, L. 155
Chauncy, N. 17
Claude, R. P. 158
Coatsworth, E. 15
Cody, D. 64
Cole, H. 155
Collingwood, R. G. 110
Collins, F. M. vii, 10, 73
Conlon-McKenna, M. 74–77, 79–80, 81

Cookson, C. 66–67
Cox, K. 54
Crew, G. 61
Croall, J. 14
Culmann, O. 109
Curtis, A. T. 15
Cushman, K. 138–139, 140, 143

Daniel, G. 23
Davin, A. 54, 64, 71, 150
de Angeli, M. 154
Dickens, C. 3, 34, 40, 95, 122
Dickinson, P. viii, 23–31
Dobard, R. G. 155, 157
Doherty, B. vii, 12, 13, 90–96, 129, 130
Doré, G. 123, 124
Duncan Edwards, P. 155
Dunnett, D. 146

Edwards, D. 14
Eliot, T. S. 44
Eyre, E. 146

Feelings, T. 150
Fellows, A. viii, 129
Field, R. 15
Fisher, J. 33, 34, 54
Forbes, E. 11
Foreman, M. viii, 60–61, 97–101
Fox, C. 12
Fox, G. viii, 21, 120
Fox, P. 151–152
Fritz, J. 153

Garfield, L. 2, 7, 12, 20, 32–34, 36–41, 65
Garland, S. 54, 56
Gavin, J. 14
Geras, A. 16, 59
Golding, W. 23–30
Goode, D. 56
Graham, J. viii, 10, 54
Gregor I. 26–27
Griffith, G. 156

Hahn, M. D. 16
Hall, L. viii, 43
Halliday, M. A. K. 37–38

Hardy, T. 45, 51
Harnett, C. 20, 54
Haviland, V. 16
Hendry, F. 158
Henty, G. A. 6, 7
Hest, A. 58–59
Heyer, G. 35
Hicks, A. ix, 138
Hoban, R. 41
Hofland, B. 3,
Hollindale, P. ix, 23, 33, 44–45, 46, 47, 49, 75, 151
Hooper, M. 21
Hopkinson, D. 157
Hudson, J. 17
Hughes, P. 54
Hughes, S. 55
Humpherys, A. 128
Hunt, P. 36, 46
Hunter, M. 13
Hynes, S. 24, 27

Inglis, F. 52

Jacobs, W.W. 106
Janeways, J. 5
Jerold, B. 123
Jerome, J. K. 106
John, T. 33

Keats, J. 50
Kennan, C. 79, 80
Kennerley, A. 93
Kerr, J. 14, 16
Kilner, G. 68
Kinkead-Weekes, M. 26, 27
Kipling, R. 9, 23, 43–46, 50

Lacan, J. 40
Lasenby, J. 12
Lathey, G. ix, 12, 32
Laycock, L. ix, 150
Leakey R. 25, 26
Lester, J. 150
Levinson, R. 56
Lewin, R. 25, 26
Lindsay, N. 106
Lively, P. 13, 43, 45–46, 50–52, 65, 156

Title Index

417793

Subject Index